Lord Eight Wind of Suchixtlan
and the Heroes of Ancient Oaxaca

T0339061

THE LINDA SCHELE SERIES IN MAYA AND PRE-COLUMBIAN STUDIES

*This series was made possible through the generosity
of William C. Nowlin, Jr., and Bettye H. Nowlin, the National Endowment
for the Humanities, and various individual donors.*

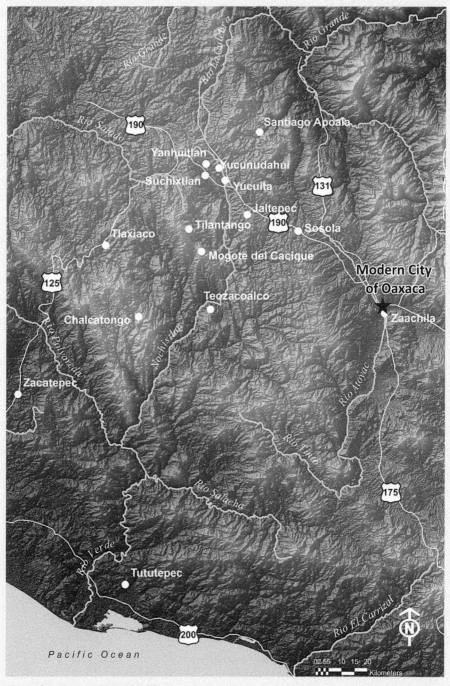

Cities of the Ancient Mixtec World

Lord Eight Wind of Suchixtlan and the Heroes of Ancient Oaxaca

READING HISTORY IN THE CODEX ZOUCHE-NUTTALL

Robert Lloyd Williams

Foreword by F. Kent Reilly III   *Introduction by John M. D. Pohl*

UNIVERSITY OF TEXAS PRESS   AUSTIN

Frontispiece map created by Elaine Day Schele, July 2008

Requests for permission to reproduce material from this work
should be sent to:
Permissions
University of Texas Press
P.O. Box 7819
Austin, TX 78713-7819
www.utexas.edu/utpress/about/bpermission.html

∞ The paper used in this book meets the minimum requirements
of ANSI/NISO Z39.48-1992 (R1997) (Permanence of Paper).

Library of Congress Cataloging-in-Publication Data
Williams, Robert Lloyd.
  Lord Eight Wind of Suchixtlan and the heroes of ancient Oaxaca :
reading history in the Codex Zouche-Nuttall / Robert Lloyd Williams;
foreword by F. Kent Reilly III ; introduction by John M. D. Pohl. — 1st ed.
     p. cm. — (Linda Schele series in Maya and pre-Columbian studies)
  Includes bibliographical references and index.
  ISBN 978-0-292-72573-7
  1. Codex Nuttall. 2. Manuscripts, Mixtec. 3. Eight Wind, 935–1027.
4. Mixtec Indians—History. 5. Mixtec Indians—Kings and rulers.
6. Mixtec language—Writing. 7. Picture-writing—Mexico. I. Title.
  F1219.56.C62532W557 2009
  972'.01—dc22   2009013444

Dedicated to many: the great Mixtec people of Oaxaca, past and present, my professors Kent Reilly and Brian Stross, family, friends, un-friends, colleagues, fellow students, teachers, Bill and Sammie McCown, Richard McCown, Madge Simmons, and my brother Twelve Flower.

CONTENTS

Foreword by F. Kent Reilly III   ix

Author's Preface   xi

Acknowledgments   xiii

Introduction by John M. D. Pohl   1

PART ONE

1   It Happened Long Ago   29

2   The People of the Codices   45

3   The Narrative Structure of Codex Zouche-Nuttall Obverse   57

4   Sacred Geography, Personified Geography   63

5   Caves in Mesoamerican Iconography | *Chalcatzingo and the Mixteca*   69

PART TWO

6   Lord Eight Wind's Introduction   93

7   The War from Heaven, Part One   101

8   The War from Heaven, Part Two   107

9   Lord Eight Wind's Family   115

10   Transition to the Future | *Eight Wind, Two Rain, and Eight Deer*   121

PART THREE

11   Rituals of Order | *Codices Zouche-Nuttall and Vienna*   135

12   The Problem of the Two Dead Lords   146

13   The Epiclassic Mixtec Ceremonial Complex   156

APPENDIX I | Biographical Sketches of Major Personnel from the Codices: Lord Eight Deer the Usurper, Lord Two Rain the King, and Lady Six Monkey of Jaltepec   163

APPENDIX II | Notes for Codex Zouche-Nuttall Pages 1–4   187

APPENDIX III | Codex Zouche-Nuttall Reverse Day Dates on Pages 46a–48a for Year 5 Reed (AD 1095) and Lord Eight Deer's Campaign as Lord of Tututepec   190

Color photo section follows page 48.
Bibliography   199

Index   209

Some seventeen hundred years ago in the mountainous western Mexican state of Oaxaca, a culture developed that left us with the rarest of commodities: books. This culture—the Mixtecs—existed in a world defined by mountains, valleys, and caves. Politically, this landscape was divided into a series of very small principalities that in many ways resembled the city-states of Renaissance Italy. The ruling lineages of this group focused on an ideology based on ancestors, marriage alliances, and warfare. The books that the Mixtecs produced were principally devoted to these genealogies and their roles in political legitimization.

Europeans first became aware of these native books, called "codices," when Hernán Cortés included two of them in his gift of New World curiosities to Emperor Charles V. They were among those items intended to elicit royal interest, delight, and amazement.

Since their introduction into the European academic landscape, these manuscripts have sparked strong interest. Though there have been many attempts at interpretation, the great breakthrough was achieved by Alfonso Caso when, in 1949, he published a definitive argument establishing their Mixtec origins (*El Mapa de Teozacoalco*, 1998). As Caso's research progressed, it became apparent that these manuscripts contained historical information. He noted:

> The Indians not only of Mexico, but from the whole of Mesoamerica possessed a true historical vocation, and they told and wrote history. (trans. Manuel Aguilar and Claudia Alarcon)

Since Caso's groundbreaking discoveries there have been many efforts to recover the specifics of Mixtec history as they wrote it. Two of their documents have been resistant to historical, chronological analysis; namely, Codex Zouche-Nuttall obverse and Codex Vindobonensis Mexicanus I obverse. In them, the Mixtec calendar has been both a key and an impediment to the recovery of their historical information. In this volume, Robert Williams has selected these most difficult and obscure Mixtec manuscripts (chiefly Zouche-Nuttall obverse) for his work. Their obscurity rests on the fact that though the codex vignettes obviously describe marriages and warfare between diverse Mixtec elites, the convoluted chronologies associated with them have been unobvious and controversial. Williams, in this important study, shows that the calendar information is far from being merely metaphorical, resting as it does solidly on the Mixtec political need to accurately record alliances, the offspring of royal marriages, and the magical foundation of Mixtec rulership. The process and methodology through which Williams demonstrates this essentially linear historical chronology rests on his elucidation of the ingenious, complex format of Zouche-Nuttall obverse. Once the reader understands that the information revealed through the codex format and contents is a combination of both history in the European sense as well as the timelessness of myth in the Native American sense, then Mixtec history comes alive vividly.

With this publication, Robert Williams takes his place among the few academics who are cognizant of the human element in the ancient Mesoamerican past. The rulers of the Mixtecs, like their European counterparts, focused on enhancing their prestige through warfare and carefully crafted marriages. Williams's linking of these elements of elite behavior with the native calendar reveals aspects of Mixtec history that dwell in myth as well as literal time. This revelation, more than anything else, underlines the often-neglected fact that the Mixtecs were human beings concerned with many of the problems of contemporary humanity. These pages reveal that Mixtec history and ideological views have their counterparts in the history and ideological foundations of all humankind.

F. KENT REILLY III
Department of Anthropology
Texas State University–San Marcos

In 1985, I studied Mayan hieroglyphic writing with Professor Linda Schele at her annual spring break Maya Hieroglyphic Workshops at the University of Texas at Austin. I taught introductory classes for her in 1987 and 1988 at that workshop. In 1989, Professor Schele asked me to found a Mixtec Pictogram Writing Workshop as an adjunct to the larger seminar because she wanted to increase the scope of the workshop to include as many Mesoamerican cultures as possible.

I subsequently taught two master classes on the Mixtec codices under Professor Schele's aegis at the University of Texas. Then followed a series of articles in 1991 about the first side of Codex Zouche-Nuttall for the periodical *Texas Notes on Pre-Columbian Art, Writing, and Culture* as well as an article in 1993 for the same journal, coauthored with Timothy Albright and Rex Koontz, titled "Eight Deer Plays Ball Again: Notes on a New Codiacal Cognate." These are in the University of Texas Department of Fine Arts online files (CHAAAC). Mr. Albright and I also presented the five-hundred-year genealogy of Lord Eight Wind Eagle Flints at the 1993 SAA meeting in Anaheim, California. We demonstrated Lord Eight Wind's descendants as recorded in several of the Mixtec codex genealogies from AD 935 until the Spanish Colonial era.

I taught the first Mixtec Seminar on Codex Selden in 1992 at the UT Maya Meetings Long Workshops, but on the proviso that an established scholar had to be engaged to direct subsequent annual sessions. Dr. John M. D. Pohl was that scholar, and in the next twelve years we established and codirected the curricula and taught the seminar. Professor Pohl's leadership enabled me to evolve my thinking regarding the largely unexplicated sections of Codex Zouche-Nuttall obverse, which had been the subject of my previous articles. My master's thesis at Texas State University–San Marcos, which due to space limitations concerned only the first eight pages of Codex Zouche-Nuttall obverse, was the direct result of my many years of study, research, and original thought about the topic. This book is an expansion of that thesis and a collection of essays on various topics in Mixtec codices.

In January of 2007, I taught an anthropology course at Texas State University titled Mixtec Codices: The Prehispanic Historical Literature of Oaxaca. The syllabus included codex material as history (the War from Heaven, the Siege of Hua Chino), biography (Lord Eight Deer Jaguar Claw of Tilantongo, Lady Six Monkey of Jaltepec–Hua Chino, and Lord Two Rain of Tilantongo), and genealogy (the first and second dynasties of Tilantongo and the second dynasty of Jaltepec). The final exam was led by the graduate students (three from Texas State University–San Marcos, two from the University of Texas at Austin). Under their leadership, the undergraduates presented sections from the codices consisting of Power Point presentations demonstrating the chronological biography of Lord Eight Deer Jaguar Claw *read* from Codex Zouche-Nuttall reverse, Codex Alfonso Caso, and Codex Bodley.

I conducted the final 2007 Mixtec Codex Seminar at UT over spring break and essentially retaught in synopsis the Texas State–San Marcos course—but in three days. Participants, including those from Guatemala, received course outlines and Power Point presentations of essential class material regarding my work and research in Mixtec codices.

The reader can see that I began this study late in life, never intending to create a long academic career based on it. Although I researched everything available to me, my approach to the Mixtec documents evolved into something unique: the ancient Mixtecs and their heroes of old Oaxaca survived for me in their manuscripts as stories, songs, sagas, dances, playlists, and dynastic propaganda/histories. The word "history" always carries the sense of "retrospective," yet the individuals and events in the Mixtec codices are delightfully current and contemporary, transferring all the excitement and drama of an archaeological culture into the modern world. The manuscript scribes still speak, but their words are only available to those who can hear with their eyes, as when reading music. The Mixtec narratives are not only history but also fascinating introductions and extended stories of a vital, dynamic people who found their own unique way of transcending time and space. Let us now undertake a journey—sometimes difficult, perhaps controversial, but always fascinating—and meet these powerful men and women of ancient Oaxaca.

ACKNOWLEDGMENTS

This present volume is the result of a study extending over the last twenty years. For this reason, I am unable to remember all who contributed to the final product. However, that being the case, I would like to thank every student who attended the annual spring break Mixtec Writing Seminars at the University of Texas at Austin. This gratitude is an accumulation of twelve consecutive years. Thanks to the graduate students, undergraduates, professors, and laypersons who took my courses there, as well as the undergraduate and graduate students who took my Prehispanic Mixtec History course at Texas State University–San Marcos. All taught me very much, and the interactions between us made me a better scholar and a better person as well.

Among my outstanding professors, whose knowledge and expertise advanced my abilities and interests, are Doctors James Neeley, Thomas Hester, James Denbow, Linda Schele, David Stuart, Martha Menchaca, Brian Stross, Fred Valdez, Julia Guernsey, F. Kent Reilly III, James Garber, Elizabeth Erhart, Richard Warms, John McGee, and John M. D. Pohl. Among colleagues past, I am especially grateful to Heather Orr, Timothy Albright, and Rex Koontz. My colleague at Texas State–San Marcos deserves special thanks for preparing the images for this book: therefore, Johann Sawyer, please understand how very grateful I am for your expertise. My constant friend, who listened always to my kvetching and offered support and advice, is David Schele. Words cannot convey my love, respect, and admiration of him.

Theresa May, assistant director and editor-in-chief of the University of Texas Press, deserves an award for editorial omniscience, graciousness, expertise, and generosity. Kathryn Charles-Wilson at the British Museum Department of Sales as well as Gabriele Daublebsky at ADEVA (Graz, Austria) are the gracious ladies who picked through and translated my many e-mails requesting assistance and permissions into common sense and good form. Ladies, you can shred or delete those e-mails now.

Madge Simmons, an educator who has not ceased to foster education even after many years of retirement, deserves special acknowledgment for her kind efforts in my behalf. Without Ms. Simmons, this book could not have come to publication. Her nephew, Richard McCown, fed me and kept me oriented as to person, place, and time.

To all these good people, and even more erased from my memory by the passing of cruel time, I am especially grateful. I hope your encouragement, faith, and pedagogy have not been wasted on such a one as me.

Lord Eight Wind of Suchixtlan
and the Heroes of Ancient Oaxaca

Introduction

John M. D. Pohl

Fowler Museum at the University of California, Los Angeles

The Mixtec Indian people are concentrated in the northern and western parts of what is today Oaxaca, southern Puebla, and Guerrero. Their land is composed of a succession of small, yet prosperous valleys surrounded by high mountains and dry deserts. The largest is called the Nochixtlan Valley. Some 10,000 years ago their ancestors subsisted by hunting and gathering. Later they became agriculturalists specializing primarily in growing maize, beans, and squash. For over a millennia they lived in small villages, but after 500 BC, their society became highly stratified as the people allowed themselves to be governed first by councils of priests and elders, and later by a class of hereditary chiefs. Between AD 200 and 1000, the Mixtecs lived in large, concentrated mountaintop communities of as many as 10,000 people, with the archaeological zones of Yucuñudahui, Yucuita, Mogote del Cacique, and Yucu Yoco being predominant in the Nochixtlan Valley of the Mixteca Alta during the Classic period (figure I.1). The principal royal families had clearly foreseen great benefits in uniting themselves. They built expansive palaces and erected great pyramids dedicated to their gods and ancestors. Then, for reasons that are hotly debated by archaeologists, the elite class abandoned these mountaintop citadels, divided the surrounding lands among themselves, and founded nearly a hundred petty city-states, each dominated by a single king and queen.

At the beginning of Mesoamerica's Postclassic period (AD 1000–1521) Nahua peoples migrated into what are today the states of Tlaxcala and Puebla to the north, while to the east the Zapotecs dominated the great Valley of Oaxaca. Seeking new and profitable opportunities for trade, the Mixtecs invited the Nahuas and Zapotecs to engage in powerful marriage alliances that subsequently unified most of southern Mexico between 1150 and 1450. Then in 1458, the kingdom of Coixtlahuaca was attacked by the armies of the Aztec Empire, whose capital was located at Tenochtitlan, or what is to-

Yucu Yoco
San Isidro

Figure I.1. In 2008 Jesús León Santos of San Isidro, Tilantongo, Oaxaca, was awarded the prestigious Goldman Prize for his successful experiments in restoring the productive capacity of the miles of terraces surrounding the Mogote del Cacique, or Hill of Flints, and the ruins of Yucu Yoco, or Hill of the Wasp-Bee, the Classic period ceremonial center that dominated the southern end of the Nochixtlan Valley between AD 200 and 950. (Photo by John M. D. Pohl)

day Mexico City. The defeat of the Mixtecs and their allies ended an era of unprecedented independence and prosperity in Mesoamerica. Once the Aztecs had taken out the alliance structure south and east of Cholula, a principal religious center, the game was up for the southern highland confederacies, and Oaxacan noble houses reoriented themselves to a Pacific coastal trade by establishing new political centers at Tututepec and Tehuantepec.

The defeat of the Aztec Empire by a Nahua-Spanish army sixty years later brought dramatic changes to southern Mexico. A new society of Mixtec caciques (colonial nobles) rose to power. Although they took the names of ranking Spanish leaders whom they regarded as their peers (for example, Felipe de Austria of Tilantongo and Domingo de Guzmán of Yanhuitlan) they also continued to preserve the legacy of their pre-Columbian past by conserving the codices of their ancestors and even creating new pictographic manuscripts to document their political affairs.

A significant issue in Mesoamerican studies remains the nature of the Late Postclassic period in southern Mexico and adjacent regions. Far from representing any cultural decline, a persistent view promoted by Gibbon-inspired notions of fallen societies, the Postclassic should instead be con-

Hill of Flints
Mogote del Cacique

constructed Terraces

sidered a time of major societal transformation that withstood Aztec conquest only to resurrect itself upon a new early colonial Spanish foundation.
Consequently, the strong distinction made between the pre-Columbian and
Early Colonial periods ought to be combined into a "Late Antiquity," the
term applied by historians to other areas of the world that witnessed comparable developments, including decentralized political systems, an emphasis on pilgrimage centers as coordinating mechanisms, and the subsequent
spread of Christianity through the missionary efforts of monastic orders
working in conjunction with an indigenous pagan elite.

Today there are more than 2.5 million Indian people still living in the
Mexican states of Tlaxcala, Puebla, and Oaxaca. Of these, 400,000 are Mixtec speaking. Many continue to live in small villages, farming their land
much as their ancestors did for millennia. Others have migrated to Mexico
City or the United States, where they have prospered. Many still return to
their traditional villages annually for religious festivals and other occasions
important to the community.

The Mixtecs were renowned throughout Mesoamerica for their miniature artistic masterpieces of turquoise, gold, silver, jade, shell, and many

other precious materials, as well as polychrome ceramics and the codices. Evidence of the social intensity achieved by the alliance networks that joined city-states during highland Mesoamerica's Postclassic is revealed in the development and spread of a pictographic communication system once called Mixteca-Puebla, but now more properly called the Nahua-Mixteca style in light of recognition of its source at Cholula and the cultural groups most responsible for its refinement. It was composed of highly conventionalized symbols. Colors were vivid, and imagery shared many of the attributes of contemporary cartoons, the exaggerated emphasis on the head and hands, in particular, being reminiscent in overall design to characters made famous by contemporary film animation studios such as the Walt Disney Company. In full figurative form the style was primarily employed to convey historical or ritual narrative, but certain symbols could also be reduced to simple icons that symbolized either an idea or a spoken word. For example, the depiction of repetitive designs of such common motifs as birds, butterflies, and jewels invokes the spirits of ancestors who were thought to have been transformed into animals or precious objects after death.

By AD 1300, the Nahua-Mixteca style had supplanted earlier pictographic and phonetically based scripts employed by the Classic period civilizations of La Mojarra, Teotihuacan, Cacaxtla, Xochicalco, Nuiñe, Monte Alban, and to some extent even the Maya. There is some evidence that the old writing systems were intentionally rejected and that the new system was adapted from the figurative symbolism used to ornament jewelry and textiles—small, portable works of art that were exchanged through bridewealth, dowry, and other forms of royal gift exchange. Far from representing any decline in literacy, therefore, the employment of this new cartoon-like horizon style became an ingenious response to the redistribution of power among Postclassic lords who communicated in as many as twelve different languages.

After the conquest of the Aztec Empire in 1521, a few learned Spaniards began to collect the pictorial books that were employed by the many indigenous peoples throughout Mesoamerica to document their religious rituals and histories. Some manuscripts were thereby spared from the fires of militant Christian evangelization, while others were copied by Indian scribes who added Spanish or native language script for explanation. There are eight pre-Conquest style codices attributed to the Mixtec-speaking people of Oaxaca, Mexico, known collectively as the Mixtec codices:

Codices Zouche-Nuttall and Egerton (British Museum, London)
Codices Bodley and Selden (Bodleian Library, Oxford)
Codex Vindobonensis (National Bibliotek, Vienna)
Codex Colombino (Museo Nacional de Antropología, Mexico City)
Codices Becker I and II (Museum für Völkerkunde, Vienna)

(Codex Colombino and Codex Becker I are two parts of the same codex, together referred to as Codex Colombino-Becker.)

Some scholars once believed that there was little or no cultural distinction between the Mixtec Group and the Borgia Group, and that the differences in content and format simply reflect a variance in intellectual application (see Pohl 2004a and Pohl and Urcid 2006 for discussion). The Mixtec Group, it was argued, is "descriptive"; in other words, the screenfolds describe historical events that actually took place and will never recur again. The Borgia Group, on the other hand, is "prescriptive"; in other words, the screenfolds prescribe events that may take place at some time in the future. However, such pan-Mixtec–oriented arguments were made by codex specialists who focus only on iconographic and stylistic similarities between codices and ignore contextually related material in ceramics, frescos, and other artifacts (Pohl 2004a). We can now determine conclusively that the Mixtec Group and the Borgia Group are culturally and behaviorally distinct, with the former being produced by Mixtec confederacies of Oaxaca, and the latter being produced by the Eastern Nahuas and the peoples they dominated in the states of Puebla, Oaxaca, and Veracruz. While there is differential emphasis in the two groups with regard to mytho-historical versus divinatory content, both were employed to determine the proper calendrical timing and kinds of ceremonies to be enacted at royal feasts.[1]

The Mixtec codices were made of animal hide and covered with a gesso-like foundation upon which figures were painted. They were folded so that they could either be stored compactly or opened to reveal all of the pages on one side. The symbols represent people, places, and things, organized to communicate religious stories, histories, and genealogies. Thanks to the writings of the colonial Oaxacan historians, we know that the codices were actually made by the ancient Mixtec ruling class:

> . . . they had many books . . . that the historians inscribed with characters so abbreviated, that a single page expressed the place, the site, province, year, month, and day with all the names of the gods, ceremonies, and sacrifices, or

victories that they celebrated, and recorded in this way by the sons of the lords . . . their priest had instructed them since infancy to illustrate the characters and memorize the histories. . . . I heard some elders explain that they were accustomed to fasten these manuscripts along the length of the rooms of the lords for their aggrandizement and vanity, they took pride in displaying them in their councils. (Friar Francisco de Burgoa, 1934 [1674])

The fact that the Mixtec codices were hung on walls implies that they were not meant to be read simply as books, but also displayed as "storyboards." A poet would then recite the text from the codex to musical accompaniment while actors performed parts of the saga in costume. The setting for these literary and theatrical presentations was the royal feast. Imagine a banquet in which the participants were literally part of the art of the performance. Their garments were painted with figures of culture heroes and gods, they drank and ate from polychrome pottery decorated with scenes from the codices, and they exchanged gifts of gold, shell, bone, and turquoise engraved with images of the founding ancestors of the highest-ranking dynasties.

According to the codices, Mixtec nobles believed that their ancestors had been miraculously born from trees, rivers, stones, mountains, and even the sky. This enabled their descendants to claim they were divinities. The ancient Mixtec word for "king" or "queen" was *yya,* but it also signified "god." By advocating kinship to the gods, the Mixtec aristocracy had irrefutably fixed their role as society's mediators with the supernatural. By being literally descended from various parts of a personified landscape, they could maintain, by divine right, proprietary claims unattainable to the lower classes. Marriage was the means by which the Mixtec aristocracy enriched themselves, perpetuated control over their people, and linked their communities into large political constellations. Codices Zouche-Nuttall, Vindobonensis, Bodley, and Selden feature different versions of the genealogies of the great patriarch Lord Eight Wind and his descendants Lady Six Monkey, Lord Eleven Wind, Lord Two Rain, Lord Eight Deer, and Lord Four Wind. By 1521, virtually every ranking noble house in Oaxaca could claim descent from these epic heroes.

Lord Eight Wind

A significant cycle of legends portrayed on Codex Zouche-Nuttall 1–8 recounts the saga of Lord Eight Wind. On the first two pages, Eight Wind is depicted as a patriarch who is magically born from the earth at two different locations: Hill of the Monkey and Hill of the Rain God. Eight Wind's narrative is then interrupted on Zouche-Nuttall 3–4 by a rendition of the War from Heaven that differs from the version on pages 20–21, which I have discussed elsewhere (Pohl 2004b).[2] Here Stone Men first attack Hill of the Rain God and capture Lady Nine Monkey. The bloody war then rages on at Hill of the Flower, where Lady Six Eagle and Lord Seven Serpent defend themselves. Next we see Lord Seven Earthquake sacrificing a Stone Man at Hill of the Jewel—Hill of Feathers, followed by a sequence of additional conflicts at Black Hill with Lord Seven Wind and Lady Eight Deer, at Town of Blood with Seven Wind Flint Eagle, and at Feather Plain with Lord Five Dog and Lord Nine Dog. On page 4, we see three red-and-white striped men, personifications of stars (or clouds), descending from the sky before Lady Eleven Serpent at Hill of the Ballcourt. Lord Four Serpent and Lord Seven Earthquake appear again, capturing two of the star warriors. After the war is resolved, the story of Lord Eight Wind resumes on pages 5–7. On page 5, Eight Wind again emerges from the earth at two additional place signs. He is blessed by the rain god Dzahui and takes his rightful place as ruler of Hill of the Monkey—Platform of Flowers. His marriage to Lady Ten Deer produces five children. Two additional wives and seven nobles who attended the marriage are portrayed on page 6. The Eight Wind saga then concludes on pages 7–8, where the patriarch, now an elder, advises Lord Two Rain Ocoñaña to form a confederation of allies to defend his claim to the throne of Tilantongo, or possibly lay claim to the kingdoms of Red and White Bundle and Jaltepec as well.[3]

The place signs are the key to attributing both the Eight Wind saga and an earlier portrayal of the War from Heaven in the Zouche-Nuttall narrative to the northern Nochixtlan Valley. M. E. Smith first identified the kingdom with which Eight Wind is associated in codices Selden and Bodley as Suchixtlan, symbolized by the sign depicting a temple platform with a flowery tree growing from it. The community is located on the lower slopes of Cerro Jasmin, the enormous Classic period citadel that dominated most of the surrounding region. Elsewhere I have argued that Hill of the Monkey is Cerro Jasmin, or at least part of it (Pohl 2004b:226–230) (figure I.2). A Mixtec toponym associated with this general vicinity is Danacodzo. *Da* is a corruption of *dza,* meaning "place." *Na* has not been interpreted. *Codzo* means "monkey." Following his emergence from Hill of the Monkey, Eight Wind travels to Apoala, 40 kilometers to the northeast, where he descends into one of two rivers there and reemerges at Hill of the Rain God (figure I.3).[4] The hill displays the frontal image of a deity with the blue, disk-shaped eyes and fanged mouth commonly associated with the Aztec rain god Tlaloc, but we know from colonial documents that the Mixtecs called this god "Dzahui." The place sign should be translated as something like "Yucu Dzahui." The largest archaeological site in the northern Nochixtlan Valley is, in fact, named Yucuñudahui, a term composed of the substantives *yucu,* or "hill"; *ñu,* meaning "town"; and *dahui* or *dzahui,* usually translated as "mist," but clearly a dialectical variant of the name of the rain god. The appearance of the place sign with both Eight Wind and the War from Heaven in Codex Zouche-Nuttall is clearly a representation of the toponym for the archaeological zone.

Yucuñudahui is located on a 400-meter-high ridge lying 8 kilometers northeast of Cerro Jasmin (figure I.4). The site is composed of a series of pla-

Figure I.2. Cerro Jasmin towers over the Yanhuitlan arm of the northern Nochixtlan Valley. The community of Suchixtlan is located on the lower slopes in the distance on the right, and the sixteenth-century church of Yanhuitlan is in the foreground on the left. The association of Eight Wind with Monkey Hill, located in the vicinity of Suchixtlan, suggests that the patriarch's place of magical birth from the earth was a component of the massive Terminal Classic–Las Flores period Cerro Jasmin urban center. (Photo by John M. D. Pohl)

Figure I.3. The Valley of Apoala is characterized by steep cliff walls framing a small, fertile plain bisected by two rivers. Pages 1 and 2 of Codex Zouche-Nuttall obverse show Eight Wind traveling from Cerro Jasmin to Apoala, where he then steps into one of the two rivers, moves through the earth, and reappears from a cave at Yucu-ñudahui. (Photo by Manuel Aguilar)

zas, mounds, and patios running along an L-shaped ridge for approximately a kilometer from west to east and nearly 3 kilometers from north to south (figure I.5). Preliminary reconnaissances were made in the 1930s by Eulalia Guzmán, Martin Bazán, and others (Pohl 2004b). Alfonso Caso briefly investigated several major architectural features at the site in 1937 and recorded significant fragments of paintings and stone carvings with Late Classic Nu-iñe-style glyphs. No further work was done until 1966, when Ronald Spores surveyed the site. Four years later Spores excavated the remains of dwellings on the western and southern peripheries of the central ceremonial complex. Michael Lind then excavated the Postclassic palace at Chachoapan, built on one of the lower slopes. Despite its prominence, Yucuñudahui was only the largest of an intensive network of Classic period sites that extended along a series of adjacent ridges from Coyotepec in the north to Yucu Ita in the south. Codex Vindobonensis 9–10 in fact portrays a large landscape profile that matches such a settlement system. Not only is Yucuñudahui prominent-

Figure I.4. Yucuñudahui. The archaeological zone consists of an extensive ceremonial center on the summit of the mountain, surrounded by a labyrinth of residential and agricultural terraces. Recognizing its significance, Alfonso Caso at one time considered excavating the site as an alternative to Monte Alban. (Photo by John M. D. Pohl)

ly featured, but probably Coyotepec and other nearby promontories as well.

In examining the War from Heaven scenes on Zouche-Nuttall 2–3, I noted that Hill of the Rain God, or Yucuñudahui, is followed by a Hill of the Flower. While flowers frequently appear as qualifiers for place signs in the codices, this particular one can be correlated with the Mixtec term *ita* in Codex Muro (Pohl 2004b:229). Thus Hill of the Flower should be called Yucu Ita. An archaeological site named Yucuita is located 4 kilometers south of Yucuñudahui. Yucuita flourished throughout the Formative as one of the largest occupations in Oaxaca, but its power was subsumed by Yucuñudahui during the Late Classic. Nevertheless, the site clearly continued to play an integral role as a secondary center within Yucuñudahui's sphere of influence. Following a preliminary reconnaissance by Ronald Spores, the site was more intensively surveyed by Marcus Winter and Patricia Plunket. Yucuita is characterized by a towering conical hill connected to a long, narrow ridge descending to the valley floor. Numerous ceremonial and residential structures were mapped over the promontory's entire extent. Excavations also uncovered large fortification walls, some over 5 meters high, as well as expansive networks of ceremonial platforms and plazas constructed over an ingenious system of drains and tunnels.

Even more compelling evidence that the first eight pages of Zouche-Nut-tall concern legends associated with the northern end of the Nochixtlan Valley is found in a remarkable series of colonial testimonies. Between 1544 and 1546, the indigenous noblemen of Yanhuitlan, a community located 2 kilometers northwest of Cerro Jasmin, were investigated by the Dominican order for practicing rituals dedicated to ancient Mixtec gods. Hoping to take advantage of political rivals, caciques from surrounding communities were quick to give testimony about the idols that they said were kept in a hidden chamber in a Yanhuitlan palace. Among the images that were specifically named were "Xacuv," or Seven Earthquake; "Sachi," or Seven Wind; "Xio," or Eleven Serpent; "Xiq," or Ten Lizard; and "Siqui," or Eleven Crocodile (Pohl 2004b). All five of these deities are depicted among the principal combat-ants in the War from Heaven portrayed in Zouche-Nuttall 3–4. Lord Seven Earthquake was the hero who sacrificed the Stone Man at Hill of the Feath-ers—Hill of the Jewel, Lord Seven Wind was one of the defenders of Black Mountain, and Lady Eleven Serpent appears at Hill of the Ballcourt. Eleven Crocodile appears by name at the same location, and according to Codex Vindobonensis 3, Lady Eleven Serpent's husband was known to have been Lord Ten Lizard. At the time of the Spanish Conquest, the larger Yanhuit-

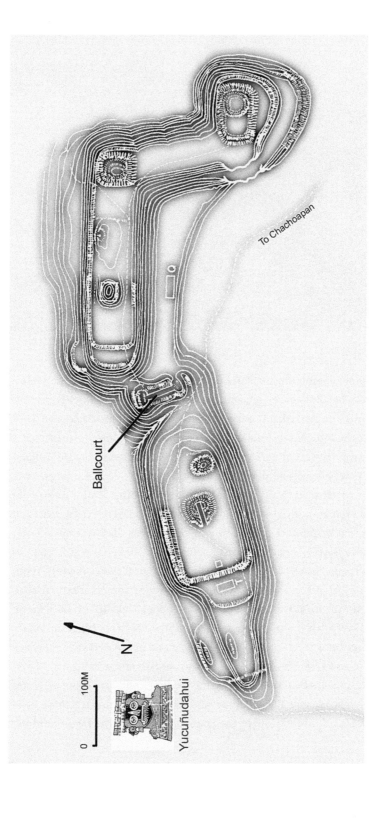

To Chachoapan

Ballcourt

N

0   100M

Yucuñudahui

lan community—including Suchixtlan, Chindua, and Andua—was regarded as the most powerful of the Postclassic kingdoms that dominated the northern end of the Nochixtlan Valley. Archaeologists have proposed that it was a direct inheritor of the venerable traditions of power and authority established in this region at the Classic ceremonial centers of Cerro Jasmin, Yucuñudahui, and Yucuita some 500 years earlier. We can see through an analysis of the legend of Lord Eight Wind that this hypothesis is verified by the ethnohistorical record as well, albeit through myth and allegory.

Alfonso Caso proposed a chronology that placed Eight Wind in the ninth century (Caso 1960:79). I published a revised chronology based in part on Caso, my own research with Bruce Byland, and the work of Emily Rabin, who was generous to share her thoughts on some of the more problematical dates with me (Byland and Pohl 1994:233–261). Rabin subsequently published a report on some of her findings confirming the placement of Lord Eight Wind in the late tenth and early eleventh centuries, and updating her proposals on the problematical dates (Rabin 2002:107–108). The problem is that some of the events in the patriarch's life appear to contain dates that are nonsequential, leading one to conclude that either the patriarch lived for an extraordinarily long time, or dates can serve other ritual purposes than simply to document genealogy. Robert Williams examines the situation in detail and proposes some provocative solutions in the present publication. Byron Hamann (1998) has shown that centuries-long genealogies conveyed through primogeniture have rarely, if ever, been accurate enough to calculate truly precise historical dates, so we should probably be thinking in relative terms anyway. Nevertheless, it is significant that the Mixtecs themselves envisioned their world as being created in the tenth century, the time when archaeologists relatively date the outset of the Natividad phase of the Postclassic in the Mixteca Alta.

I find the legend of Lord Eight Wind especially fascinating because his biographers chose not to associate him with a Late Classic Nuiñe dynasty

Figure I.5. (Facing page) Yucuñudahui site map illustrating the principal pyramid and plaza complexes. The elite residential area extends for more than a mile across an adjacent ridge known as Yucu Tnoo, or Black Hill. The ceremonial center dominates the northern end of the Nochixtlan Valley, together with Yucuita, in the same way that Yucu Yoco, Yucu Yuhua, and Mogote del Cacique dominate the southern end of the valley. (Redrawn by John M. D. Pohl after Spores 1984)

at Yucuñudahui but rather the mountain itself and, in the case of Cerro Jasmin, a platform from which grows a flowering tree. It is as if Mixtec nobles wished to connect themselves to the Classic by venerating the ruins, but not the original inhabitants who were actually responsible for constructing them. It is a break with the past administration, but not the landscape they once dominated.

It is also important to remember that the painters of the Mixtec codices were attempting to accommodate broader agendas than simply documenting history. I have proposed that the dates may determine a chronology, but they also signify principal feast days during which the events portrayed in the codices' creation stories were reenacted. Moveable feast cycles characterized ritual life in Oaxaca and are described throughout Mixtec colonial accounts. The sixteenth-century lords who were charged with idolatry in Yanhuitlan were accused of holding four feasts annually. Ten were held at Tilantongo. Many Mixtec feasts were sponsored on local mountaintops at the ruins of Classic period citadels such as Yucuñudahui, Yucuita, Mogote de Cacique, and Yucu Yoco, where the ancestral foundation events depicted in the codices were thought to have taken place (Pohl, Monaghan, and Stiver 1997; Hamann 2002). Caves in adjacent cliffs held the mummies of the principal royal lines, and feasts and associated market fairs were carried out in conjunction with the veneration of the founding ancestors (figure I.6). In contrast to their Eastern Nahua confederates, the Mixtecs and Zapotecs consequently saw little utility in a fixed feast system given the profound environmental differences that characterize Oaxaca (Pohl 2003a:147).

Different Histories, Different Agendas

Ronald Spores has always expressed concern over the relevance of the codices given the notable lack of a place sign for Teposcolula, one of the wealthiest and most powerful kingdoms in the Mixteca Alta at the time of the Spanish entrada (Spores 1967, 1984; Spores and García 2007; Terraciano 2001). Considering the amount of archival material on the administration of the colonial *cacicazgo,* it does present a conundrum. However, it is not entirely true that Teposcolula is absent from the accounts. Two boundary signs for the kingdom appearing in the colonial Codice de Yanhuitlan—Ravine of the Column and Market of the Bird—are depicted as locations visited during the course of a peregrination by the eleventh-century Lord Eight Deer on Zouche-Nuttall page 69. It is also possible that we simply have not identified the correct place sign for the palace; it should be a hill sign with a jewel, signifying Teposcolula's Mixtec name, Yucundaa, but there may be another name associated with the site as well. On the other hand, it may be significant that there is an equally notable lack of colonial documentary material for many of the *cacicazgos* of the Nochixtlan Valley (Terraciano 2001).

Figure I.6. Reconstruction of a boundary festival and market at the ruins of Yucuñudahui, celebrated by surrounding communities including Chachoapan, Yucuita, Chindua, Andua, and Suchixtlan. The Mixtecs continued to plaster over the main plaza at the ruins of the Classic site but purposefully neglected the pyramids and platforms, leaving them as grassy hills. Testimonies recorded during fifteenth-century idolatry trials at Yanhuitlan refer to celebrations on nearby hills involving *voladores*, or "flyers," who appear descending from the central pole in the distance. This celebration commemorates the rituals dedicated to the War from Heaven and the bringing of sacred bundles and other cult objects from the sky, as portrayed in Codex Zouche-Nuttall. (Illustration by John M. D. Pohl)

The bias in pre-Columbian codical emphasis on the Nochixtlan Valley in the northeastern Mixteca Alta, on the one hand, and colonial documentary emphasis on the western Mixteca Alta from Tlaxiaco to Teposcolula on the other may not be coincidental. We see in the Eight Wind story a reflection of a purposeful, even structured formula by which Mixtec aristocrats connected themselves to the remote past by showing their ancestors, priests, and oracles emerging out of the "pre-sunrise" world of the Classic period (Hamann 2002). Archaeological survey of the western Mixteca Alta has demonstrated that although the Late Preclassic Ramos phase at Huamelulpan rivaled or even surpassed comparable developments at Monte Negro and Yucuita, the region did not experience the same level of growth during the subsequent Classic Las Flores phase (Balkansky et al. 2000). Consequently, we can see why the Mixtecs attributed their tenth-century dynasties to Nochixtlan Valley citadels. They really were the ranking Classic period capitals of the Mixteca Alta at the time, and they dominated what would later be recognized as some of the most fertile bottomland in New Spain (figure I.7). Elsewhere I have discussed the subsequent legend of the War from Heaven as an explanation in allegorical terms for the abandonment of Classic sites and the founding of the earliest Postclassic kingdoms. The ensuing eleventh- and twelfth-century conflicts over the inheritance of Tilantongo and Jaltepec—involving Lord Eight Deer, Lady Six Monkey, and Lord Four Wind—then represent an Iliad of the Mixtec people that was played out in the southern Nochixtlan Valley. It is their direct descendants who are subsequently credited with establishing the principal alliances throughout the greater Mixteca Alta, the Baja, the Costa, and the Valley of Oaxaca.

In 1528, Yanhuitlan displayed a codex in a Spanish court that depicted a succession of twenty-four rulers who had governed the kingdom over the previous 500 years. Although the manuscript is now missing, its description

Figure I.7. (Facing page) Map of the principal archaeological zones of the Nochixtlan Valley. The two primary stories portrayed in Codex Zouche-Nuttall obverse are associated with two different versions of the War from Heaven. The first story (ZN pages 3–4) concerns Lord Eight Wind, whose biography focuses on major Classic–Las Flores period sites located in the northern end of the Nochixtlan Valley. The second story (ZN pages 20–21) focuses on the legend of Lady Three Flint, whose biography focuses on major Classic–Las Flores period sites located in the southern end of the Nochixtlan Valley. (Illustration by John M. D. Pohl)

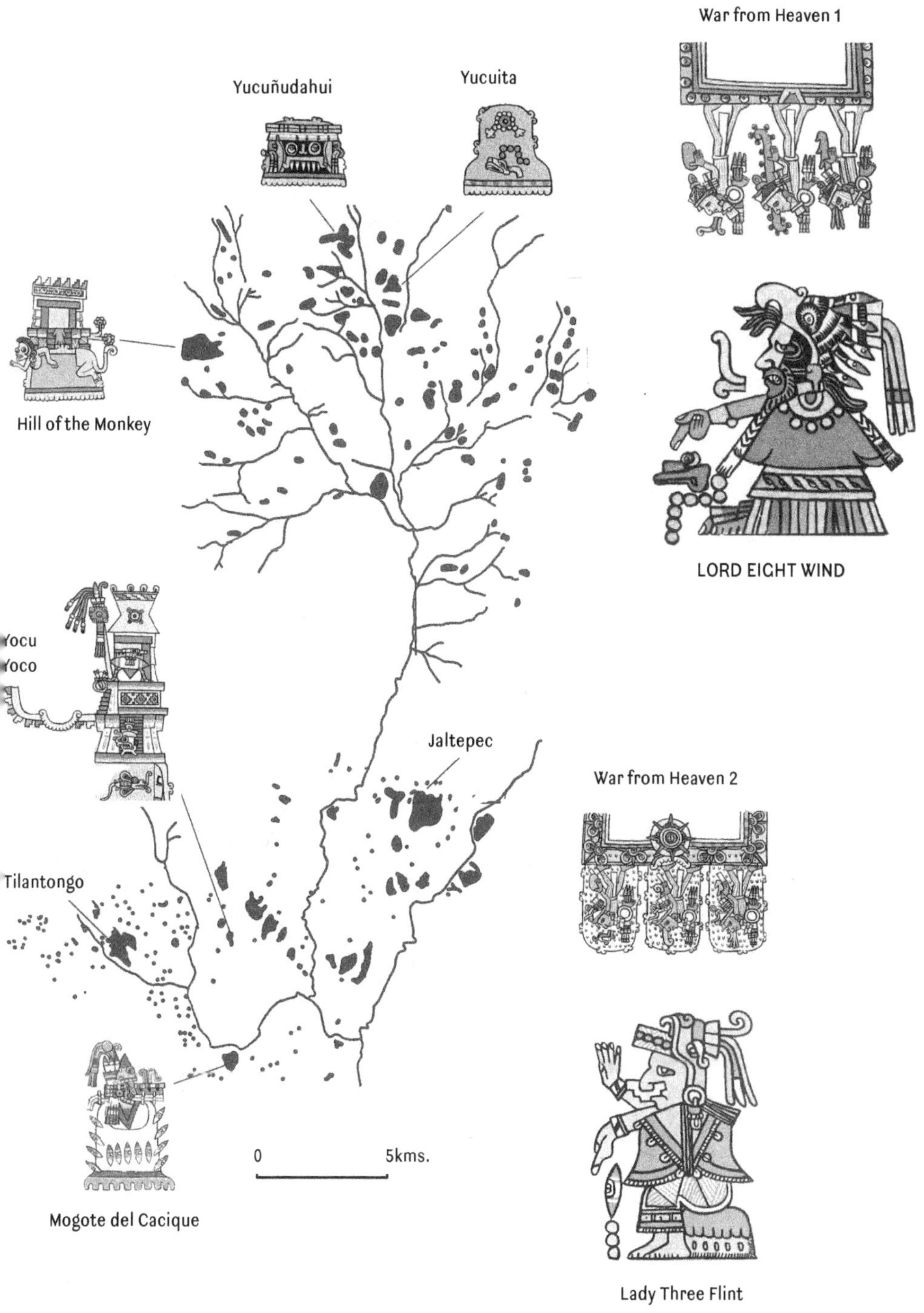

Yucuñudahui

Yucuita

War from Heaven 1

Hill of the Monkey

LORD EIGHT WIND

Yocu
Yoco

Jaltepec

War from Heaven 2

Tilantongo

Mogote del Cacique

0   5kms.

Lady Three Flint

in the court testimonial places Yanhuitlan's earliest ancestors at around AD 1028, the period of Eight Wind. Significantly, the famous legend of the birth of the first ancestors at Apoala was actually recorded at Cuilapan in the Valley of Oaxaca. This kingdom had been ruled by a Mixtec lord of Yanhuitlan who married into the Zapotec royal line of Zaachila. The alliance and the invocation of the legend suggest that Mixtec and Zapotec ethnicity among the nobility was not emphasized through language and behavior, but rather through the invocation of religious stories that differentiated their families. Codex Bodley obverse portrays a genealogy of Tilantongo through twenty-three rulers—from Lord Four Crocodile, who lived around AD 950, to Lord Four Deer, who was ruling in 1519. The account begins with a sequence of marriages between kingdoms that dominated the southern end of the Nochixtlan Valley. The first genealogy ends with the death of the male heirs during the War from Heaven at Yucu Yoco. In 990, Tilantongo creates its first dynasty through marriage with a surviving female. However, when this dynasty also fails at the end of the eleventh century with the suicide of Lord Two Rain, the saga of Lord Eight Deer is recounted to explain the institution of a second Tilantongo dynasty that continued relatively uninterrupted through the time of the Conquest. Several different kingdoms are shown as having intermarried with Tilantongo during the intervening centuries, including Teozacoalco, Tulancingo, Tlaxiaco, Chalcatongo, Jaltepec, and Yanhuitlan.

Other genealogies were structured to associate the families of two or three royal houses into extended alliance corridors. Codex Zouche-Nuttall, for example, follows the Tilantongo genealogy through Eight Deer but then switches to recount first the dynasty of Eight Deer's son at Teozacoalco and later a new dynasty at Zaachila through the marriage of the Teozacoalco Lady Four Rabbit to the Zapotec Lord Five Flower. Partners in these alliances subsequently supplied one another with heirs during times of successional crisis. Eight Deer was not necessarily the preferred heroic ancestor, however. On Codex Bodley reverse the royal houses of Tlaxiaco and Achiutla are portrayed as consistently intermarrying with each other from the thirteenth through the sixteenth centuries. In this case, Tlaxiaco and Achiutla traced their heritage back to Eight Deer's son-in-law and assassin, Lord Four Wind. The two royal houses later became so closely connected that by colonial times they were considered to be a single *cacicazgo*. The Lienzo de Zacatepec indicates that the first lord of that kingdom was appointed by Lord

Four Wind, and he was very likely his son as well (Smith 1973:110–119). There were apparently significant linkages between the kingdoms of Jaltepec, Yanhuitlan, and Cuilapan. A colonial genealogy called "the Yale document" may trace the ancestry of the cacique of Cuilapan back to Jaltepec's Lady Six Monkey, Four Wind's mother and Eight Deer's principal rival for control over the southern Nochixtlan Valley. Codices Selden and Bodley reverse in turn allow us to extend the genealogy of both Tlaxiaco and Jaltepec back to the miraculous birth of the first ancestors from both the rivers of Apoala and a ceiba tree at Achiutla.

The legends in the codices were mythic, propagandistic, theatrical—but they were very real to the people who composed them and are therefore worthy of anthropological analysis in attempts to understand the past from an indigenous perspective. Furthermore, evidence that the alliance corridors charted through them had become so institutionalized by the sixteenth century that they could define territoriality is indicated by the distribution of the three dialectical groups that continue to divide the Mixteca Alta today (figure I.8). The Northeastern Alta dialect extends from Apoala through Yanhuitlan, Jaltepec, and Etla to Cuilapan. The Eastern Alta dialect extends from Coixtlahuaca through Teposcolula and Tilantongo to Teozacoalco, whose eastern boundary is contiguous with Zapotec-speaking Zaachila. The Western Alta dialect extends from Ñumi through Achiutla and Tlaxiaco, south through Zacatepec to the Mixteca Costa. As the Postclassic progressed, political constructions became ever more intricate and widespread throughout Oaxaca as lesser-ranking kingdoms sought to increase their status by intermarrying with the highest-ranking royal lines.

In the fifteenth century, Teozacoalco played a particularly significant role and even became the dominant partner in its alliance with Tilantongo. Given the competitive factionalism that characterized Mixtec dynastic affairs, we should not be surprised to see that the most powerful *cacicazgos* at the time of the Spanish entrada were not necessarily the oldest. Survey of the western Mixteca Alta demonstrates that by the late fifteenth century the region had experienced an unprecedented level of expansion, with kingdoms such as Teposcolula, Tlaxiaco, and Achiutla evolving into prosperous city-states that far surpassed their counterparts in the Nochixtlan and Oaxaca valleys in size and complexity (Balkansky et al. 2000).

Wealth and power did not necessarily coincide with prestige in Postclassic southern Mexico. The ranking houses of Tlaxcala are certainly not

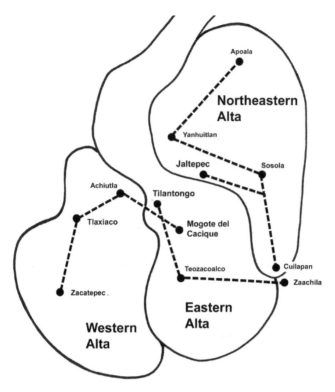

Figure I.8. Dialectical areas appear to correspond to primary Mixtec alliance corridors. (Illustration by John M. D. Pohl)

the largest or most complex archaeologically (García Cook 1981:273–274). Zaachila was said to be the highest-ranked royal house of the Zapotecs, and yet the ruins of its palace are hardly impressive compared to Yagul (Blanton et al. 1982:129). By the same token we know virtually nothing about Yagul's royal family from the historical sources, suggesting that its nobles may have held secondary rank. We should also consider the possibility that we are dealing with a traveling nobility comparable to medieval European princes who moved from one residence to another, living off stores until they were depleted, after which the farming population labored to replenish them in preparation for their return. We know that Zapotec nobles, for example, maintained palaces both within their own territories and at Mitla. By comparison, Nine House appears as both a lord of Teozacoalco and Tilantongo in codices Bodley and Selden, even though Tilantongo apparently had its own ruler as well.

Who or What Was Lord Eight Wind?

Codex Zouche-Nuttall depicts a history, but a unique kind of history in that it reflects how the Mixtecs themselves viewed their social and political cosmos without the bias of western European interpretation. In fact it is the longest continuous history known for any indigenous people in the Western Hemisphere. Marshall Sahlins (1983:517) proposed that historians trained from a western European perspective have been arguing over two polar ideas. Many support the analysis of an elite history, narrated with its partiality to higher politics, while others favor the study of the would-be life of communities. Actually both positions merely reflect the evolution of thought since the first empirical treatments made by the Classical Greeks. Sahlins proposed, therefore, that many traditional societies did, and still do, maintain a different kind of historical tradition that might better be described as "heroic history."

In such societies "heroes" are seen as persons who were considered extraordinary during their lifetime, who were honored after death by public worship, and who were usually ascribed some degree of divinity. Heroic history, then, is usually elite genealogical history. It is not evenly distributed in the society, as it is in and of itself a symbol of politico-religious authority reserved for the ruling class. If, as Sahlins originally proposed, different cultural orders have their own ways of reckoning historical action, consciousness, and determination, it should be possible to identify some aspects of Mixtec social organization on the basis of what they thought necessary to communicate. Above and beyond the fact that the ancient Mixtec nobility were so obviously concerned with time-reckoning and genealogical accounts, what is most notable is the emphasis on place signs and therefore the geography of creation stories like that of Lord Eight Wind. Elsewhere I have proposed that one cannot discuss the politics of Mixtec kinship hierarchies without also discussing the way in which the kinship segments defined by the genealogies had distributed themselves over the landscape. Like the elite kinship structure, the division of the land was justified by mytho-historical events involving founding ancestors of the various kin group segments, described in colonial sources as *linajes,* or lineages (Pohl 1984:133). I therefore propose that:

1. Lineage maintained social order and defined the kinship segments of the society.

2. Lineage was tied to the land through some form of genealogical record on the division of the territory by the society's founding ancestors.

3. The land was therefore used to prove the genealogies and kinship group affiliation, for aside from violent seizure or community fission (acts depicted in the codices as well), the very fact that an individual or group was occupying it was used to demonstrate that it must have inherited it through established rules of property transference laid out by the first ancestors.

4. Thus all land owners must have had to trace the title to their territory through their genealogy. By doing this, they were coincidentally reaffirming lineal affiliations with other parts of their segment, and of their segment to other segments.

Nowhere are these principles more graphically portrayed in allegory than in the portrayal of Eight Wind as literally a personification of the earth itself. From this perspective the fact of whether Eight Wind was an actual historical personage or not is irrelevant to anthropological study, for he had been transformed into something more of a structural principle in the rationalization of the Mixtec social hierarchy and land distribution of the Late Postclassic period than a historical individual. But by the same token we know that he was also the subject of religious veneration, and given our understanding of how the codices were used in feasts and other ritual displays, he must have been the focus of considerable dramatic attention. It is the latter perspective that intrigues Robert Williams. There have been many commentaries written about the codices, but for the most part they have been simply annals or lists of events. In this regard, Williams departs from the more standard approach and provides us with a literary interpretation that I hope will point the way to more humanistic insights into the minds of ancient nobles that are equally worthy of our scholarly endeavors.

Notes

1. In my 2004 article "The Archaeology of History in Postclassic Oaxaca" (2004b), I responded to critique of my research in the southern end of the Nochixtlan Valley and provided new site identifications that prove conclusively that Tilantongo's Postclassic dynasty claimed its heritage from an earlier regional Classic urban center of some 7,000–12,000 people extending between Yute Coo, Mogote del Cacique, Yucu Yoco, and Yucu Yuhua, rather than Monte Alban, as others have pro-

posed (Pohl 2004b). Unfortunately, the volume editors, Hendon and Joyce, never sent me a proof of the article before going to press, and some confusion over Yucu Yoco, or Hill of the "Bee," and Yucu Yuhua, or Hill of the "Bet," resulted when the manuscript was spell-checked electronically and "bet" was changed to "bee." The second paragraph on page 221 therefore should read: "A few weeks later, my survey team encountered ruins on Hill of the *Bet*. . . ." The caption for figure 9.1 (p. 223) should read: "The site is contiguous with Yucu Yuhua or Hill of the Enclosure (also known as Hill of the *Bet* or Hill of Chocolate)." Another addendum is that the caption for figure 9.2 (p. 225) should be corrected to: "To the *east,* Yucu Cui descends to the Yute Coo or River of the Serpent from which Nine Wind's ancestors were magically born." Finally, the editors identified me as an independent researcher in their list of contributors to the book, but in fact I was Peter Jay Sharp Curator and Lecturer in the Arts of the Ancient Americas at Princeton University and have never been an independent scholar.

2. Two Rain was the last surviving member of Tilantongo's first dynasty. His father, Lord Five Earthquake, married Six Monkey's sister, Lady Four Death. When Four Death didn't produce an heir, he married Lady Two Grass, with whom he had Two Rain. Two Rain apparently went to live with his great-great-grandfather Lord Eight Wind. Following his conference with the patriarch he appears at Yucu Yua/ Hill of the Ballcourt or Tlachitongo, located a few kilometers south of Cerro Jasmin (Pohl 2004b:230, 233, 235). Ten Eagle of Jaltepec had lost three sons in war, perhaps fighting against Five Earthquake, his nephew. In any event, he decided to marry his daughter Lady Six Monkey to Lord Eleven Wind of Red and White Bundle rather than Two Rain of Tilantongo. Old Eight Wind was apparently angry that Two Rain was not to marry Six Monkey and sent his son Three Lizard to attack Ten Eagle. The attack failed and Three Lizard was captured and killed.

Later Two Rain committed suicide. He appears in Codex Bodley driving an arrow into his chest, after which one of Six Monkey's priests, Lord Snake/Digging Stick, directs his spirit to ascend into heaven. Possessing no legitimate heir, control of Tilantongo was left to Lord Twelve Earthquake and Lord Eight Deer, the sons of Tilantongo's high priest, Lord Five Crocodile. When Twelve Earthquake was assassinated, Eight Deer blamed Lord Eleven Wind, who was not only the oldest living member of the extended family but also lord of Tilantongo's rival, Red and White Bundle. After Eight Deer conquered Red and White Bundle, Eleven Wind and Six Monkey were both killed. A year later, Eleven Wind's first-born sons, Ten Dog and Six House, were also executed. Their mother was in fact Eight Deer's half-sister. Doubtless they represented a personal threat to Eight Deer's claim as the founder of a new dynasty. Six Monkey's own son, Lord Four Wind, on the other hand, was either spared or escaped. He later married Eight Deer's daughter and was even present at Eight Deer's assassination many years later. By the time of the Spanish Conquest, nearly every Mixtec royal house could claim direct descent from Eight Deer, Six Monkey, or Four Wind.

3. In Codex Borgia, the geographical locatives signifying hills, rivers, and valleys, so characteristic of Mixtec codices, are almost entirely absent. The reasons for the differing sensibility in landscape and ritual between the Mixtec and Nahua codices are due to variant forms of social and ritual behavior reflected in elite settlement patterns. For the most part, Eastern Nahua ritualism was focused on densely settled urban centers that did not demand the kind of toponymic referencing that we see for the Mixtec (Pohl 2003b:244).

4. Legends are still told in the Tilantongo Valley of ancient lords who could move through the earth to bring water to communities—an idea that does have a basis in observable fact. Some of the longest cave networks in the world, extending over 20 kilometers, have been mapped in Oaxaca, the Sistema Huatla being the most famous. They feature underground rivers, lakes, and waterfalls.

Bibliography

Balkansky, Andrew K., S. A. Kowalewski, V. Perez Rodriguez, T. J. Pluckhahn, C. A. Smith, L. R. Stiver, J. Beliaev, J. F. Chamblee, V. Y. Heredia Espinoza, and R. Santos Perez

2000   Archaeological Survey in the Mixteca Alta of Oaxaca. *Mexico Journal of Field Archaeology* 27(4):365–389.

Blanton, Richard E., Stephen A. Kowalewski, Gary Feinman, and Jill Appel

1982   *Monte Alban's Hinterland, Part 1: Prehispanic Settlement Patterns of the Central and Southern Parts of the Valley of Oaxaca, Mexico.* Prehistory and Human Ecology of the Valley of Oaxaca, Vol. 7. Edited by Kent V. Flannery and Richard A. Blanton. Memoirs of the University of Michigan, No. 15. Ann Arbor: Museum of Anthropology.

Byland, Bruce, and John M. D. Pohl

1994   *In the Realm of 8 Deer: The Archaeology of the Mixtec Codices.* Norman and London: University of Oklahoma Press.

Caso, Alfonso

1960   *Interpretación del Codex Bodley 2858.* México D.F.: Sociedad Mexicana de Antropología.

de Burgoa, Francisco

1934   *Geográfica descripción.* 2 vols. Publicaciones, Vols. 25–26. Mexico: Archivo
[1674]   General de la Nación.

García Cook, Angel

1981   The Historical Importance of Tlaxcala in the Development of the Central Highlands. In *Supplement to the Handbook of Middle American Indians,* Vol. 1, pp. 244–276. General Editor: Victoria Reifler Bricker. Volume Editor: Jeremy A. Sabloff with the Assistance of Patricia A. Andrews. Austin: University of Texas Press.

Hamann, Byron

1998   First-Born Son of a First-Born Son? Discontinuous Succession in the Co-
        dex Selden. *Indiana Journal of Hispanic Literatures* 13:53–58.

2002   The Social Life of Pre-Sunrise Things: Indigenous Mesoamerican Archae-
        ology. *Current Anthropology* 43(3):351–382.

Pohl, John M. D.

1984   The Earth Lords: Politics and Symbolism of the Mixtec Codices. Ph.D.
        dissertation. UCLA Archaeology Program. Manuscript in author's
        possession.

1998   Themes of Drunkenness, Violence, and Factionalism in Tlaxcalan Altar-
        Ofrenda Paintings. *RES* 33:184–207.

2003a   Ritual Ideology and Commerce in the Southern Mexican Highlands. In
        The Postclassic Mesoamerican World, edited by Michael Smith and Fran-
        ces Berdan, pp. 172–177. Salt Lake City: University of Utah Press.

2003b   Royal Marriage and Confederacy Building among the Eastern Nahuas,
        Mixtecs, and Zapotecs. In *The Postclassic Mesoamerican World,* edited by
        Michael Smith and Frances Berdan, pp. 243–248. Salt Lake City: Univer-
        sity of Utah Press.

2004a   Screenfold Manuscripts of Highland Mexico and Their Possible Influence
        on Codex Madrid. In *The Madrid Codex,* pp. 367–413.

2004b   The Archaeology of History in Postclassic Oaxaca. In *Mesoamerican
        Archaeology,* edited by Julia Hendon and Rosemary Joyce. Malden, Mas-
        sachusetts: Blackwell Publishers.

Pohl, John M. D., John Monaghan, and Laura Stiver

1997   Religion, Economy and Factionalism in Mixtec Boundary Zones. In
        Códices y documentos sobre México, Segundo Simposio Volumen I, edited
        by Salvador Rueda Smithers, Constanza Vega Sosa, and Rodrigo Mar-
        tínez Baracs, pp. 205–232. México: Instituto Nacional de Antropología e
        Historia.

Pohl, John M. D., and Javier Urcid Serrano

2006   A Zapotec Carved Bone. *Princeton University Library Chronicle*
        67(2):225–236.

Rabin, Emily

2002   Toward a Unified Chronology of the Historical Codices and Pictorial
        Manuscripts of the Mixteca Alta, Costa, and Baja: An Overview. In *Ho-
        menaje a John Paddock,* edited by Patricia Plunket, pp. 100–132. Puebla:
        Fundación Universidad de las Américas.

Sahlins, Marshall

1983   Other Times, Other Customs: The Anthropology of History. *American
        Antiquity* 85(3):517–544.

Smith, M. E.

1973   *Picture Writing from Ancient Southern Mexico: Mixtec Place Signs and Maps.* Norman: University of Oklahoma Press.

Spores, Ronald

1967   *The Mixtec Kings and Their People.* Norman: University of Oklahoma Press.

1984   *The Mixtecs in Ancient and Colonial Times.* Norman: University of Oklahoma Press.

Spores, Ronald, and Nelly Robles García

2007   A Prehispanic (Postclassic) Capital Center in Colonial Transition: Excavations at Yucundaa Pueblo Viejo de Teposcolula, Oaxaca, Mexico. *Latin American Antiquity* 18(3):333–353.

Terraciano, Kevin

2001   *The Mixtecs of Colonial Oaxaca: Ñudzahui History, Sixteenth through Eighteenth Centuries.* Stanford, California: Stanford University Press.

PART ONE

1   It Happened Long Ago

The Far Places of the Earth: Ancient Oaxaca

When some of us want vacation, education, or adventure, we think in terms of space; that is, we travel a distance across the planet to achieve our goals. Anthropologists, art historians, and archaeologists travel spatially and ideologically across the planet to achieve the goals of social science, but, like sci-fi heroes, these adventurers in history also travel through time as well. The purpose of these great adventures of mind and knowledge is to illuminate modern humanity and its civilizations by connecting them securely to the past. Therefore, history is recovered before history was written, and given to us so that we may understand, at least to some degree, who and what we are, where we came from, how we got here, and, perhaps, where we are going.

These scientists of societies merely continue a noble human tradition in the pursuit of their endeavors. That is to say, it would seem that we human beings always try to preserve and pass on knowledge of what came before. This activity is ancient: it preceded the invention of alphabets and writing. It is rooted in memory and language, and transmitted from generation to generation, often by remembered stories. Storytelling is a vital activity that ensures the survival of succeeding generations. It is a gift to our children, a foundation stone of culture.

Long ago, in ancient Oaxaca, the Mixtec Indians did as we all do; namely, they passed on their memories of the past to succeeding generations. However, they were not Europeans; neither were they from the Middle East, nor from the Far East, nor from Africa. When Mixtecs developed their own form of writing to encode and transmit history and their knowledge of it, there was no European precedent. They did it in their own way using narrative pictograms painted elegantly on the panels of fan-folded books. With the passing of time and cultural changes, the culture-dependent hieroglyphic writing of earlier times (perhaps Olmec, then Zapotec and Mayan) ceased in general use, and pictograms, which were not language-dependent and were to some extent transcultural, persisted. Oral histories—genealogies, histories of great heroes, wars, and marriages—unfolded in the fan-folded panel pages of the codices. These were (and are) great treasures because the Mixtec Indians of Oaxaca were masters of codex painting, and the codices are even more precious now because so few of them remain. By the happenstance of history, eight Mixtec manuscripts survived the European invasion subsequent to the discovery of the "New World." Of the pre-Conquest Mayan books, only four are extant, and from the extensive pre-Hispanic Aztec corpus, none. Several examples of ceremonial and prognostication codices in the Borgia Group do survive and are the subject of intensive study by certain scholars, notably Elizabeth Hill Boone.

This present book is an attempt to tell Mixtec "stories": their history as they understood it. These people were not us. They had no sharp dividing line in their minds between what we call the "physical" and the "metaphysical." They were deeply religious. This quality of indigenous cognition in culture prevailed whether in Native American peoples north, central, or south. Theirs was an integrated, interactive universe in which spirituality and daily life were continuous, contiguous processes. As explained by John Lame Deer, a Miniconju Sioux, Native Americans

> live in a world of symbols where the spiritual and the commonplace are one. To you, symbols are just words, spoken or written in a book. To us, they are a part of nature, part of ourselves—the earth, the sun, the wind and the rain, stones, trees, animals, even little insects like ants and grasshoppers. We try to understand them not with the head but with the heart, and we need no more than a hint to give us the meaning. (quoted in Newton and Hyslop 1992:9–10)

We are going to read those rarest of all things: stories, history, biographies, and genealogies from original, pre-contact books written by a literate society of Native Americans living in what is now the Mexican state of Oaxaca.

Although the Mixtecs of old Oaxaca would be pleased to know that we still read their books and learn from them, they did not write them for us. Therefore, the world they recorded seems both strange and wonderful, and perhaps, as does our modern world, at times frightening. One of the Mixtec codices, Codex Vindobonensis Mexicanus I (commonly referred to as Codex Vienna), deals with marvelous things described by the royal Mixtec scribes, who tell us of their world as they understood it, and as their gods manipulated it.

It is actually two documents: an older obverse and newer reverse. The first three pages of the Vienna obverse document provide a good introduction to this present study. With a little imagination, and a great deal of abbreviation, it says this: "It happened long ago when sky and earth were one, the gods sanctified Oaxaca." We are going to travel in time and space to *that* Oaxaca—where the ancient Mixtecs lived and where their modern descendants still reside. In a sense, the Mixtecs provide us with insight into one specific Native American pre-Conquest culture that, to some extent, reflects the level of developmental potential of all native cultures prior to the Europeans' arrival. The insight they give us is breathtaking.

Although this book includes chapters on various topics that augment the subject matter revealed in the Mixtec codex stories, the proper subject of this book is the first eight pages of Codex Zouche-Nuttall obverse (Vienna's sister document). The protagonist of these first eight pages is Lord Eight Wind Eagle Flints of Suchixtlan. Therefore, the purpose of this material is to detail the history of Lord Eight Wind and to define him as his Mixtec descendants understood him.

Eight Wind was a mighty demigod/priest, the founder of an enduring lineage, and a great instrument for social change—alive and dead. He was born in AD 935 and lived for ninety-two years. His great-grandson called him back from the dead when Eight Wind would have been more than 140 years old, and this consultation started a war. His life spanned one of the most turbulent periods of change in Mixtec history, and his family was extant through the matriline when the Spanish arrived in Oaxaca in AD 1521. Because he was positively and powerfully remembered among the later Mixtec scribes of the northern Nochixtlan Valley in Oaxaca, his story begins the political history of his people, and through him the Mixtec histories enter into the arena of world civilizations. His story also involves the biographies of other great Mixtecs who lived later: his granddaughter, Lady Six Monkey, warrior queen of Jaltepec; his great-grandson, the ill-fated Lord Two Rain Twenty Jaguars of Tilantongo; and Lord Eight Deer Jaguar Claw, the usurper of Tilantongo, who was unrelated to them but who became king by his own hand.

These great individuals and their deeds live for us in vivid pictogram text, and Lord Eight Deer Jaguar Claw—having the most extensive biographical material in the Mixtec codices—will have more than a passing appearance. As was Lord Eight Wind of Suchixtlan, Lord Eight Deer of Tilantongo was the man of his day. Therefore, in one way or another, these great heroes are pivotal figures in Mixtec history.

Sadly, we can never understand the Mixtec histories exactly as they wrote them because much of the narrative oral history between pictogram tableaux in the codices is lost forever. This demands comparison of various codices because, occasionally, we can find cognate scenes among Mixtec manuscripts elaborating similar data. Sometimes we encounter folklore that does the same. However, in general, most of the details of the memorized stories highlighted in the codices are unavailable to us. For this reason, there is a problem—not only of incomplete content, but also of interpretation.

The Problem of Interpretation

Codex Zouche-Nuttall obverse (museum numbered pages 1–41) is known as the most mysterious and resistant to interpretation of all codices in the recognized canon of Mixtec manuscripts, including its "sister" manuscript, Codex Vienna (Pohl, pers. comm., 1999). The manuscript is composed of two documents: the older "reverse" (ZN pages 42–84) is the political biography of Lord Eight Deer Jaguar Claw of Tilantongo. The newer Codex Zouche-Nuttall obverse (pages 1–41) consists of three narrative sagas connected by various events and genealogies. Each saga is discrete from preceding and succeeding texts, although the War from Heaven unfolds from two different perspectives in Sagas 1 and 2. Comment on the codex obverse is scanty. In her introduction to the 1987 edition of Codex Zouche-Nuttall, Troike observes:

> Scholars have made brief studies of sections of topics in the Zouche-Nuttall, but out of deference to [Alfonso] Caso's role as virtual founder of the field, no one wrote a commentary to the codex. As a result, the contents of the manuscript have never been explained in any detail, and without such an explanation as a guide to the difficulties in the pictorial text, the codex is not utilized as frequently as other Mixtec texts. (26)

Troike implies that Caso wrote no commentaries on Zouche-Nuttall obverse because of the manuscript's opaque text. It is simply resistant to interpretation.

Because this array of narrative in the obverse of Codex Zouche-Nuttall is not only mysterious and extremely diverse, it is desirable in the following pages to analyze, interpret, and detail the first of them, the history of Lord Eight Wind of Suchixtlan (pages 1–8). However, Lord Eight Wind Eagle Flints' story explores a complex problem existing in several narratives, all of which are necessary for a successful, comprehensive interpretation. Perhaps these sectional narratives are sequential songs or poems. This book explores several major points of interpretation.

To begin, the first eight pages present Lord Eight Wind Eagle Flints as a historical personage throughout both parts that describe his life (ZN pages 1–2, 5–6a). In the literature, only one historical date assignment has been made relative to the second part of Eight Wind's biography (Byland and Pohl 1994:238). The Mixtec scribes tell us the first fifty-two years of his life were spent as a supernatural *santo,* and the last forty years of it as a patriarch and lineage founder—a history that will be recounted in the following chapters.

Second, native chronology will be employed and subsequently interpreted as written in the narrative itself. The chronology of pages 1–8 displays twenty-six dates, including the one established by Byland and Pohl. These dates provide a reasonable chronological sequence that places the biography of Lord Eight Wind into the context of a human lifespan. Of even more significance is that this chronology demonstrates that Eight Wind's biography records founding events of the Epiclassic culture of his people, the Mixtecs. He lived from AD 935 to AD 1027, and this span is adequate to define the Epiclassic period (a transition involving social reformation from the Late Classic to the Early Postclassic) for the Nochixtlan Valley Mixtecs.

Third, the entire text establishes 165 years of pre-Hispanic history of the Mixtec people, which their royal scribes wrote as beginning in AD 935 (page 1) and ending in this particular narrative in AD 1100 (page 8), well into the Mixtec Postclassic period and the biography of Lord Eight Deer Jaguar Claw. The recovered history is political, ceremonial, military, biographical, and genealogical.

Fourth, despite the fact that both codices Zouche-Nuttall and Vienna have been known as related documents from the time of Zelia Nuttall's 1902 commentary in the Peabody Museum edition of the manuscript bearing her name, it is necessary to draw comparisons between them not previously explored in the extant literature. These comparisons demonstrate that they are linked by at least one historical date, two ceremonies, one shared chronological sequence, and many personnel. The shared date is especially important because Codex Vienna obverse and, to some extent, Codex Zouche-Nuttall obverse have been considered documents without historical dates, thus recording only allegorical or nondurational time (Pohl 2004a:390). At least two of these native manuscripts—Vienna (and, by implication, Zouche-

Nuttall)—are linked not only by persons and places they both record, but also because they were linked at the time Hernán Cortés arrived in Mexico in 1519. Therefore, at least one shared native date is both reasonable and expected.[1]

This study also attempts an exercise in an unusual type of ethnography, especially since the Mixtec scribes writing long ago are employed here as cultural informants. The subject is one of vital interest because, since the Spanish entrada into Oaxaca in 1521, the Mixtec Indians (and all Native Americans, no matter their location and source of contact with Europeans) have been rendered people without history. The admirable Mexican scholar Alfonso Caso (who determined the ethnicity of the Mixtec codices) was very clear about this in his article "The Map of Teozacoalco," published in 1949.

> It is very common when speaking about the history of America to say that it be-gan with the [European] Conquerors and the first Spanish chroniclers and that [beforehand] the Indians have no written history: [implying] therefore, that the surviving written accounts that refer to the remote past of native peoples were recorded only when the Indians learned to write in Spanish after the Con-quest. . . .
>
> This opinion is completely false. The Indians not only of Mexico, but from the whole of Mesoamerica, possessed a true historical vocation, and they told and wrote history. . . .
>
> Unfortunately, both in Yucatan (Mani) and in Mexico (Texcoco), Landa and Zumarraga burned a large number of indigenous manuscripts, actions that de-stroyed forever many historical works. . . .
>
> It is a cruel injustice that, after burning the Indian histories, [the Spanish] denied that the Indians wrote them.

I can only add one thing to Dr. Caso's remarks: the Spanish denied that the Indians could even *write.*

I use the word "unusual" to describe this book as an exercise in ethnogra-phy because the native informants have been deceased for 600 or 700 years, and they wrote about historical events occurring more than a thousand years ago: events which, in some cases, were almost 400 years before their time. These anonymous royal scribes are our informers and our primary sources.

"Ethnography" also applies to the Mixtec manuscripts in an unusual sense because the artifacts themselves speak and inform, not a living hu-

---

1. Zelia Nuttall first advanced the connection with Cortés in 1902; nevertheless, not all scholars agree with it.

man being functioning as informer so as to have his words translated and written in an alien language. In a real sense they are vocalizations of deceased humans who function as timeless informers of culture. The manuscripts are written in icons: symbols like language, but without phonemes and grammar. They are provocateurs of image, environmental symbols imbued with a transcultural load of meaning. I, now or recently so, can have the phenomena represented affect me, but I as native informer's subject must be affected by them in the ancient sense, somehow discovering the elements of original meaning and appreciating their transformation and translation across time within myself. The observer is, in a sense, written by them because the observer's meaning is empowered with a new consciousness transmitted from antiquity. Words spoken or written are deleted in one genre (codices), impelled by a different genre (communication to an observer), but experience of original songs and impulses is conveyed and created by unusual evocation in yet another (interpretation by an observer). Tyler's correlation of ethnography and poetry is insightful: "ethnography is a cooperatively evolved text consisting of fragments of discourse intended to evoke in the minds of both reader and writer an emergent fantasy" (1986:125).

The Mixtec manuscripts are narrative, performance discourse. Perhaps they and their evocative content are culture's poetry, for true representations of environmental phenomena and to some extent cross-cultural translation are shared a-linguistically by all who encounter them, even those who do not recognize the word "Mixtec" as signifying both a people and an Otomangean language. Non-Mixtec observers are empowered to share the native cultural system of meaning and integrate it with their own. This transaction is both effective ethnology and divorced from it as original native narrative experience becomes contemporary in content and context. This is not paradox: it is the apprehension and appreciation of meaning embodied in Mixtec history as they tell us the great deeds of their heroes, their gods, their fathers and mothers, their illustrious royal progenitors.

Significance of the Problem: A Focus

This text explores certain problems about the chronological and ideological interpretations of Codex Zouche-Nuttall pages 1–8 as a document of Native American history written by Native Americans. The central figure of this history is Lord Eight Wind Eagle Flints, who has been interpreted as both a historical figure (Byland and Pohl 1994:238) and as a supernatural figure whose life is told in terms of ceremonies, with no clear distinction between history and myth itself (Furst 1978b:4b). He exemplifies Dennis Tedlock's term, "mythhistory" (1985:64). Therefore, in the literature, Lord Eight Wind seems both fish and fowl: sometimes one, sometimes the other, giving us a certain truth to explore. The native chronology associated with him—especially for the first part of his life—seems metaphorical; thus he stands in Homeric or Virgilian fashion as floating free from time itself.

Mixtec use of dates as historical markers has been established, however, and is clarified in the literature by the work of Emily Rabin. In the majority of their surviving manuscripts (Zouche-Nuttall reverse, Vienna reverse, Bodley, Selden, and what can be deciphered of the Colombino-Becker I fragments, now called Codex Alfonso Caso), the Mixtecs recorded chronologies fixing events securely in time. The difficulty in other texts lies in determining when chronology is literal, when it is allegorical, and when it is used as an admixture of both (Troike 1978:555). Here is a clue: the Mixtecs recorded absolute time in their 365-day vague solar calendar, and they recorded absolute and/or metaphorical time in the 260-day sacred calendar. The one known example of both integrated calendars used as metaphor is Year 1 Reed Day 1 Alligator, which always means "beginning" yet is not necessarily exempt from calendrical time-measuring. More explication of this subject appears in the section titled "Method: Calendars, Chronology, and Scribal Errors."

Codex Zouche-Nuttall obverse consists of three sagas connected by genealogies. Lord Eight Wind's pages are first (pages 1–8), the Ladies Three Flint pages second (pages 14–22), and the Four Lords from Apoala third (pages 36–39). In Lord Eight Wind's saga/biography, twenty-six dates are used in the course of eight pages (3.25 dates per page). In the Ladies Three Flint saga, only fifteen dates appear in the nine pages, and at least two of those are allegorical (1.4 dates per page). The third saga has five dates on four pages (1.25 dates per page).

Because the first saga relies more on temporal markers, it is fair to ask if Lord Eight Wind's story fits within the framework of a possible human lifetime. In the course of this investigation two more questions are asked: what is the order of the historical events recorded, and what is the purpose of the first eight pages of Codex Zouche-Nuttall? A necessary but ancillary series of questions concerns the relationship of, and interaction between, events in both manuscripts, Zouche-Nuttall and Vienna.

The three sagas of Codex Zouche-Nuttall obverse are dramatic performance narratives (Byland and Pohl 1994:9) and sometimes little-understood statements by an indigenous people about the foundation of their complex culture centuries prior to contact with Europeans. This analysis provides recovery, definition, and insight into a portion of Mixtec history literally written in Mixtec style.

Stated in brief, the Classic period Mayans wrote their elite histories from approximately AD 100 to AD 1000. The Postclassic period Mixtecs wrote theirs about events that occurred from AD 935, and slightly before, until and after the arrival of the Spanish in Oaxaca in AD 1521. Interpretation of the Mixtec manuscripts provides historical sequences of events for a transitional period of Mesoamerican history beginning in the Epiclassic era, a time of great cultural reformation.

Mixtec history was interconnected as to eras, as is all history. Although this text focuses on the biographical history of Lord Eight Wind Eagle Flints, his history is continuous with history of later times. That is how the Mixtecs understood it, and although their viewpoint does not make this present task easy, it does make it interesting because we readers acquire both data and insight exactly as the ancient scribes set it down.

Definition of Terms

Technical terms will be defined in text as they occur. However, for general purposes, Mesoamerican cultural eras occur within a specific timeline that can vary somewhat from source to source (table 1.1). As mentioned, the Mixtec transitional era called "Epiclassic" corresponds roughly to the life of Lord Eight Wind Eagle Flints, our protagonist. Individuals' names are their birthdays (number and day) in the sacred calendar; therefore, birth-name numbers are spelled out in text, while actual dates such as Year 1 Reed Day 4 Flint employ numerals.

The phrase "Middle America" refers to a geographical zone that includes territory from the Isthmus of Panama northward through the Sonoran and Chihuahuan deserts of northern Mexico and the southwestern United States (Evans 2004:19). However, "Mesoamerica" refers to a culture area that begins somewhat south of the U.S. border and ends north of the Isthmus of Panama (Evans 2004:19). This study focuses on Mesoamerican territory in the modern Mexican state of Oaxaca. A laudable tendency among recent commentators is to use original Mixtec language names for various towns

Table 1.1. Mesoamerican Cultural Eras

Early Formative	1600–1200 BC
Middle Formative	1200–900 BC
Late Formative	900–250 BC
Preclassic	250 BC–AD 100
Classic	AD 100–800
Early Postclassic	AD 800–1200
Middle Postclassic	AD 1200–1400
Late Postclassic	AD 1400–1521

mentioned in the codices (Troike 1978; Pohl, variously; Jansen and Jimenez 2005). "Añute" is Mixtec for the town of Santa Magdalena Jaltepec; "Yuta Tñoho" is Santiago Apoala; "Nuu Tnoo" is Santiago Tilantongo; and the Mixtec themselves are "Ñuu Dzaui," or "Rain People." Non-Mixtec terminology is a combination of later Nahautl and Spanish colonial nomenclature and is retained here because it is commonly used on official maps and in previous scholarly work.

Sources of Data

Primary data sources are drawn from photographic facsimiles of the Mixtec codices themselves, and these manuscripts are described and illustrated in text and listed in the bibliography. Secondary sources include various authors and their publications, cited in text and listed in the bibliography.

Geographical data about Oaxaca comes from electronic documents available on the Internet, cited in the bibliography as "electronic documents." Some illustrations by Dr. John M. D. Pohl (Princeton University Art Museum) from the undated FAMSI Web site section titled "Pohl's Mesoamerica" are used with permission and identified in text.

Interpretation of Mixtec codices must be to some extent inferential since they are mnemonic pictogram texts written in sequential tableaux and intended to supplement oral tradition as memorized and recited by royal bards. In reference to this book, some interpretation is original and based on my research not only in codex pictorial tableaux, but also on the physical structure of the artifacts themselves. I assert that the application of cautious inference based on intrinsic evidence is valid because were we to restrict this investigation only to scientifically verifiable data, many interesting areas of valid research would be negated, and such evidence as is presented rendered vague or inaccessible (Paddock 1985b:358).

Method: Calendars, Chronology, and Scribal Errors

I have mentioned previously that codex interpretation involves an important native technology; namely, the Mixtec use of the Mesoamerican calendar. Methodology used herein employs the Mesoamerican calendar round corresponded with the European calendar to establish events recorded on pages 1–8 of Codex Zouche-Nuttall (and other native manuscripts) as historical events in the lifetime of the protagonist, Lord Eight Wind Eagle Flints. In doing so, Lord Eight Wind's position in the Mixtec culture of the Epiclassic (the transition from Classic to Postclassic for the Mixtecs) and Early Postclassic will be explicated chronologically, his family detailed, and the foundational culture of the Mixtec Indians of Oaxaca demonstrated as a chronological progression of historical events, many of them religious ceremonies.

As already mentioned, there is debate on the allegorical versus absolute nature of Mixtec temporal markers, and this discussion appears in the literature (Furst 1978:69–72; Pohl 2004:390). In fact, Furst (1978ak:69, citing Caso 1954:12–13) has asserted that the Mixtec date Year 13 Rabbit Day 2 Deer has no European calendar equivalent at all. Therefore, much has been said about nontemporal, nondurational time (Jansen 1988:156–192). I have also noted that most Mixtec manuscripts—Zouche-Nuttall reverse, Bodley, Vienna reverse, Selden—have no difficulty recording literal chronology. However, agreement between manuscripts—and even events in one manuscript—can be problematical.

Codex Vienna, by virtue of its qualities as both a book of ritual and of extensive maps of the Mixtec world (see figure 1.2, a map page from Zouche-Nuttall), does contain dates that are difficult to sequence chronologically and difficult to identify in metaphorical context. They are associated with persons, man-made and natural places in the landscape, and ceremonies. Zouche-Nuttall obverse is often compared to the Codex Vienna obverse as a "sister" document, and the assumed, vague metaphorical content of the latter is attached to the former (Furst 1978:4b). However, as will be demonstrated, both manuscripts share a recorded historical date for at least one critical event: a lineage-founding ceremony.

Calendars

A detailed study of Codex Zouche-Nuttall obverse pages 1–8 was written by Jill Leslie Furst and titled "The Life and Times of Lord Eight Wind Flinted Eagle" (1978b). Two elements of her discussion are immediately relevant. First, she details the relationship between codices Vienna and Zouche-Nuttall, and, second, she observes that the Mixtec concept of time was "cyclical." This latter point is critical because she qualifies it by saying of the Mixtec calendar that "it may not have been a calendar in the Western sense of the word" (Furst 1978b:12a). I concur with her statement, but not precisely in the sense she intended. Our culture identifies or finds historical events by dates; apparently the Mixtecs found or identified dates by historical events. Their texts are event-driven. The difference is subtle, but critical. Although acknowledging the cyclical nature of time-counting, we tend to see history as linear, progressing from past to present to future along "time's arrow."

Cyclical time-counting, however, is standard in pre-Hispanic Mesoamerica. There is nothing unusual about it. The precedent Mayan long count calendar round system expires and resets itself every 5,126 years and is thus cyclical in an expansive chronological framework. John Pohl (2004:368–418) notes that the Maya employed two basic calendars. One was a 365-day solar *haab* that measured time relevant to the annual agricultural cycle, divided into eighteen months of twenty days each. The second, concurrent calendar to the *haab* was the 260-day *tzolkin*, or ritual calendar, imbued with allegorical content. These two were mathematically coordinated and reset every fifty-two vague solar years (Schele and Miller 1986:16–17).

The Mixtec calendar had both these solar and ritual components, there being seventy-three 260-day ritual cycles per every fifty-two-year solar cycle of 365 days per year. The Mixtecs counted days and metaphorical content in the 260-day ritual calendar, and years as specific chronology in the solar one. Occasionally they used the day-count 260-day calendar to record the specific length of events with or without allegorical content. The appendices dealing with Codex Zouche-Nuttall reverse demonstrate both allegorical and precise day-counting of events as they appear on Codex Zouche-Nuttall reverse.

Unlike the Maya system, however, the Mixtec repeating cycles have no long count added to tell them in progression or regression one from another. Also, there is no evidence that the Mixtecs measured twenty-day months.

Codex Borgia, a manuscript in the Mixteca-Puebla style but of unknown provenance, does indicate the observance of a thirteen-day *trecena,* or week. Each day beginning with the number "one" began a thirteen-day *trecena.* Otherwise there is no evidence that the early Mixtecs were interested in recording vast cycles of time, as were the Classic period Maya.[2] Rather than dealing with religious time cycles covering millions of years (as at the Maya town of Quiriguá), the Mixtecs recorded the duration of their history over hundreds of years. Ancient things merely happened "long ago."

Integration of solar and ritual calendars indicates that Mesoamerican calendars were temporal recording technologies with both historical and allegorical content running "parallel" to one another. Anyone would be hard-pressed to name any modern calendar without both chronological and metaphorical content. Therefore, one does not necessarily exclude the other, and we will see that the majority of dates recorded in Codex Zouche-Nuttall pages 1–8 are in most instances historical temporal indicators of solar years, even if loaded with ritual, augural allegory to enrich data in the ritual 260-day calendar. They are chiefly markers for ceremonies and rituals, most of which are "hard" history.

Chronology

The twenty-six year-dates on Codex Zouche-Nuttall pages 1–8 are usually sequential in occurrence, with one exception noted in text. The criterion for interpreting dates is this: when a year-date occurs within a progressive sequence of dates but has no relevance to that sequence, it is either ritual-allegorical, an inset flashback or flash-forward, or a scribal error. The technology implied by an accurate calendar does not exempt it from recording historical events, no matter the allegorical content embedded within it. Allegory is, after all, a means of enriching data in mnemonic texts.

Building on preceding work by Emily Rabin, Byland and Pohl (1994:231–264) produced a chronological sequence of historical events applicable to all Mixtec manuscripts, specifically codices Zouche-Nuttall, Bodley, Selden, and Alfonso Caso (Colombino-Becker I fragments). This sequence covers fourteen fifty-two-year cycles from AD 883 to AD 1610, inclusively. Their seminal work has become standard, and much of it is used for this analysis and

---

2. Ethnographic evidence indicates, however, that after the Aztec conquest, later sixteenth-century Mixtecs believed in previous creations (Hamann 2002:5).

interpretation. In the context of their chronology, the events related in the codex pages scrutinized in this book occur in the historic AD Mixtec cycles as follows: Cycle 2, 935 to 986; Cycle 3, 987 to 1038; Cycle 4, 1039 to 1090; Cycle 5, 1091 to 1142. It is important to note that these codices are not strict chronicles—that is, they do not record events in each successive year, and often gaps of several years occur between events.

Scribal Errors

Mixtec scribes appear to have made mistakes in enumerating dates and day names of individuals. These errors are usually uncorrected, presumably because doing so was difficult.[3] For errors consisting of too many number-circles, existing images and foundational gesso had to be scraped and repainted (Jansen and Jimenez 2005:30b). Because codex scenes were mnemonic devices for oral recitation, it was probably easier for scribes and bards to simply correct erroneous dates from memory.

One obvious example of scribal date correction occurs on Zouche-Nuttall reverse page 50, column D (figure 1.1): the six units for a House year have been scratched out and replaced with seven units, although it is unclear why another unit simply was not added to the existing six. In the example cited, the entire date has been shifted up in position on the page.

An apparent error in recording a personal day name occurs in Codex Selden (6-IV). Lord Eleven Wind (the future husband of Lady Six Monkey of Jaltepec) is named Ten Wind; then, in subsequent narrative his name is corrected. I do not know why another unit was not simply added to correct the error. This same scene begins in Selden register 6-III with what seems to be yet another scribal error. The correct year, 6 Reed, is drawn as 5 Reed (Pohl 1994:70). So, two scribal errors occur with the same event but without subsequent repetition. This seems suspicious, and perhaps in context of this particular narrative the numbers 10 and 5 had a favored, allegorical significance that eludes us now.

Therefore, the possibility exists that the scribal errors mentioned above are not errors at all, but rather a kind of pun understood as glossed into text. So one must do just what the Mixtec bards very likely did from memory and

3. Classic period Maya did not correct scribal errors in their inscriptions either, presumably for the same reasons.

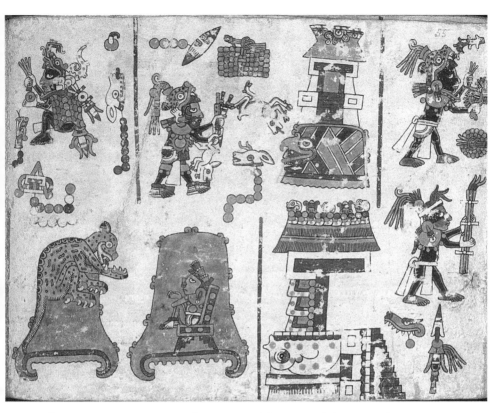

Figure 1.1. Codex Zouche-Nuttall page 50 (British Museum folio no. 55). The corrected year date is in column D (reading right to left). (© Trustees of the British Museum, The British Museum Company, Ltd.)

make one-digit corrections if necessary, though sparingly. It is not necessary to do this often.

Comparing and contrasting cognate scenes in other codices, or subsequent scenes in the same manuscript, can help to identify scribal errors. Codex Bodley, for example, reverses the names of Lord Five Alligator's wives. However, for unique scenes this comparison technique is unavailable. Therefore, when examining dates in chronological sequences, the investigator must be alert, and when a single date occurs remarkably out of context in a sequence, the existence of one too many or one too few units in year numeration can be inferred. This procedure is followed here cautiously (Oudijk 1998:19). For Zouche-Nuttall pages 1–8, there appear to be two scribal errors

Figure 1.2. Codex Zouche-Nuttall page 22 (British Museum folio no. 23). This map mural page is read from right to left and shows people, dates, events, and places in the vicinity of Monte Negro. It is specifically the introduction to the first dynasty of Tilantongo. (© Trustees of the British Museum, The British Museum Company, Ltd.)

involving one numeral and perhaps a third example, too. These are mentioned in text. Even if they are not errors, they do not invalidate the historical sequences recorded through some twenty-six dates therein. When these errors are noted, the recorded number is stated with the correction following it in parentheses; for example, Year 5(6) Reed. A complete numeration of the fifty-two years is provided in table 3.1.

2 The People of the Codices

Mixtec Indians

Prior to the arrival of the Toltec people in approximately AD 700, the Mixtecs were culturally complex, their forebears possibly influenced in Middle Formative times (1200–900 BC) by the Olmecs, who imported greenstone from what is now present-day Oaxaca (Tate 1995:49c). The Mixtecs were then dominated by the Zapotecs. As Zapotec control waned after the collapse of Teotihuacan and Zapotec Monte Alban in the seventh and eighth centuries AD, Mixtecs overshadowed them, formed marriage alliances with them, allied with the Tolteca-Chichimeca in the time of Lord Eight Deer Jaguar Claw, and then became subjugated by the Aztecs in the late fifteenth century. Resisting Aztec and Zapotec alliances with ardor, the later Mixtecs also resisted Spanish incursions until conquered by them in AD 1521.

Mixtec polities were small village-states and scattered throughout the landscape (Jansen and Jimenez 2005:42b). They were closely situated to one another, politically connected, and economically stabilized by a complex system of marriage alliances (Spores 1974:298). Kingdoms were socially stratified into castes. The highest caste included hereditary kings and queens; the second, the lesser nobility; third, the plebeians; and fourth, the bonded serfs. Rulership was absolute and continued until death or abdication (Spores 1974:301). Kings and queens were expected to provide for community protection, adjudicate disputes involving nobility, and serve as appellate courts for strife among commoners. They provided accoutrements and instruments for religious ceremonies, and sustenance and accommodation for nobles summoned to ceremonial and political occasions.

In his dissertation, "The Earth Lords: Politics and Symbolism of the Mixtec Codices" (1984), John M. D. Pohl demonstrates a tripartite administrative system for the Mixtec village kingdoms of the Postclassic period. In the codices, he notes, these levels of administration are visually displayed before representative architecture: kings in front of palaces, four governing priests in front of a temple or shrine, and the *yaha yahui* shaman in front of market areas. These shamans were a special kind of wizard with the ability to fly through the air—among other capabilities. As we will see, the two heroes who are subjects of this study, Lord Eight Wind Eagle Flints and Lord Eight Deer Jaguar Claw, were both *yaha yahui.* Local names for these wizards in the modern Mixteca and in Zapotec lands are *hechizero* and *negromantico* (Urcid, in Pohl 1994:67). In government, these priests were associated with human sacrifice and markets, as well as control of the economy and tribute collection (Pohl 1994:53). Pohl succinctly identifies the prime hero of Codex ZN pages 1–8, Lord Eight Wind Eagle Flints, as *yaha yahui,* as well as Lord Eight Deer Jaguar Claw and Lady Six Monkey's son Lord Four Wind.

The magical abilities attributed to the *yaha yahui* are extensive, including being able to fly through solid rock and to fly around the canyons of the Mixteca at night while appearing as balls of light (Pohl 1994:44). Of the many meanings for *yahui,* one is "comet" or "shooting star" (Arana and Swadesh 1965:133, cited in Pohl 1994), and descriptions of their flights sound similar to observed meteorological phenomena recorded in several parts of the world at various times (Huntington 1977 [1900]). Legends of a "devil" flying as a bright light from a mountain cave to another mountain in the Texas Big Bend survive in local folklore (Miles 1976:17–26). This is relevant when we consider the personification of meteorological phenomena—rain, lightning, and thunder—by Zapotecs (mentioned in chapter 8). These personifications appear in Codex Zouche-Nuttall's representation of the War from Heaven on pages 3 and 4. Such ideas had extensive purchase among peoples in the ancient Americas.

In most cases, given that royal families were focused on local causes and not on extensive extraterritorial politics, there was no conflict between means and goals, as would be expected in larger, unified states. Spores (1974:301) writes that stresses and destabilizing influences typical of unified royal state systems did not develop in the later Mixtec polities. As will be seen in our reading of Codex Zouche-Nuttall's first saga, this stability was earned by the exercise of great power from associated wars during the lives of lords Eight Wind Eagle Flints and Eight Deer Jaguar Claw. These wars and their resolutions ultimately produced an internally stable society.

Byland and Pohl (1994:198–199) also note the presence of significant numbers of religious oracles in the Mixteca—numbers higher than in any other part of pre-Hispanic Mesoamerica. These oracles, as sociopolitical function-aries, were held in extreme regard (Dahlgren 1966, cited in Byland and Pohl 1994) and played significant roles in maintaining social order among the Mixtec royalty. Francisco de Burgoa wrote about three of the most impor-tant of these oracles (1934 [1674]). First of these is the goddess of the dead, Lady Nine Grass of Chalcatongo. A prominent figure in the codices, she con-trols, among other things, marriage alliances. She also had the non-exclu-sive ability to speak with the mummies of deceased ancestors. The Mixtecs also gave significant importance to the oracle of the sun, Lord One Death, and his temple at Achiutla. Lord One Death also figures prominently in the codices and has the same name as the actual solar deity. The third oracle of prominence, "the great seer at Mitla," was the high priest there (Byland and Pohl 1994:194) and was of Zapotec origin. The Mixtec manuscripts do not appear to mention him, although Mitla is mentioned. A possible exception to this is Codex ZN page 33b, where Lord Seven Rain (attired as Xipe Totec) stands in the temple at Mitla and presides over the marriage between a Za-potec, Lord Five Flower, and a Mixtec, Lady Four Rabbit. This event occurred in the thirteenth century AD. Archaeologists excavated Lord Five Flower's tomb in recent times.

Oaxaca

The modern state of Oaxaca is located on the southwest portion of the Isth-mus of Tehuantepec at the southern extremity of Mexico. It borders the states of Guerrero to the west, Puebla to the northwest, Veracruz to the north, and Chiapas to the east. Oaxaca is an area of 95,364 square kilometers, and at the beginning of the twenty-first century its population was estimated at 3,597,700: approximately 300,000 of these are Mixtecs. Geographically Oax-aca is located in the mountains and valleys of the Sierra Madre del Sur.

The Mixteca itself occupies the western third of Oaxaca and has three dis-tinct areas. The Mixteca Alta is mountainous, high, and cool, with moderate rainfall and deep valleys. The Baja is lower in elevation, hot, and semiarid. The Mixteca Costa is a region of hot, humid coastal lowlands bordering the Gulf of Tehuantepec (Spores 1969:557a). From Cholula and its Tolteca-Chi-chimeca culture to Oaxaca with its dominant Mixtec and Zapotec cultures, marriage alliances helped to establish trade networks (corridors) and politi-cal interaction spheres in pre-Columbian times.

The area of cultural focus related in Codex Zouche-Nuttall's first saga is the Nochixtlan Valley of Oaxaca, specifically the northern part of it. This valley is about 450 kilometers southeast of Mexico City on the Pan-American Highway. Spores writes (1969:558c) that it is the largest stretch of mostly open and level land between the Valley of Oaxaca (100 kilometers to the south) and the Nexapa Valley at Izucar de Matamoros and the Tehuacan Valley, nearly 200 kilometers to the north.

The Nochixtlan Valley is composed of four major cultural areas: Yanhuitlan, situated in the northwestern portion; Yucuita, in the north (near Yucuñudahui); Nochixtlan, in the east; and Jaltepec, in the southeast. All follow river confluences. From north/northwest to southeast the Nochixtlan Valley is about 25 kilometers long, in width varying from 5 to 10 kilometers. Topographically the area consists of numerous narrow valleys interrupted by high mountain ranges and lesser promontories, including buttes and piedmont spurs (Spores 1969:558c). Level areas are located only in the central portions of these smaller valleys, and some have been created by man-made terracing. Spores (1969:558c) considers the Nochixtlan Valley to be the single most important area in the Mixteca during its extensive history of occupation.

Ronald Spores's detailed archaeological work in the Nochixtlan Valley in the 1960s provides significant insight into settlement patterns there and length of occupation—an observation integral to kinship/marriage patterns described subsequently. These data will be summarized in a later chapter.

Today Oaxaca is known as the area wherein the two great cultures of Zapotec and Mixtec peoples developed and founded enduring communities that persist into modern times. Pre-Hispanic Mixtec culture influenced other cultures outside Oaxaca, and one instrument for this diffusion was the body of manuscript literature (codices) written not in alphabetic script, but in pictogram text.

Currently, the indigenous American people known as Mixtecs still reside in modern Oaxaca. Communities of Mixtecs have been established in recent times in the United States, notably in California, where they have their own Mixtec-language radio programs (KFCF 88.1 FM in Fresno, California [*The Sacramento Bee,* 10/20/2002]). "Mixtec" is the name of both the people and their language.

Writing Traditions and Mixtec Codices

Pre-European Mesoamerican cultures developed at least thirteen writing systems, including the Olmec (ambiguous, but some evidence exists on cylinder seals and the Cascajal Block), the Epi-Olmec (also called Isthmian) (Tuxtla Statuette, La Moharra Stela), Zapotec, Teotihuacano, pre-Classic Maya, Nuiñe, Classic period Maya, Mixtec, Xochicalco, Cacaxtla, and Aztec. These systems represent ancient and diverse languages. Mixe-Zoquean is likely Olmec and Isthmian. Mixtec is among the Oto-Manguean languages, and the Uto-Aztecan group of some three thousand languages and dialects includes the Aztec Nahuatl spoken and written at Tenochtitlan. Totonacan language is a likely candidate for the mysterious megacity Teotihuacan.

To date, Mayan hieroglyphic writing is a demonstrable closed writing system; that is, it encodes a specific language and dialects. Nuiñe and Isthmian may be also. The others appear to be open writing—pictogram systems not tied to specific language writing—or, as in the case of Zapotec examples, an admixture of open and closed systems. Aztec and Mixtec writing also may be combinations of open and closed systems.

Open-system pictogram writing is indigenous to Mesoamerica, specifically to cultures in central and southern Mexico. Although Jansen and Jimenez (2005:11) associate its development with Teotihuacan, its origins probably began much earlier, in Middle Formative times, with the Olmec on the Gulf Coast of the northern and north-central parts of the Isthmus of Tehuantepec, as did hieroglyphic writing. Very likely, both forms existed together as displays of public art consisting mainly of royal propaganda.

Subsequently, in Zapotec and Mayan cultures, hieroglyphic writing recorded elite histories, but those texts accompanied elaborate iconography: pictograms augmenting hieroglyphic texts and providing information not contained in the hieroglyphs. One example of this is a carved wooden lintel from Tikal, Temple IV (Lintel 3), dated June 26, AD 741 (9.15.10.0.0 3 Ahau 3 Mol) (figure 2.1). The small hieroglyphic texts at the upper right- and left-hand portions of this lintel record (among other things not well deciphered) a ceremony that is augmented in the large, elaborate pictogram icon. The icon includes carrying poles which bore the king of Tikal on a kind of litter or palanquin. Further elaboration of the hieroglyphic text occurs as individual components of the ruler's costume. This transforms the ruler's regalia into "a literal text, an extreme version of the particularistic historical character of costume" (Joyce 2000:13).

The Highland Guatemala Maya, specifically the Quiche, did not employ a hieroglyphic writing system. As Pohl (2004a:369–370) states, "Rather, it appears that the highland Guatemala Maya used a pictographic communication system exclusively and that this system was largely derived from that developed by the Eastern Nahuas, Mixtecs, and Zapotecs of southern Mexico." Evidence now emerging from the northern Peten in Guatemala shows an interesting combination of pictogram and hieroglyphic pre-Classic era

Figure 2.1. Tikal, Temple IV, Lintel 3, an example of hieroglyphic texts enhanced by pictograms. (Pen-and-ink drawing by John Montgomery, from the author's collection)

Mayan writing; according to Mary Miller, murals at San Bartolo that were painted on stucco display an "incredible complex of early paintings" ("Earliest Mayan Writing Found Beneath Pyramid," CNN.com, January 2006). Other archaeologists noted that "some of the glyphs are pictorial." David Stuart is cited in the article as saying that this text (dated at 300 BC) was exemplary of writing and public art as "part of a package."

After the Classic period collapse, even those Maya who employed hieroglyphics relied upon them less and less, more frequently using pictograms. Hieroglyphic writing for Mayan cultures appears to have been a Classic period expression that diminished over time, at least for public monuments. Writing in pictogram tableaux became the lingua franca, so to speak, for many different cultures in Mesoamerica. Pictograms were translingual and so had utility among diverse peoples: an important quality for societies with economies based on trade and marketing systems scattered over territories with sometimes mutually unintelligible languages. Jansen and Jimenez note (2005:11–12) that areas where pictograms developed as writing systems had tonal languages wherein words pronounced in different tones have different meanings, as is the case with Chinese.

Mixtec Codices and Pictographic Literature

The Mixtecs became masters of pictogram writing. Of the eight fan-fold manuscripts that survive, five are considered major codices, although this designation varies between scholars. They are, from latest to earliest, and without dispute as to importance:

> Codex Selden, a post-Conquest palimpsest painted over an older pre-Hispanic manuscript
> Codex Bodley, from the Late Postclassic period, perhaps Early Colonial period
> Codex Zouche-Nuttall (two documents—an older reverse and newer obverse)
> Codex Vindobonensis Mexicanus I (Codex Vienna) (two documents—an older obverse and newer reverse)
> Codex Colombino-Becker I, composed of partly destroyed fragments now named Codex Alfonso Caso when assembled according to Caso's schema (Jansen and Jiménez 2005)

All but Codex Selden are pre-Hispanic.

The content of the codices is mythological (religious), historical/biographical, and genealogical. The codices were composed by royal princes and used not merely for personal reading, but for performance narratives during ceremonial occasions; that is, they were scripts for dramatic presentations sung and danced by costumed and masked individuals. They were opened and hung as fresco-like displays on walls, and their various scenes and characters were used to decorate pottery and clothing.

Except for Codex Vienna, investigated by Lauren Touriens in two articles published in 1983 and 1984, the European history of these artifacts is largely unknown or speculative. Hernán Cortés wrote that he sent two native books to Europe as curiosities (Prescott 1934 [1843]:65), and Touriens established that Codex Vienna was one of these. The other has been long suspected to be Codex Zouche-Nuttall, which surfaced at the Library of San Marco in Florence, Italy, in 1854 (Nuttall 1902:1–5; Troike 1987:17); however, the precise era of its arrival in Europe is still debated. In her introduction to the Peabody Museum edition of the codex named after her, Zelia Nuttall (1902:9–11) provides the clearest rationale accounting for Zouche-Nuttall's presence in Italy and its discovery at the Florentine library.

She remarks on the similarity of the manuscript discussed here with its "sister codex," Vienna, because of the similarity of personnel and events in both, and maintains that shortly after the Conquest both manuscripts were in Florence. Thinking the codices Aztec, Zelia Nuttall asserts that Codex Zouche-Nuttall is: (1) one of two books mentioned in the inventory of 1519 as among presents given to Cortés by Montezuma's envoys; (2) these two manuscripts were received in the spring of 1520 by Charles V of Spain and subsequently distributed to various sovereigns along with other New World curiosities; and (3) finally, Codex Zouche-Nuttall and Vienna were in Florence but separated as gifts, with the former remaining at the Library of San Marco in Florence (1902:10). If this is the case, it is possible that the two Mixtec manuscripts came into Aztec possession when Emperor Montezuma I conquered the Mixteca in the 1400s.

Alfonso Caso thought Zouche-Nuttall had been painted about AD 1438 (1979:18), which fits well for the document's obverse side. The histories and genealogies painted there are well-designed to reinforce land ownership and rule by Mixtec royals. This objective also explains why the authors of Zouche-Nuttall obverse were pointedly interested in connecting their earlier histories to the life of Lord Eight Deer Jaguar Claw of Tilantongo (the older codex reverse) and the tree-birth event shown in Codex Vindobonensis Mexicanus I obverse. The resulting unified history is a legal document stating the right of Mixtec families to territories and would have been of keen interest to Mixtec kings and queens and their descendants, whether resident in the Mixteca or not, as well as to Aztec tribute collectors.

The similarity noted by Nuttall of personnel and content between codices Zouche-Nuttall and Vienna has been subsequently reinforced (Furst 1978a:2). Comparing and contrasting data from the obverse documents of both these manuscripts is necessary for interpretation.

Codex Zouche-Nuttall Obverse, Pages 1–8

As previously stated, the primary subject of this study is the first eight pages of Codex Zouche-Nuttall obverse. The entire manuscript is painted on both sides of sixteen gesso-coated, fan-folded leather strips glued together and totaling 1,296.95 centimeters in length (12.97 meters). Page width varies from 18.3 centimeters to 25.2 centimeters (Troike 1987:38–39). The codex obverse (museum numbered pages 1–41) displays pictogram text that relates historical and mythological events told in three sagas interspersed with genealogies.

The obverse is complete, but the older reverse is unfinished, the text becoming incomplete on page 84, leaving one and one-half unwritten columns and two unwritten pages. Microscopic examination reveals that paint from the obverse seeped through small cracks and holes, and overlays small portions of the painted figures on the reverse (Furst 1978b:5a; Troike, pers. comm., 1987). Therefore, the obverse is newer than the reverse. Pages 1 and 2 introduce the first saga, page 14 introduces the second, and page 36 the third. Although the texts of both sides of Codex Zouche-Nuttall are pre-Conquest documents, they may be newer versions of still older codices that do not survive (Winter 1989:78).

Among the Spanish who noticed the presence of Mixtec codices and their use was Friar Francisco de Burgoa, who in AD 1674 wrote that the codices were displayed along the length of rooms (see Pohl's introduction to this volume). This "portable mural" display is depicted in the 1875 painting *The Senate of Tlaxcala,* by Rodrigo Gutiérrez (*Mexico: Splendors of Thirty Centuries,* 1990:505). The artist obviously knew of the tradition of codex display and reproduced one as individual murals rather than as a fan-fold book. Perhaps he had seen the Kingsborough reproductions published in a preceding generation.

The Protagonist of Codex Zouche-Nuttall, Pages 1–8

The codex narratives scrutinized in the following pages illustrate a dramatic fact: royal people alive in Epiclassic Oaxaca's Nochixtlan Valley played a vital, formative role as agents effecting social change. The protagonist central to this sometimes cataclysmic social drama was a patriarch, politician, and religious leader named Lord Eight Wind Eagle Flints. Zelia Nuttall mentions him in her 1902 introduction to the Peabody Museum reproduction on pages 27–28, but her commentary is descriptive rather than interpretative.

Lord Eight Wind was first born from the earth at Cavua Colorado in AD 935. For fifty-two years he lived as a supernatural wonderworker and participated influentially in altering the existing social paradigm, exercising power from the era of Classic period Zapotec civilization (Pohl 1991:22b). The change in social paradigm involved, in effect, lineage franchise, whereby a new order of lineage nobles, said to be born from the trees at Apoala, constituted the sine qua non of rulership in the Mixteca (figure 2.2). After his elevation to twice-born status as Tree Born noble and Earth Born, Lord Eight Wind completed a cycle of fifty-two calendar years. He lived the remaining forty years of his life at Monkey Hill/Suchixtlan as the founder of an enduring lineage passing through his daughters and persisting until the arrival of the Spanish in AD 1521.

The system against which Eight Wind reacted included not only Classic period rulers at a place called Wasp Hill, but also subjugation of the original peoples of the Mixteca, who are referred to as "Stone Men," or Tey Ñuu.[1] The second part of this sixteen-year war conducted against the nobility of Wasp Hill is narrated on ZN pages 4, 20, and 22. It is also related in Codex Bodley (pages 3 and 4, 34–36) for the southern Nochixtlan Valley. The Stone Men and their involvement with the Epiclassic Mixtecs will be detailed when their narrative is interpreted, and subsequently where necessary.

Lord Eight Wind's contribution to the new Mixtec cultural and social dynamic had far-reaching implications. We know he founded an enduring

---

1. The Stone Man War appears on Codex ZN page 3. The subsequent truce between the Stone Men and the new tree-born rulers appears on the last half of page 4 as well as on Codex Vienna page 35a.

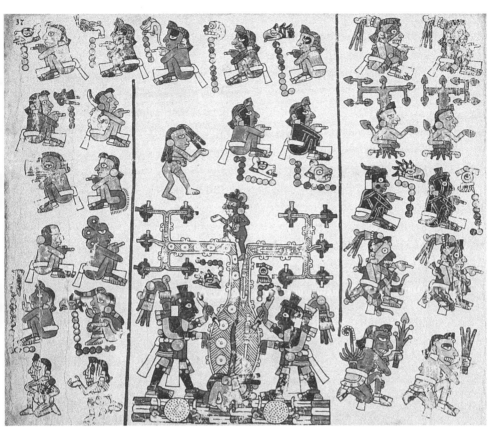

Figure 2.2. The tree birth shown on Codex Vindobonensis Mexicanus I (Vienna) page 37. (© Akademische Druck- u Verlagsanstalt, Graz, Austria)

lineage, but as lord of Rain God Hill for at least seventeen years, he may have been instrumental in giving the Mixtecs their very name: People of the Rain.

The Mixtec historical manuscripts detail actions of politically and personally motivated individuals against a preexisting, overriding social system. As Pohl has written, these "stories were composed to break with the old social order through a miraculous act of renewal, without giving up claims to territory itself" (2003a:64). The Mixtec scribes who wrote Codex ZN pages 1–8 as retrospective events were also careful to record unexpected consequences of Eight Wind's enduring deeds. In particular they recorded a dynastic conflict in the time of his great-grandson, Lord Two Rain Twenty

Jaguars of Tilantongo, against Eight Wind's granddaughter, Lady Six Monkey of Jaltepec, and the resulting lineage war against the rival polity of Hua Chino (also called Red and White Bundle).

This dynastic political drama is mentioned on Codex ZN obverse page 8 and detailed on Codex ZN reverse pages 80–84. It was to be resolved, as the scribes tell us, by the powerful and charismatic warlord, Eight Deer the Jaguar Claw of Tilantongo, who usurped rule there after Two Rain Twenty Jaguar's death.

This great warlord, Eight Deer, attempted the most dramatic social changes since the time of Lord Eight Wind himself. In this regard I will elaborate subsequently on material I first demonstrated in a seminar at the University of Texas at Austin in March 2004 concerning the connection between Zouche-Nuttall's obverse and reverse as the scribes of a later time (obverse) connect earlier events to those told by scribes before them (reverse). This scribal technique produced a unified history of two great heroes, Lord Eight Wind (obverse) and Lord Eight Deer (reverse). Historical hindsight provided by the Mixtec scribes is illuminating regarding the cultural permanence of these two powerful men. First, Lord Eight Wind's actions and the social changes they provoked survived, and he is displayed as acting beyond the grave. In the second instance, Lord Eight Deer the Usurper's far-seeing social changes affecting the unification of the families of the Mixteca into what seems to be a paramount chiefdom or protostate, and the suppression of the Oracle of the Dead at Chalcatongo did not; nevertheless, his hard-earned fame and prestige did.

3   The Narrative Structure of Codex Zouche-Nuttall Obverse

Each page of every Mixtec codex usually displays painted tableaux that can be interpreted individually as stating temporality in years and days. In these tableaux are symbols defining places, actors who are chiefly elite personnel, and actions such as marriage, conquest, peregrination, and diverse religious ceremonies.

Taken collectively these tableaux demonstrate narrative sequences and reveal highlights of historical events, biographies, and detailed genealogies. The pictogram tableaux are mnemonic devices, spotlights on ritual moments and narrative performance, and, like a movie storyboard, reveal only certain highlights of action. The connecting data between them is lost. Prior to the arrival of Europeans, those trained to do so passed on these memorized stories from generation to generation.

The reader's progress through pictogram text is usually guided by red lines that determine the movement of narrative. This line-guided movement is boustrophedon, up-and-down or side-to-side—literally, "as the bull plows." Different scribes used a variety of pictorial conventions to suit their needs, including abbreviation or conflation, variation of reading order, omission of red guide lines (as in Zouche-Nuttall's last narrative sequence on pages 36–39), and use of page-length red lines to separate one narrative sequence from another, to name a few. In the case of ZN pages 1–2, the scribes have not provided a set of red guide lines because these two pages of painted tableaux introduce their subject (Lord Eight Wind) and proceed chronologically. However, as with all of the major intact Mixtec codices, reading begins in the lower right (for documents reading from right to left) or lower left (for documents reading from left to right).

Events such as marriage have various representations according to local custom but usually husband and wife face one another on a mat, and are perhaps enthroned with a vessel filled with liquid between them. Their children are usually pictured next, in order of importance, with or without temporal indicators.

The following illustrations (figures 3.1–3.3) picture the temporal indicators of year bearers and day signs, and toponyms. Table 3.1 gives the sequence of years in numerical progression through a fifty-two-year cycle. Colored circles attached to years and days establish their enumeration; i.e., Year 5 (colored circles) Flint, Day 6 (colored circles) Alligator.

Figure 3.1. The four year bearers and the A-O year sign. (Drawings by John M. D. Pohl)

HOUSE

RABBIT

REED

FLINT

Table 3.1. The Fifty-Two Years in the Mixtec Calendar and Their Numbers in Sequence

No.	Year	No.	Year	No.	Year	No.	Year
1.	1 Reed	14.	1 Flint	27.	1 House	40.	1 Rabbit
2.	2 Flint	15.	2 House	28.	2 Rabbit	41.	2 Reed
3.	3 House	16.	3 Rabbit	29.	3 Reed	42.	3 Flint
4.	4 Rabbit	17.	4 Reed	30.	4 Flint	43.	4 House
5.	5 Reed	18.	5 Flint	31.	5 House	44.	5 Rabbit
6.	6 Flint	19.	6 House	32.	6 Rabbit	45.	6 Reed
7.	7 House	20.	7 Rabbit	33.	7 Reed	46.	7 Flint
8.	8 Rabbit	21.	8 Reed	34.	8 Flint	47.	8 House
9.	9 Reed	22.	9 Flint	35.	9 House	48.	9 Rabbit
10.	10 Flint	23.	10 House	36.	10 Rabbit	49.	10 Reed
11.	11 House	24.	11 Rabbit	37.	11 Reed	50.	11 Flint
12.	12 Rabbit	25.	12 Reed	38.	12 Flint	51.	12 House
13.	13 Reed	26.	13 Flint	39.	13 House	52.	13 Rabbit

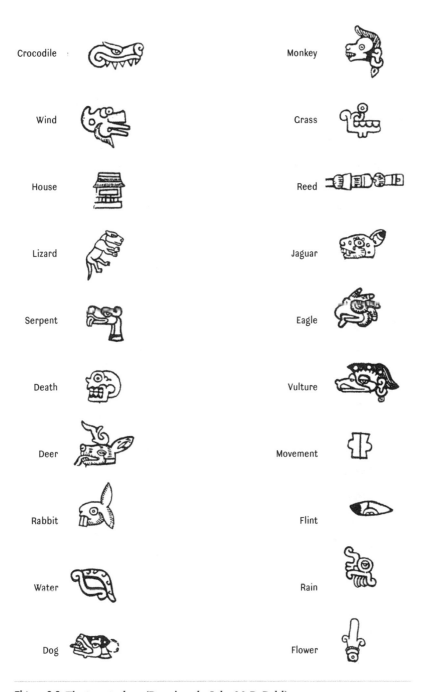

Crocodile		Monkey	
Wind		Grass	
House		Reed	
Lizard		Jaguar	
Serpent		Eagle	
Death		Vulture	
Deer		Movement	
Rabbit		Flint	
Water		Rain	
Dog		Flower	

Figure 3.2. The twenty days. (Drawings by John M. D. Pohl)

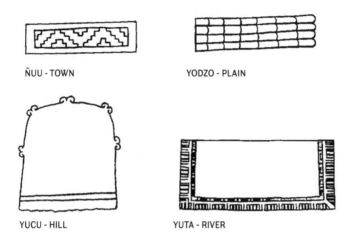

ÑUU - TOWN

YODZO - PLAIN

YUCU - HILL

YUTA - RIVER

Figure 3.3. The four basic toponyms. (Drawings by John M. D. Pohl)

Although complex in content and variable in reading order among its diverse sections, the narrative structure of the entire Codex Zouche-Nuttall obverse is simple in plan: three sagas are each followed by events and genealogies. Full-page vertical red lines divide one section from another. The following schematic outline lists the codex obverse contents, focusing in detail on pages 1–8.

I. Saga of Lord Eight Wind Eagle Flints, pages 1–8
   A. Biographical introduction, pages 1–2
   B. The War from Heaven, pages 3–4
      1. War with the Stone Men, page 3
      2. War with the Striped Men, page 4
   C. Lord Eight Wind and his family, pages 5–6a
      1. Lord Eight Wind at Monkey Hill, page 5a
      2. Lord Eight Wind rain god ceremonies, page 5a–b
      3. Lord Eight Wind's three wives and children, pages 5c–6a
   D. Two processions, pages 6b–7c
   E. Lord Eight Wind's mummy and Two Rain, pages 7d–8a
   F. Lord Two Rain's mummy, page 8b
   G. Ceremonies and genealogies, pages 9–13

II. Saga of the Ladies Three Flint, mythological events and genealogies, pages 14–35 (not analyzed in this book)

III. Saga of the Four Lords from Apoala, genealogy, pages 36–41 (not analyzed in this book)

Structure of the Codex

Generally speaking, the Mixtec scribes exercised significant freedom to record their narratives within this structural framework. If reading order is established without using red lines placed on the page in various ways to guide the eye, then either similarity of dates, chronological sequence of dates, or perhaps mnemonic systems familiar to the original bards but unknown to present-day scholars are intended. The first two sagas of Zouche-Nuttall obverse end with a full-length red line separating them from the pages that follow. The narrative text is *res gestae* (Boone 2000:70–77), or event-driven, and qualified by literal and allegorical temporal markers recording solar years and days within them.

The physical structure of the Zouche-Nuttall manuscript itself was utilized by the scribes in creative ways. The rigid in-fold, out-fold form that creates the pagination is fixed; that is to say, one cannot fold pages contrary to their original directions without breaking them, establishing a rigid folding format.

This format is used advantageously in two instances to augment narrative sequences in Codex Zouche-Nuttall obverse by creating "parentheses" whereby two pages can be eclipsed or omitted from recitation. Both these parentheses are histories of the War from Heaven sequences, first on pages 3 and 4 in Lord Eight Wind's story, and also on pages 20 and 21 in the Ladies Three Flint narrative. In the first example the war story is told from the political perspective of the northern Nochixtlan Valley settlements; in the second, from the political point of view of the southern Nochixtlan Valley (Pohl, pers. comm., 2004).

As I demonstrated during the Mixtec Pictogram Writing Workshop (University of Texas, March 2004), in both cases these war pages can be deleted by taking advantage of the folding scheme, connecting in the first instance page 2 to page 5 to produce a continuous biography of Lord Eight Wind. In the second instance, double-page 19 connects to page 22, omitting pages 20 and 21 (the second telling of the war) in order to demonstrate that the founding of the first dynasty of Tilantongo (page 22) was similar in prestige to the founding of the earlier, and subsequently exterminated, dynasty at Wasp Hill (ZN double page 19).

The reciting bards had the option of including the war narratives or omitting them, depending on the occasion. The conclusions drawn from these data are obvious: although of extreme importance, the War from Heaven sequences were secondary stories inserted into two primary stories for purposes of elaboration. A similar example in Western literature is the Ajax story inserted into Homer's *Iliad*. The importance of the War from Heaven as an event is obvious: it is twice-told in Codex Zouche-Nuttall from the point of view of two different polities. It is also twice-told in Codex Bodley, first on pages 3 and 4, then on pages 34–36.

The first war narrative does not mention the Wasp Hill lineage exterminations at all, but emphasizes Lord Eight Wind's activities at Yucuñudahui (Rain God Hill) and the subsequent conflict with the Stone Men. The first section that includes the war narrative also emphasizes Lord Eight Wind's participation in the founding of a new lineage franchise at Apoala—that is, the Tree Born nobles who became rulers of Postclassic Oaxaca.

For both areas of the Nochixtlan Valley, the war had extreme dynastic implications as an old order of rule at Wasp Hill was swept away by a long, terrible war and replaced by new ruling families. The culture was altered by violent change beginning in the Epiclassic era and entered the Postclassic transformed by new kinship ties.

4 Sacred Geography, Personified Geography

The Hill Is a God

The gods pictured on the obverse of Codex Vienna interacted with a living, personified geography: the very landscape itself was alive and named accordingly. Codex Zouche-Nuttall pictures Pregnant Hill, Bird Hill, and the Place Where the Sky Was. It is no surprise to find named places in the codices that can still be found in the modern Mixtec landscape. One such is the Hill (*yucu*) of the (*nu*) rain god (*Dzahui*): Yucuñudahui (see Pohl's introduction to this volume and figure I.4).

This place in the northeastern Mixteca is prominent in both Zouche-Nuttall obverse and Vienna obverse. However, the old manuscripts depict this geographical feature in an unusual category; it seems from the pictograms that the hill itself *is* the rain god, Dzahui. This implication, reinforced by the fact that Dzahui himself seldom appears in the narratives in human form, is obvious. In most codex representations Dzahui is the hill with rain god characteristics: goggle eyes, fanged teeth, black body paint, and so on. Rain god substations, so to speak, display this facial effigy, which is in such representations as a carved stone, wood, or large decorated ceramic head (ZN page 37) and is the subject of ceremonial dramatic presentations.

The Rain God Hill is, itself, a mnemonic device, like codex tableaux, intended to jog the memories of living humans and instruct them in the vast complexities of history and religious ideology. Byron Hamann makes this very point brilliantly:

> The social lives of objects and places cannot be separated from the social lives of humans, and one aspect of this cohabitation is the role of objects and places in human pedagogy. . . . In explicit pedagogy, objects and places are used as "mnemonic pegs," prompts for telling stories that explain the relevance of the past for present social life. . . . Meaning-coded things also impact human cognition as implicit, silent (if physically structuring) backgrounds, for day-to-day existence. (2002:352–354)

Yucuñudahui is the prominent feature of an actual bifurcated landscape. The community of Chachoapan has been located at the base of the mountain at least since Postclassic times. An arroyo divides it. The ceremonial center ruins atop the mountain are at least Classic era constructions and, as my recovered chronology demonstrates, Late Classic and Epiclassic as well. Zouche-Nuttall, page 2, shows Yucuñudahui as the subject of an ordering ritual conducted by the fire-drilling Lord Eight Wind Eagle Flints. The duration of this elaborated performance is seventeen years, from Year 3 Reed to Year 7 Flint. The tableau also shows several fabricated constructions—temples, buildings, ballcourts—situated at the foot of the mountain. Similar ordering rituals occur in the pages of Codex Vienna, nine (perhaps ten) in all. Virtually all of the rituals show unnamed tertiary actors measuring stone for building purposes. Of these Vienna rituals, all display building activities as an integrated part of the rituals themselves. The conclusion is that during the time of our protagonist, Lord Eight Wind Eagle Flints, not only was Yucuñudahui ordered by fire-drilling ritual, but he either constructed or incorporated the community at the foot of it as well.

The God-Hill as a Resource

The point will be made later that Yucuñudahui itself was a political resource and important enough to be fought over. It was the center of the religious focus of the original non-Mixtec inhabitants (Stone Men) of the Nochixtlan Valley, and it was the "source" of rain itself, courtesy of the god Nine Wind Quetzalcoatl (Vienna 47b), who held water and sky above it in previous times. Zouche-Nuttall makes the point (as we will see later) that Lord Eight Wind himself was an important resource in this place and subsequently in other places as well. The scribes tell us also that Yucuñudahui supplied something else of extreme importance: the sacred plants.

Plants

Codex Vienna and its sister manuscript, Zouche-Nuttall, are treasure troves for ethnobotanists. Important plants are everywhere within the elaborately painted pages. Ceremonial tobacco-pouring is present in both codices and also in folk history as an important component in rituals of rulership (Furst 1978a:65). A maize ceremony with warriors featured on Vienna page 26a may reflect ancient rites associated with the god of spring fertility, Xipe Totec (Furst 1978a:200). Pulche, a fermentation from the maguey plant, is ritualized on Vienna page 25a, and the goddess associated with it is prominently featured in the terminal tableaux of ZN obverse pages 3 and 4. Communication with nonhuman beings and transformation of elite humans was an integral part of Mesoamerican religions—and at least partially induced by the consumption of certain plants. One such ritual involving sacred mushrooms is pictured on Vienna page 24, and similar rituals survive in modern Oaxaca (Furst 1978a:203).

Plants and Rivers

The ritual use of plants as integrated with human lifeways occupies a substantial part of the Codex Zouche-Nuttall obverse symbolism associated with Lord Eight Wind Eagle Flints. Further, Codex Vienna obverse establishes that certain plants, specifically three combined together into a white-wrapped bundle, were used in the "ordering" or sanctification of the Mixtec geography and its man-made features. Of particular interest is the fact that one of the lineage rivers at Apoala is a source of these three plants, as is Yucuñudahui, and that Lord Eight Wind is himself closely identified with them. As will be elaborated later, it would appear that Eight Wind's ordering of Yucuñudahui represents him as being the sacred plants intrinsically. The important fire-drilling apparatus and an associated ceremonial bundle also emerge from one of the Apoala lineage rivers. Thus these three mysterious plants emerge from the Apoala River (Vienna 24b), the same one from which Lord Eight Wind emerges (ZN page 1), and from which the necessary fire-drilling apparatus does also (ZN page 18b)—and ZN page 2 implies that Eight Wind is the plants.

The Sources of the Nobles

Trees in Mesoamerican religions generally have extreme prominence because of their identification with the world tree, or axis mundi: a cosmic device that transcends the planes of existence. A world tree has its roots in the underworld, its trunk and branches in the middle world, and its crown in the sky. From Olmec times, rulers have been identified with and considered to be world trees, which can be represented in Mesoamerica as maize plants. At times, lineage clans can be represented as plants or trees (ZN page 20a–b).

The Mixtecs give us a literal view of this important ideology when they tell us how their kings and queens came to be. Ethnography records that lineage founders were born from trees at Apoala and Achiutla. Lord Eight

Wind was first an earth-born noble (ZN page 1), but by being present at the Tree Birth ceremony at either Apoala or Achiutla, he was granted twice-born status and was thereafter a tree-born noble (Vienna 35a). He subsequently founded his lineage at Suchixtlan (ZN page 5).

In the Codex Vienna page 37 tableau the gods Lord Seven Rain and Lord Seven Eagle carve the trunk of the great birth tree. Seven Eagle engraves female spindle whorls on one side, while Seven Rain engraves male atlatl darts on the other; therefore, the birth tree is capable of bringing forth both sexes. The tree itself is a goddess, the Lady Nine Reed (Furst 1978a:136), but wears a male attribute: a blue tubular earplug. Furst (1978a:133) notes that this earplug is otherwise an exclusively male ornament and is worn by no other female actor on Vienna obverse. This combination of male/female attributes is reflected (as Furst comments) in the carvings on the trunk itself.

In AD 1593, seventy-two years after Pedro de Alvarado entered Oaxaca, Fray Antonio de los Reyes noted that the Mixtecs had folktales about how the nobles came out of, and were cut off from, trees that grew by the river *yuta tnoho* at Apoala (*yuta tnuhu*) (de los Reyes 1976 [1593], cited in Furst 1978a:134). By showing us that Lord Eight Wind emerges from this same river (ZN page 1), the codex makes the attribution plain: although born from the earth, he is also born from the great lineage river Yuta Tñoho.

Fray Francisco de Burgoa recorded a later version of this folklore in the seventeenth century (1934 [1674]:I, 274, cited in Furst 1978a:135). According to this version, the Mixtec nobles were born from two trees growing on the riverbank at Apoala. This legend mentions that the trees were nourished by the *underground water* that produced the rivers. In retrieving the sacred plants from beneath Apoala (Vienna 24b), Lord Seven Wind goes into a cave in the river there—the same river cave from which Lord Eight Wind emerges on ZN page 1 and from which the fire-drilling bundle emerges on ZN page 18b. We can see that this ethnography recorded by the Spanish friars preserves an integrated ideology that is perhaps illustrated in the codices under discussion. Yet, in post-Conquest times, Apoala was not a grand place. Citing colonial sources, Jansen (1988:99–100) writes that in the sixteenth century Apoala was not an important town but, rather, was controlled by Yanhuitlan. In that era Apoala had perhaps 352 houses among 700 married couples, 314 unmarried people, and 537 children—all of whom paid annual tribute amounting to sixty pesos of gold dust along with thirteen hens, an amount of salt, beans, bead works, and balls of yarn.

Another birth-tree source for nobles is also mentioned in the ethnography: namely, Achiutla or, as it is called, "Hill of the Sun" (Pohl 2005b:116a). The legend of the Achiutla tree birth says, in abstract, that the first man and woman were born from "two beautiful sabino trees" at Achiutla (Castellanos 1910:21–22). In the considered opinion of John Pohl (pers. comm., 2006), this legend corresponds to and confirms the tree-birth scene displayed in Codex Selden, as discussed below.

Codex Selden, the royal document of Jaltepec, was composed in the native style but is a palimpsest written over an older document after the Spanish arrived. On telling the story of Jaltepec's first dynasty (which failed for unspecified reasons) the god of the Sun, Lord One Death, and the god of Evening Star, One Motion, split the earth, and Lord Eleven Wind was born from it. He married the Lady Seven Eagle at Oracle Head in Cave, and they ruled that place (Selden 1-I). Their child was Lady Ten Eagle, who married Lord Four Eagle from Snake River (the same place where Lord Two Rain's mummy will be interred in a later story), and their daughter was Lady Eight Rabbit (Selden 1-II). In order to produce a royal husband for Lady Eight Rabbit, two elderly priests, the Lords Ten Lizard and Ten Flint, conduct two ceremonies, the first one at Apoala, whereupon the rulers of that place, Lord Five Wind who lives in the sacred river there (grandson of Lord Nine Wind Quetzalcoatl) and Lady Nine Alligator (daughter of the first two rulers of Apoala), receive gifts (Selden 1-III); the tree then appears at Achiutla and gives birth to the bridegroom, Lord Two Grass (Selden 2-I).

In this Selden version of tree birth, the tree stands above the river on a masonry platform. In the river are three stones which were made in the sky (Vienna 49). Two serpents emerge from the masonry place and entwine the tree: one has vapor or clouds upon its back; the other has water and stars on its back. We remember from Codex Vienna page 47b that Lord Nine Wind Quetzalcoatl first held up sky and water near Yucuñudahui. That same power or those same qualities are called upon for this tree birth. The sky itself is two partial U-bracket shapes above Achiuta in this Selden tableau: sky above, water below, and two snakes entwining the tree, representing both elements called into being at a stone-masonry place by the priests Ten Flint and Ten Lizard.

The first tree birth was engendered by the gods at Apoala, but the second was engendered by two elderly priests at Achiutla. This Selden performance ritual carefully displays the elements the priests used, just as the Vienna ritual displays the gods carving male/female elements into the tree trunk. At the event itself, both priests are displayed to either side of the tree, pouring tobacco from their hands onto two ritual objects topped by grass knots. One object is an earth-spirit stone (*ñuu*) on top of what appears to be a circular grass mat lying on edge; the other object is a stone with a serpent's face bleeding onto one of the underwater stones. All three levels of the Mesoamerican world are represented in the tableau: underwater underworld, earth, and sky. On one side of the tableau, in the sky, is the date Year 10 Reed Day 2 Grass, and on the other side is a garment topped by a gold pectoral and displaying a jeweled collar emerging from its lower side. The only remaining Lady Nine Reed personification of the tree is an eye peering from its trunk just beneath the split where Lord Two Grass emerges. It is in this elaborated milieu that the tree gives birth.

The contrast of the Vienna tree birth with that in Selden is a vivid demonstration of the extension of performance ritual outward from one initial source at an earlier time to serve the needs of royalty later in another place. The elements of creation are all present, and the goddess Nine Reed Tree draws from elements of sky, earth, and water to produce nobles to rule the very land, underworld, and sky from which they are born. As with the Maya before them, they are the lords of creation.

5 Caves in Mesoamerican Iconography
Chalcatzingo and the Mixteca

Geographical Review

As mentioned in the previous chapter, the geography of earth and sky, and of the forces of nature is generally personified as graphic toponyms in the Mixtec codices. This nomenclature has persisted among Mixtec people to this day, and frequently a place in their landscape—whether natural or man-made in ancient times—is recalled by a name descriptive of its corresponding toponym mentioned in one codex or another.

The power or force of this custom reflects the way Mixtecs—or at least their elite—saw themselves. Since the kings and queens, princes and princesses among the pre-Columbian and post-Columbian Mixtec peoples of Oaxaca were descended from divine or semidivine ancestors originally born from the earth, then it is fair to say that these families *were* the landscape that gave them birth and the right to rule (Pohl and Byland 1990:116). Other progenitors were born from the trees at Apoala or Achiutla, or came down via cloud-ropes from cave openings in the sky. Some were born twice: first in the earth from a cave (Lords Eight Wind and Nine Wind Quetzalcoatl) and then from the trees (Eight Wind) or from a stone knife in the sky (Nine Wind). It is then also fair to say that for some royal Mixtec families, caves and things associated with them were an inherent part of their genesis.

This chapter examines some of the earliest cave iconography (ca. 700 BC) at the Olmec outlier Chalcatzingo and analyzes it in relationship to elite empowerment. The discussion then turns to similar iconography as represented in the Postclassic Mixtec documents. The purpose is to demonstrate similitude of such iconographies in Mesoamerica for approximately 1,400 years between two cultures separated not merely by time but also by distance. Inasmuch as developed writing is unavailable in regard to early monumental iconography, the later Mixtec codices can be insightful aids in understanding the precise employment of cave ideology by royalty of any era, at least as it had been received and developed by the Postclassic Mixtecs themselves.

The methodology for this study—at least for Olmec cultural representations—was established by Kent Reilly (1996:29c) in what he terms "the Middle Formative Ceremonial Complex Model." This is an analysis of "artifacts, symbols, motifs, and architectural groupings" to ascertain the rituals, ideology, and political organization of various, diverse societies "forming the demographic and cultural landscape of Middle Formative period Mesoamerica." Therefore, the contention that this paradigm can be used insightfully to some extent for understanding the transference of iconographic ideology from culture to culture in Mesoamerica through time is relevant.

Caves as Icons of Empowerment

The importance of caves and caverns (whether entirely natural, modified, or artificially constructed) cannot be overstated when considering Mesoamerican iconography. They appear in the earliest recorded monumental art and persist as viable components in contemporary life there today (Freidel, Schele, and Parker 1993:205; Manzanilla 2000:105). Relative to the three levels of Mesoamerican cosmos—underworld, terrestrial, and celestial—caves are underworld portals and form part of a paradigm that maintains the world in a complex of associations; specifically, rain, fertility, supernatural beings, birth, death, mountains, the establishment of sacred space, temples, and, as we shall see, the empowerment of the elite who manipulate these important things and qualities.

Regarding the Mesoamerican cosmos, Carrasco (1990:51) remarks: "The Mesoamerican universe, in its various formulations, had a geometry consisting of three general levels: an over world or celestial space, the middle world or earthly level, and the underworld." He states further that each realm was subdivided into smaller, powerful "units," each saturated with supernatural power. This power moved through all cosmic levels. The lower levels, the terrestrial and aquatic underworlds, included mountains and were abundant with seeds, water, and precious stones upon which human life depended.

Caves are represented in diverse ways in Mesoamerican iconography: either by direct depiction of a cavern portal as a reptilian earth monster's maw, gaping jaguar mouth, or as a serpent's mouth, vividly represented in

Postclassic Codex ZN page 36. These representations will be amplified later. Caves are also places of origins, genesis, and creation. The Aztec people said they came from a complex of seven caves at Chicomoztoc (Brundage 1979:131). The womb itself has cave associations, and there are graphic similarities in the codices. In this regard, Hayden (2000:175) cites Sahagún, who repeats what he heard from Mexica (Aztec) women: "in us is a cave, a gorge . . . whose function is to receive." Hayden then continues: "When a woman was about to give birth, the midwife took her to the temazcalli, the steambath, which represents an artificial cave, a place of birth."

With such powerful and evocative associations it is not surprising to learn that Mesoamerican peoples, even from the beginnings of civilization in the Olmec heartland on the northern part of the Gulf of Tehuantepec nearly 2000 years BC, constructed their sacred space in the terrestrial realm by creating watery underworld portals and, as we assume from the archaeological remains at Olmec La Venta, the prototypal ballcourt also, with its strong underworld, cavernous associations. Such mysterious places would naturally empower those who could partake of or be generated by their transcendent qualities. The Pyramid of the Sun at great Teotihuacan was itself constructed over an artificial cave (Schele 1996:111), and this pattern seems universal and repeated wherever people designed to partake of and manipulate those powers, allowing them to function in all planes of existence.

Chalcatzingo

Chalcatzingo is located about 100 kilometers southeast of Mexico City near the eastern border of the state of Morelos. Middle Formative period burials and ceramics have been identified there, as well as Late Classic to Middle Postclassic artifacts from the Tetla area, chiefly by David C. Grove and associates, who initiated and completed an intensive excavation and analysis of the site from 1972 to 1974. Today Chalcatzingo is occupied chiefly by rural agriculturalists. The Middle Formative archaeological remains consist of terraces. The later Tetla occupation consists of a ceremonial zone with large mounds and a ballcourt. Collectors have removed many of the ancient monuments from this zone, and today the site is a stone mine (Grove 1987:13b). Only monuments with iconography relevant to this study are considered here.

Chalcatzingo Monument 1

This bas-relief monument (called El Rey) is incised on the vertical surface of a large boulder and faces north. Its dimensions are 2.7 x 3.2 m. The site is near the El Rey drainage runoff ditch, and locals associate it with a "rain serpent" and stormy weather—this from a local informant who witnessed the discovery of the monument after a violent storm in 1932 (Grove 1987:1a).

El Rey iconography is a unified tableau presented in three registers. In the upper or celestial register there are three rain clouds, each represented by three cloud units (a total of nine clouds) grouped together and shown as three distinct clouds per unit, with slashed lines representing rain falling from them (figure 5.1).

Beneath these clouds are thirteen objects in the shape of exclamation points, identified by Grove as raindrops. If we number the sets of clouds from one to three moving from the viewer's left, then there are five drops beneath cloud group 1, one drop between cloud groups 1 and 2, three beneath the central group (cloud group 2), and four beneath the cloud group 3. The number 13 is evocative of elemental calendrics, and a similar observation has been made by Angulo V. in another place regarding this monument (1987:137a).

Two pieces of vegetation—which I take to be stalks of maize (and not bromeliads, as noted in the edited volume by David Grove)—are also seen falling from the sky, one to either side of cloud group 2. Because stylized rain is closely associated with each cloud directly, and these exclamation-point objects are located in the same register as the falling maize stalks, I am inclined to identify them as raindrops and as maize seeds because of their unusual form and maize association. This identification is consistent with the concept of agricultural fertility and also with later maize god iconography identified at La Venta, where sprouting maize seeds are represented as the "trefoil motif" in association with elite regalia (Reilly, pers. comm., 2004). Reilly (1996:38b) also identifies the trefoil motif as associated with the "world tree." In each interpretation, vegetation is represented, and elite associations reinforced.

It is also important to mention that this celestial register displays at its lower level three round, target-shaped objects. Although it is tempting to identify them with "the three-stone place," a fourth occurs elsewhere in the iconography. The Codex Vienna identifies at least twelve stone qualities in the sky.

Figure 5.1. Chalcatzingo Monument 1. (Photograph by Linda Schele, used by permission of the Linda Schele Archive)

The terrestrial register shows a personified cave represented as a doubly indented bracket (one-half of a quatrefoil shape), open-mouthed to the viewer's right. Jorge Angulo V. (1987:135b) identifies this zoomorph as having both feline and reptilian features, and remarks that the creature's eye not only contains a St. Andrew's Cross but is topped by a design similar to the eye-crest of a harpy eagle—both celestial symbols. It has three maize plants sprouting from it, an eye located at its upper surface, and a double merlon at the central point of the bracket's left exterior side. He also notes vegetation and zoomorphic images on other monuments in the Monument 1-A grouping, specifically monuments 6, 7, 8, 11, 14, and 15. The open mouth of the personified cave image in Monument 1 also displays double merlons at the edge of upper and lower jaws outside the mouth opening, thereby giving the impression that they are extruded teeth. Taube (1996:89) identifies double merlons with the vegetal color green, and in the same volume Schele notes their association with sacred precincts (1996:121a).

The underworld is the interior of the personified cave itself, and this is indeed a dynamic image. An elaborately attired person is seated on a rect-angular throne within it, facing toward the cave mouth to the viewer's right. The throne-rectangle is designed in a scroll or lazy-S motif, used in Olmec art to represent clouds or rain (Chalcatzingo, Monument 9, pictured in Reil-ly 1996:101c).

The seated figure holds a lazy-S bar in his arms, and at the back of his head is a large headdress. The headdress also contains two raindrop/maize seed symbols and two quetzal birds at the back interspersed with two con-centric circle motifs topped by eyebrow-like brackets. Another circle and eyebrow is located at the top of this crown. A plant sprouts from the front central part of the headdress, and another from the figure's forehead (which appears to be covered by a turban). A combination circular and triangular earplug is in place, the figure's shoulders are covered by a short cape, and he wears a knee-length kilt and sandals. The skirt has raindrop/maize seed symbols, but the front-hanging belt (rather like a loincloth) is eroded beyond symbol identification. Everything about these accoutrements indicates an intimate association with rain and agricultural fertility.

Power is further shown by the great scrolls emanating from the zoomor-phic cave mouth. While this can be surely associated with wind, later rep-resentations of scrolls and people indicate speech or singing. It is unclear whether this anthropomorphic figure is a human elite or a supernatural, but considering the power claimed by rulers, it is likely that this confusion for us was not present in those who saw it originally; namely, the ruler had these supernatural abilities and connected with all three planes of existence. This connection, and implied transcendence, is reinforced by ideological associations between ruler and the axis mundi, or world tree, which can be demonstrated not only among the Olmecs but also among earlier and sub-sequent Mesoamerican civilizations (Reilly 1996:27c, 31a).

Implicit in the exercise of elite power is shamanism, noted by Reilly (1996:30a) as an "ancient, worldwide religious tradition . . . based on the belief that the spirits of ancestors and the controlling forces of the natural world, or gods, can be contacted by religious specialists in altered states of consciousness." Shamanism appears different in different cultures, depend-ing on the level of cultural organization; therefore, it cannot be confined to an individual, a collection of individuals, or an institutional organization. Shamans are believed to have the ability to transform into powerful animals that can function in one or more levels of the universe. Often this transformation involves an alteration of consciousness achieved through the use of plant-derived hallucinogens and changes of reality undertaken in caves.

Let us now turn our attention to another Chalcatzingo monument, the striking and dramatic Monument 9 (figure 5.2).

Monument 9 is an arresting image of the zoomorphic earth monster with an open, quatrefoil-shaped mouth. This is a frontal view of the same zoomorphic cave opening seen in side view on Monument 1-A. It is surrounded or outlined by three tiers or rows of "lips" following the quatrefoil pattern, which may represent a pyramid as seen from above (Michael McCarthy, pers. comm., 2004). Its dimensions are 1.8 x 1.5 meters, and the opening is large enough for a small, barely or completely undressed person to pass through.

This monument was looted from Plaza Central Structure 4 at Chalcatzingo (originally built in the Cantera phase, 700–500 BC) sometime in the

Figure 5.2. Chalcatzingo Monument 9. (Image © Justin Kerr and used by permission)

1960s. It was originally situated above a tomb. Reilly (1996:165a, b) notes that this monument relates directly to La Venta Monument 6 (the Sandstone Sarcophagus), which was carved to represent the Olmec earth dragon. In La Venta Monument 6 the deceased person rode on the back of, or within, the dragon to the underworld. Reilly notes that with Chalcatzingo Monument 9, the deceased in the tomb below passed through the open maw, thus passing from life to death. It is also likely that the open portal, placed strategically above a tomb, was a mode of access to or communication with the deceased, a common practice in many Mesoamerican cultures (Steele 1997).

It is important to note that this monument was broken, and that its upper left portion above the nose and left eye was reconstructed with concrete and subsequently stained with tea to make the newer reconstruction's color compatible with the remaining image (Reilly, pers. comm., 2004). Thus the two bars above the monster's nose may actually be three, but it is impossible to tell. Otherwise, the symbolism of this monument relates directly to that found in Monument 1-A, excluding wind elements and, perhaps, rain. The creature's nose is formed of a lazy-S, and vegetation images are seen at the trefoil corners of its gaping maw.

Although associated with a tomb, this device was also a functional portal; after all, it was *above* the tomb, not in it. As with Monument 1, it is possible that it is more than a portal—namely, a place-identifier, or a kind of toponym of the cave itself. In any event, the individual buried below it was imbued in life with those qualities displayed on Monument 1: the elite whose ability to command authority in all three levels of creation while alive is now in the underworld. In effect, Monument 9 suffers nothing by lacking some of the iconographic symbolism of Monument 1, because it is a *pars pro toto* (a part represents the whole) example of the earlier work, although a large one. Through such a portable cave, the power resident in one supernatural place is therefore transferable to another useful location.

Chalcatzingo Monument 13

This broken monument (known as "The Governor") measures 2.5 x 1.5 meters and is incised on a "thick, flat slab of stone" (Grove 1987:122b) that was originally rectangular (figure 5.3). The surviving fragment displays a "cleft-headed, baby-faced person seated within the full-face mouth of an earth-monster." Grove notes further that the earth monster figure is executed in the same manner, or style, as monuments 1 and 9—that is to say, the sur-

Figure 5.3. Chalcatzingo Monument 13. (Photograph by F. Kent Reilly III, used by permission of the Linda Schele Archive)

viving portion shows part of the original trefoil design. Vegetation images sprout from the monster-mouth's exterior, and the remaining portion of one eye is elongated instead of oval. It is topped by a large flame eyebrow. Grove implies that it is identical with the earth monster/cave shown on Monument 9. It is therefore likely a representation of that same cave.

The individual seated within the cave is in profile and faces left with both arms extended down toward the knees. The person is clothed. Angulo V. (1987:141a, b) notes such similarity between monuments 13, 9, and 16 (a decapitated statue) that he feels they might have formed a visual unit or tableau when originally carved and displayed. He also remarks that the individual shown on Monument 9 has, according to his seated position, great similarity to the Gulf Coast La Venta monuments 8, 10, and 73. Chalcatzingo monuments 9 and 13 show the earth monster/cave full-face, and since associated humans are shown within a cave, we note also the similarity to the La Venta throne monuments, which display the royal personage seated within or emerging from a cave niche. In all cases the cave niches display iconographic symbolism indicative of the exercise of elite power, whether to control the natural environment or, by extension, to control polities within that environment. The human or human-like figures displayed on the Chalcatzingo monuments cannot be parsed into either human or supernatural, yet it is clear from their implications that the individuals partake of both identities. Chalcatzingo iconography contains archetypal images that can be seen in later Mesoamerican cultures as clearly divine or supernatural. Although examples abound, one appears in this context: Monument 5 (figure 5.4).

This bas-relief clearly depicts a serpentine monster either devouring or regurgitating a human. However, closer examination shows that only the human's left leg is inserted into the creature's mouth, evoking the later story of the god Tezcatlipoca, who lost his left foot when he dangled it into the water and had it bitten off by Cipactli, the crocodilian personification of the underworld waters. Iconographic associations between rain, wind (as in Monument 1), and human figures can be seen as prototypal images of various rain gods, such as Chaac, or gods of the wind, such as Lord Nine Wind (Mixtec) and Ehecatl (Aztec). The point here is simply that all of these elements, which we have briefly catalogued in a limited choice of Chalcatzingo monumental art, are cultural images transmitted as viable icons in later

Figure 5.4. Chalcatzingo Monument 5. (Photograph by F. Kent Reilly III, used by permission of the Linda Schele Archive)

Mesoamerican civilizations. The concept that Mesoamerican art is thematically conservative but stylistically diverse or creative according to culture is well established. We propose now to demonstrate this by moving forward in time more than one thousand years and examining the same iconographic concepts inherited and employed by the Postclassic Mixtec elites of Oaxaca in their painted picture books.

Mixtec Cave Iconography

In the Classic period the dynamic Mixtec people were, at first, vassals of the Zapotec Confederacy centralized at Monte Alban. John Pohl writes,

> By AD 400, what had been rival villages for centuries during the Preclassic had now become regional administrative centers ruled by lesser ranking families who were incorporated into a system of power sharing through exclusive inter-marriages, gifts and rewards. Monte Alban's kings were thereby able to transform distant regions into rich tribute paying provinces ultimately controlling much of the state of Oaxaca and beyond. (FAMSI Web site, 2001)

When powerful Monte Alban collapsed in the Middle Classic period, the Mixtec people had marriage alliances with Zapotec royalty, chiefly at Zaachila, and emerged on their own, very likely by revolt and warfare (Pohl 1991:23a). They had a political system based on principles inherited from the Zapotec-dominated era. This influence is seen especially in their retention of a system of oracles, including the Zapotec's Lord Seven Flower (called Bezelao), as well as Zapotec supernaturals such as Lord Seven Rain, a Xipe-Totec archetype who was the patron of Zachilla (ZN page 33b). As we shall see, they inherited the iconography of elite interaction with the natural and supernatural world via caves, and closely identified their elite with the world tree and, by implication, shamanism.

Empowerment Rituals

Mixtecs attribute various forces, qualities, and functions to caves; namely, spirits, supernatural beings, weather, religious ceremonies (some associated with the assumption of status), ancestor burial cults, and, in modern Oaxaca, blood-letting rituals (Steele 1997).

This section elucidates representations of caves and associated empowerment rituals as they appear in codices Zouche-Nuttall (ca. AD 1430 for the obverse) and Bodley (parts of which are perhaps as late as AD 1521). Though separated from the princely authors/scribes of Codex Zouche-Nuttall by perhaps 230 years, Codex Bodley is painted in the original native format and style. Both documents, however, are retrospectives of the events they portray. Supportive examples from other Mixtec codices—especially the Colonial era Codex Selden—will be employed as well. In this way it may be possible to demonstrate how iconography displayed in Middle Formative period Chalcatzingo came to be employed in the Mixtec culture more than a thousand years later.

Mixtec Cave Scenes and Lord Eight Wind

Codex Zouche-Nuttall obverse (museum numbered pages 1–41) begins (pages 1–8) with the narrative saga of lineage founder Lord Eight Wind Eagle Flints. He is born from the earth, and the narrative tells that he is lineage founder in at least three places where he emerges from caves (pages 1 and 2): Cerro Jasmine, Apoala, and Yucuñudahui (Rain God Hill). The second dynasty of Jaltepec (Codex Selden page 5) claims him as well. These first eight pages display no fewer than twelve cave openings in association with Lord Eight Wind's history. The narrative scenes themselves are discussed in detail in chapter 6.

This historical narrative of Lord Eight Wind's life displays many of the characteristics demonstrated in the Middle Formative period monuments at Chalcatzingo; namely, those associated with elites and the power that goes with their status. In the case of the Mixtec narrative tableaux, however, we have more to follow because the narratives are more complete and uninterrupted; excepting partial erosion by time, they are unmutilated (except for the Codex Alfonso Caso [Codex Colombino-Becker I]). The vegetative associations are present, and Lord Eight Wind is clearly identified as being venerated at the cave on Rain God Hill, as we would expect. ZN page 5c even shows him receiving water directly from the rain god (Pohl and Byland 1990:121).

Although the historical saga of Lord Eight Wind is not told completely at this point, I have demonstrated that he, as an earth-born noble, functioned in the three realms of creation: the underworld (from which he was born and with which he continually interacts), the terrestrial world, and by virtue of his association with the rain god, the celestial as well. Another feature of his life is that he used caves as transportation. A Mixtec gentleman, Ruben Luengas, told me in 1998 that old folks in the Mixteca still mention caves as "roads" from one place to another, but that the danger of getting lost in them is great. I must also restate at this point that Lord Eight Wind is revered in the Mixtec books as a lineage founder. As mentioned previously, the post-Conquest era Mixtecs at Jaltepec recorded in Codex Selden that he founded their second dynasty, which was still viable at the time of the Spanish entrada. Codex Zouche-Nuttall (5c) mentions his marriage and his offspring's connections with the first dynasty of Tilantongo, and Codex Vindobonensis Mexicanus I (Codex Vienna, 35-II) mentions him as among the great lords who were present when the lineage nobles were born from the world tree (axis mundi), and as one of those tree-born nobles himself. Codex Selden associates him with the toponym tree at Suchixtlan.

In this regard, I do not overlook a relationship of transcendence between caves and axis mundi. Powerful shamanic rulers of the Mixteca (such as Lord Eight Deer) make close associations between their dynamic persons, caves, trees, and mountains (which are frequently personified). Lord Eight Deer himself (of whom we will learn more later) was the Mixtecs' great culture hero, and every major codex mentions him. He was attentive to associations with caves and supernatural trees. He was not only a conqueror, but a priest, politician, and lineage founder.

Another important ideological feature of the Mixtec codices is that all bodies of water have established otherworldly/underworld symbolism and are usually shown as contained in upturned devices resembling U-brackets. Visually, these are literally upended caves. Often, as in ZN page 44, these underwater/underworld areas contain the residences of the gods, represented as temples, masonry platforms, and enclosures. The cave at Apoala has a name: "the Serpent's Mouth" (ZN page 36). Apoala was also the place where nobles were born from the great tree or trees (this also happened at Achiutla) that had been carved by the gods with both male and female symbols (Codex Vienna 37b).

Lord Eight Deer at Tututepec, According to Codex Zouche-Nuttall

As interesting as the foregoing narrative tableaux are in that they associate caves, a prominent lineage founder who acts in the three planes of the cosmos, and royal authority, yet another fascinating scene occurs on the reverse (side 2) of Codex Zouche-Nuttall (pages 42–84) concerning the initial political career of the great culture hero Lord Eight Deer of Tilantongo. At age twenty, in Year 1 Reed on Day 7 Vulture (AD 1083), Lord Eight Deer conquers his way to Tututepec and is empowered in a complex, three-part ceremony beginning in a cave. The identifier for the first part of this ceremonial empowerment complex occurs in the cave itself. Lord Eight Deer sits on a blue stone in the cave; a non-Mixtec person sits cross-legged before him and speaks. Two deer hoofs and an animal (perhaps a coyote) followed by two more deer hoofs are ascending toward Lord Eight Deer and are connected to his feet by a black line. Eight Deer wears his jaguar suit and helmet, an earplug, a blue collar with gold bells, and a quiver from which displays of colored feathers can be seen to protrude. The ascending deer hoofs and coyote, besides being a qualifier for this ceremony, connect visually via the black line to the second ceremonial qualifier seen directly below them: a ballcourt/bird sacrifice. The ballcourt itself is four-colored (the green section has faded to golden-brown), and the event therein is qualified by the presence of a circular, woven grass mat and knot (both faded from green to brown). The white-painted individual seated before Lord Eight Deer in the first part of this ceremony is seen now in part 2 at the lower right drinking from a cup. Lord Eight Deer—now in different attire and wearing a beard— stands to the viewer's right and receives a ballplayer's collar and gold bell/ bangle from an individual identified as Lord Six (or Seven) Snake.

The third part of this Tututepec empowerment ceremony closely follows the second. Lord Eight Deer (still wearing a beard, but attired in yet another costume) and Lord Six (or Seven) Snake stand above Star Temple on Tututepec Hill. The aforementioned ballcourt is at the base of Tututepec Hill. A blood-stained altar is glimpsed through the temple's door. Not shown on this page (45) but occurring immediately on page 46, therefore appearing just behind Lord Eight Deer, is a priest attired as the supernatural Lord Nine Wind—all indicators of human sacrifice. This assumption of authority at Tututepec is preceded and followed by Lord Eight Deer's conquest events.

Perhaps this sequence can be better understood if we realize that the first dynasty of Tilantongo (Eight Deer's home) was unstable (Byland and Pohl 1994:121–127). Its last ruler (Lord Two Rain) dies heirless thirteen years later (Byland and Pohl [1994:242] call his death "mysterious"), and Eight Deer himself was not of direct royal bloodline. This is why the codex scribes painted this historical retrospective. They indicate by this narrative that Lord Two Rain of Tilantongo had been refused the traditional marriage alliance with the royalty at Jaltepec (ZN page 44) and that Eight Deer's father (Lord Five Alligator), who was high priest and head of the Council of Four at Tilantongo, had died the previous year (Codex Bodley 8). The reverse of Codex Zouche-Nuttall shows Eight Deer's political biography (none of his marriages are shown) and begins with his parentage statement and conquest events he achieved in his preteen years.

This cave empowerment ceremonial complex (cave, ballcourt, temple) essentially represents the three planes of existence—underworld (cave), terrestrial (ballcourt, implying the underworld manifested in the terrestrial), and celestial (the temple and Lord Nine Wind). The cave-installation ceremony is important because Eight Deer's later career—of which this is only the beginning—moves him into position to assume rulership at Tilantongo and, subsequently, of the whole of the Mixteca and associated non-Mixtec polities (ZN pages 54–74). By implication, one of Eight Deer's political motives will include retribution concerning severance of the alliance between his own polity at Tilantongo and neighboring Jaltepec.

Lord Eight Deer at Tututepec, According to Codex Bodley

Although all major Mixtec codices are retrospectives, Codex Zouche-Nuttall, Codex Vindobonensis Mexicanus I obverse, and the fragments now called Codex Alfonso Caso (Codex Colombino-Becker I) are pre-Columbian. Codices Selden and perhaps parts of Bodley are post-Conquest documents painted in the original Mixtec style. Codex Zouche-Nuttall, while surely Postclassic, is not securely dated but is separated from Codex Bodley by maybe two hundred years, and between them two distinct traditions are represented. It is reasonable to expect variation and, in some cases, amplification of their narrative cognates. This is the case in both codices' representations of Lord Eight Deer's biography.

Codex Bodley (9–10) presents us with interesting insights on the history and empowerment of Lord Eight Deer at Tututepec. After the death of his father, Lord Five Alligator (Bodley 8-V), Lord Eight Deer is seen leaving a cave (year 3 Flint, or AD 1080, when he was seventeen years old): this cave has a remarkable resemblance to the half-trefoil caves seen in Middle Formative period Chalcatzingo monuments. It even has the Mixtec equivalents of double merlons, as well as eyes and gaping maw. He travels directly to another personified cave (shown in profile) where he makes offerings. Codex Zouche-Nuttall mentions that prior to this (pages 43–44) he conquered several towns at the age of eight years, and yet another town when he was sixteen years old; both conquests occurred prior to his father's death.

Continuing in year 3 Flint, Lord Eight Deer visits the elders Lady Four Rabbit and Lord Ten Flower, who are related to the first dynasty of Tilantongo (Caso 1960:38b). The story now continues on page 10-V (bottom of page), where Lord Eight Deer is seen going to yet another cave, shown in cut-away view, associated with the elders. Only Lord Eight Deer's name-pictogram is shown within it. It also contains a temple. Continuing with the text on Bodley 10-V, Lord Eight Deer visits Lord One Death, Oracle of the Sun, at Achiutla. This oracle will always be prominent in Eight Deer's political career.

The year is now 4 House—one year later, or AD 1081—and Lord Eight Deer journeys to a town where he is seen in a ballcourt activity (Bodley 10-IV) with Lord One Motion, the god or oracle of the planet Venus. Two oracles (One Death Sun God and One Motion Venus God) are shown acting together in lineage activity on Codex Selden page 1, where they propel an atlatl dart (male element) into a cave (female element), which then gives birth to Lord Eleven Water, founder of the first dynasty at Jaltepec. However, in the Bodley narrative, Lord Eight Deer and Lord One Motion, having formed an alliance in the ballcourt ceremony, conquer a town together.

The narrative continues on Bodley 9-IV. The year is 6 Reed (AD 1083), two years later, and Eight Deer is twenty years old. He attacks another town, offers gifts to Lady Nine Grass (the oracle of Chalcatongo), seated in a temple, visits the rulers of Apoala (according to Caso 1960:39a), then travels to Tututepec, where he sits atop its toponym. The empowerment ceremony shown in Codex Zouche-Nuttall as happening in a cave/ballcourt/temple ceremony is represented in a *pars pro toto* image of the animal and deer hoofs ascending toward the seated figure of Lord Eight Deer.

No fewer than three caves are associated with ceremonies in this expansive Bodley cognate, and all are associated with the central figure of Lord Eight Deer, oracles of power, and the assumption of rulership. For the scribes of Codex Bodley, who were writing in a different tradition from those who recorded Codex Zouche-Nuttall, the events prior to Eight Deer at Tututepec, especially those associated with the powerful elders and oracles, were their important historical events. Both traditions emphasize Eight Deer's prowess as a warrior from childhood to early adulthood. In the Bodley cognate Lord Eight Deer is always shown wearing his full jaguar attire, indicating that he *is* the jaguar's power. This is a vivid reminder that Lord Eight Deer's personal name is "Jaguar Claw." When Codex Bodley displays him seated in power at Tututepec, Eight Deer wears a different garment but retains his jaguar helmet.

Lord Eight Deer's Later Career

At the end of Lord Eight Deer's career, he conquers a place called Huachino and, for lineage reasons, spares one of its princes, a youth named Lord Four Wind (ZN page 83), the son of Lady Six Monkey of Jaltepec, and thus a descendant of Lord Eight Wind Eagle Flints. The Bodley cognate narrative (page 34 of the codex) reveals different details of the events.

The narrative begins in the lower band, reading from right to left, starting with year 11 House (AD 1101). This is the sequence of events beginning on page 34: (1) Lord Eight Deer attacks Huachino; (2) the scions (Lords Ten Dog and Six House) of the ruler of that place (Lord Eleven Wind) by a former wife become captives. The narrative continues on page 35 at the page fold: (3) Lord Four Wind (the captives' younger half-brother and the son of Huachino's ruler and Lady Six Monkey of Jaltepec) is shown seated in a cave looking out or down on his bound half-brothers; (4) a fire-serpent priest holding an excised heart descends from the cave mouth directly between seated Lord Four Wind and the bound captives. The Zouche-Nuttall cognate scene (83–84) shows the two captives being executed by Lord Eight Deer: Ten Dog is bound to a round rock, given ineffective weapons, and clawed to death by two men wearing jaguar gloves; Six House is bound to a scaffold and bled to death by being shot with atlatl darts.

In this cave empowerment ceremony, the animal sacrifice is omitted, and the narrative tableaux proceeds directly to human sacrifice; however, the point is that Lord Eight Deer of Tilantongo makes an alliance with the young Lord Four Wind of Huachino and empowers him seated in a cave. The outstanding feature about this empowerment/sacrifice ceremony is the presence of a *yaha yahui* (fire serpent) priest descending from the cave mouth directly before the bound captives and holding an excised human heart. These priests could fly through sky and earth, and they performed human sacrifice. Pohl (1994) remarks that the title was also associated with persons who later became lineage founders, as did Eight Deer, so we can assume without impediment that this figure is Eight Deer himself as pictogram metaphor. Eight Deer literally empowers the boy Four Wind by the sacrifice of his two half-brothers.

Lord Four Wind was barely more than a boy when Eight Deer captured Hua Chino and ritually sacrificed his parents—Lady Six Monkey of Jaltepec and Lord Eleven Wind of Huachino and his half-brothers. It is possible to assume that Four Wind (his surviving younger brother was One Alligator, who later ruled at their mother's town of Jaltepec) was an important link to the Jaltepec dynasty. Eight Deer himself was very likely refused marriage with Lady Six Monkey because of his non-elite lineage. An alliance with the old, distinguished lineage of Lord Eight Wind Eagle Flints and Eight Deer's town of Tilantongo had been custom, so this present alliance was the next best thing—a child of that dynasty who could be controlled by Eight Deer.

This cave presentation/human sacrifice ceremony was not only a bestowal of authority, but also the creation of a desired confederacy between the two polities. The two sacrificed half-brothers were also recognized as an important dynastic link, but to the lineage of Huachino and Wasp Hill. Their elimination completed the lineage extermination of that rival dynasty and divorced the two descendants of Jaltepec (Four Wind and One Alligator) from Huachino forever.

Both of these historical narratives—Eight Deer's empowerment at Tututepec at the beginning of his political career, and Four Wind's subsequent empowerment by and alliance with Eight Deer eighteen years later—speak of a special kind of power. They illustrate not only the use of important geographical features—specifically, caves—to impart authority by virtue of the transcendent qualities they possess innately, but also by this very ability to bestow alliance status upon recipients by sharing it in ceremonial confederation.

These scenes also have another kind of power because they demonstrate the qualities attributed to caves as sacred spaces influencing Mixtec history through individuals who claimed to partake of potent, mysterious, underground, underworld attributes, whether by birthright or by association. Apparently, although he lacked royal descent, Eight Deer's status as the first son of a high priest of the Council of Five at Tilantongo was sufficient for him to receive specific elevations in position (ZN page 52) subsequent to his assumption of rule at Tututepec. After that, his insightful and aggressive abilities would enable him to engineer a way to successfully fill the power vacuum at Tilantongo and repair the rift in alliance between his hometown and neighboring Jaltepec.

The historical saga of Lord Eight Deer is fulsome even in so few tableaux; therefore, our search for outstanding symbolism should conclude with a restatement of the Mixtec cosmos. It follows an ancient Mesoamerican pattern of celestial, terrestrial, underworld that is discernable among the Olmec of antiquity, the Classic period Maya, and beyond. In this scheme, caves are more than entrances to another realm beneath the earth. Sometimes caves can be an entrance from sky to earth, with a sky-cave opening represented in a distinctive way similar to that illustrating cave mouths in sacred mountains. Caves transcend the planes of existence. Page 18 of Zouche-Nuttall shows an underwater/underworld cave—and it actually contains the sky or an opening to it—an evocative image suggestive of the sky reflected in a lake.

The codices depict ceremonies for those who are able to tap into these powerful features. Caves connect *all* three levels of existence and are occupied by otherworldly beings. We have also mentioned information from a local informant that caves are underground highways used to travel from one place to another. Page 36 of Zouche-Nuttall shows the Apoala cave named the Serpent's Mouth. Four men are entering it. Page 37 shows them exiting in another place. The oracle Lady Nine Grass of Chalcatongo had access to the underworld via a cave. Within it were mummy bundles of ancestors available for consultation regarding important decisions. It may be implied by association that Monument 9 of Chalcatzingo could have served a similar function for that Middle Formative to Classic period people.

Caves, then, are gateways between worlds, and mysterious, powerful things happen in them. They are the loci for transactions that happen in all spheres of creation. Jaguars were great, even mighty creatures to the Mixtecs—Lord Eight Deer is proof of that. According to their surviving iconography, the Olmecs before them had observed that jaguars hunted both land and water, and lived in caves. Our Mixtec hero Lord Eight Deer was always associated with jaguar attributes and was even named for the animal's claw, an instrument he used in human sacrifice. His representation on Codex Bodley almost always has him attired in jaguar accoutrements, suggesting a complete identification between this sacred animal and the great culture hero. Codex Selden, on the other hand, only mentions Eight Deer as the father of two Tilantongo princesses who marry the royal sons of Jaltepec (Four Wind and One Alligator); even with such slight shrift, Eight Deer is shown in jaguar attire lest the implication of his power be diminished.

Conclusions: Politics and Power

The ideological cave iconography displayed on earlier Olmec monuments at Chalcatzingo and elsewhere in Olmec civilization is a tantalizing indicator of how such graphic ideology was actually employed by elite rulers to achieve their goals. Inasmuch as caves form an important part of these ideograms, their symbolism becomes diverse in association and content, according to the purposes desired by those who employ them. Agricultural fertility involving control of the elements, the creation of supernatural mythologies, the relationship to and actions of these supernatural elements in the everyday world, and the empowerment of elite rulers imply there was no distinct dividing line between the physical and what we would call the "metaphysical." This is true for many ancient cultures (such as the Maya) that survive in today's world. In effect, these iconographies were a kind of religious and political technology employed to serve the goals of those who shaped and directed society. Although such symbol systems have been deeply and effectively analyzed by modern scholars, much about them and their use must perforce remain mysterious to us.

The Mixtec historical documents, on the other hand, provide a more expansive look at the societal use of iconography (specifically, cave iconography) in a later Mesoamerican culture which appears to have been as forceful and dynamic as the Olmecs who preceded them. This is indicative of an Epiclassic/Postclassic Ceremonial Complex, at least among the Mixtecs. This study of the Mixtec pictogram books is useful and insightful because narrative tableaux represented on their pages are neither interrupted, disordered, nor destroyed. This is said even in light of the fact that many of the *tonindeye*—or "lineage histories," as the Mixtecs call them—have been lost to time and circumstance, and even though one of the five precious, major Mixtec documents remaining (Codex Alfonso Caso) has been almost eradicated by an unknown hand.

The earlier Olmec monuments are truly imaginative, superb works of art—the equal of any art from any culture. We can see in them the beginnings of writing, calendrics, and perhaps astronomy as well. The Mixtec pictogram books, however, name historical figures, record their deeds, and depict events that can be advanced and regressed according to an accurate calendric system. We know their family histories; in fact, the Mixtecs have the longest written royal histories in the world. The Maya, whose gods live in the sky, proved that Mesoamerican cultures had a more than passing interest in astronomy. I am certain the Mixtecs did, too, because we have the One Motion (Venus)/Sun (One Death) association on page 1 of Codex Selden—and, of course, many codex pages display icons of the celestial realm and the descents of elite personages from them. Temples are named for the celestial realm: Temple of Heaven, Temple of the Star, Stars Temple, and so on.

Cultural "back streaming" is a difficult and often misleading undertaking. However, it is not treacherous to observe the progress of artistic, cultural themes through time and remember that an idea which began as a seed could, and very likely did, grow not only into a cultural tree, but into cultural forests of societies. Those who followed the great Olmecs partook of their seminal greatness—Maya, Zapotecs, Mixtecs, and Aztecs. They did it by iconographically transforming their perceived levels of the cosmos into terrestrial reality and then used it to maintain stability in a world that was often hostile and chaotic.

The very transformation of chaos into order was the business of those born to power and rule. They were the scions of underworld, earth, and sky, and it was their particular ability to use their positions to translate supernatural paradigms into the structured progress of everyday life—whether agricultural or political. The unknown person shown on Chalcatzingo Monument 1 may not have been so very far removed in purpose from mighty Lord Eight Deer the Jaguar Claw of Tilantongo.

We can now turn our attention to Codex ZN pages 1–8 and its story of the protagonist of this text: Lord Eight Wind of Suchixtlan.

PART TWO

6   Lord Eight Wind's Introduction

Figure 6.1. Codex Zouche-Nuttall page 1 (British Museum folio no. 1), tableaux 1, 3, and 4. (© Trustees of the British Museum, The British Museum Company, Ltd.)

Pages 1 and 2: Synopsis of Tableaux

Although page 1 of Codex Zouche-Nuttall obverse has three tableaux, the single large tableau on page 2 is the dominant scene, with the page 1 tableaux subordinate to it. The five dates among the four tableaux on these two pages cover a span of fifty-two years, from AD 935 (Year 1 Reed Day 1 Alliga-

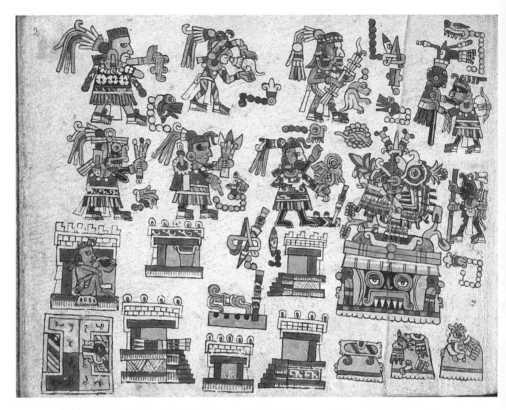

Figure 6.2. Codex Zouche-Nuttall page 2 (British Museum folio no. 2), tableau 2 in this two-page sequence. (© Trustees of the British Museum, The British Museum Company, Ltd.)

Table 6.1. Sequenced Chronology and Reading Order of Zouche-Nuttall Obverse Pages 1 and 2

Page/Tableau/Event	Mixtec Date	European	Date AD
1/1. ♂ 12 Alligator born	1 Reed 12 Alligator		935
		+42 days	
1/1. ♂ 8 Wind born	1 Reed 8 Wind		935
		+28 years	
2/2. At Yucuñudahui	3 Reed 4 Motion		963
		+17 years	
2/2. At Yucuñudahui	7 Flint 1 Motion		980
1/3. At Apoala	7 Flint 1 Motion		980
		+7 years	
1/4. At Monkey Hill	1 Reed 1 Alligator		987

tor) to AD 987 (Year 1 Reed Day 1 Alligator). The date itself is metaphorically associated with "beginnings," especially of dynasties (Furst 1978a:90–92). Four sites or locations are illustrated: Toto Cuee Cave (page 1, tableau 1), Yucuñudahui (Rain God Hill) (page 2, tableau 2), Apoala (page 1, tableau 3), and Monkey Hill/Suchixtlan/Cerro Jasmin (page 1, tableau 4).

The introduction has one primary actor, Lord Eight Wind, and two secondary actors, Lords Twelve Alligator and Eleven Flower—all of whom face in the direction the pictograms are to be read (to the reader's left). There are fourteen tertiary actors in the four tableaux, although none in the first. They function as ceremonial attendants who face against the reading direction, to the reader's right.

The actions displayed on these two pages are: the births of Lord Eight Wind and Lord Twelve Alligator (page 1, tableau 1); Lord Eight Wind's appearance at Apoala (page 1, tableau 3); Lord Eight Wind's appearance at Monkey Hill (page 1, tableau 4); and the ordering ritual at Yucuñudahui conducted by Lord Eight Wind, Lord Twelve Alligator, and Lord Eleven Flower (page 2). On page 1, directly above the lower left-hand tableau (tableau 3) is a blank space. This is suspicious. Examination of high-resolution photographs from the British Museum under various filters discloses that this space once displayed a human figure, now erased (Johann Sawyer, pers. comm., 2008).

Lord Eight Wind, Myth and History

The recovery of Lord Eight Wind's biography is complicated by the fact that the Mixtecs believe that all of their great ancestors, heroes, and lineage founders have supernatural qualities. This is surely the case with Lord Eight Wind. Ancestors are often called "gods" in the literature, when in point of fact they more resemble the concept of *santos*: holy and extraordinary people whose lives are embellished by supernatural deeds (Troike 1978:558). John Pohl (1994:55) writes: "In Pre-Columbian times the kings were the equivalent of saints. They bore titles of divinity and claimed sacred rights to control of the land by virtue of their direct ancestors, the nuu, who were born literally from specific geographical features (see Pohl and Byland 1990)."

The first two pages of Codex Zouche-Nuttall obverse are Lord Eight Wind's introduction and deal with the first fifty-two years of his life, a period when he undertook and accomplished extraordinary deeds. By the time his biography resumes on page 5, after the War from Heaven (pages 3 and 4), he is beginning the second part of his life transformed as a mortal lineage founder.

Because the codex is a Postclassic manuscript retrospectively recording Epiclassic events, he is called "Eight Wind" for the day of his supernatural birth from Toto Cuee Cave in the Cavua Colorado (Byland and Pohl 1994:88, 120). Subsequent appearances in the various tableaux show him emerging from cave openings, even in temples and other buildings.

Lord Eight Wind's eagle costume identifies him as a specific kind of *santo,* a class of priest referred to as *yaha yahui.* These special wizards are said to have several extraordinary abilities: they can speak with the dead (Fray Antonio de los Reyes (1976 [1593]:79), control local economies, become invisible, and fly through both air and earth. As to this latter feat, one meaning of *yaha* is "eagle." Lord Nine Wind Quetzalcoatl is seen in two of his forms as both *yaha* and *yahui* in Codex Vienna (page 48). These priests, sometimes symbolized by the maguey plant, are described as "fathers of the tribe or race" (Byland and Pohl 1994:88). Fray Gregorio Garcia (1729 [1607]:327–328) notes the legend of two brothers named Nine Wind—a legend that is preserved in Mixtec folklore. Although it is recorded as coming from two illiterate Mixtec farmers from the towns of San Juan and Santa Crux Mixtepec in 1976 (León-Portilla and Shorris 2001:619), it is actually preserved in a Spanish version in the Monastery of Cuilapa that is mentioned by Antonio de los Reyes (1976 [1593]). One brother—the older one, Nine Serpent Wind—could turn himself into an eagle and fly through the air. The younger brother, Nine Caverns Wind, could transform into a small winged serpent and fly with such skill that he could fly through rocks and walls. He could also be invisible. Clearly, Lord Eight Wind Eagle Flints partakes of some of these Nine Wind avatar characteristics, particularly in his ability to move through caves in the earth with great ease.

This is not a casual association. As demonstrated previously, from earliest times in Mesoamerica, caves are illustrated as portals to another world. In Middle Formative period Chalcatzingo, an Olmec influenced outlier, the earliest stone monuments show caves as entrances to the underworld and as the proper spheres of action for powerful elites with supernatural abilities (Grove 1987). Individuals who appear from, or who enact events in, caves have been variously labeled as wizards, priests, or shamans. Because Mesoamerican art tends to be thematically conservative but stylistically variable, it is not surprising to note that the prominent cave image at Chalcatzingo on Monument 9, dated at ca. 700–500 BC, is figured similarly to a prominent cave at another location in Codex Bodley (9-V), ca. AD 1500—almost two thousand years later.

Lord Eight Wind's predominating association with caves as supernatural portals both qualifies his abilities and provides secure identification as a yaha yahui priest. This association persists until he reaches age sixty-nine, after which two tableaux do not display him with caves: page 5c, his marriage to Lady Ten Eagle, and page 7d, where he is shown in post-mortem events as though alive, and seated in the temple at Monkey Hill/Suchixtlan/Cerro Jasmin.

This particular site is identified in Codex Selden as a place with white flowers, and this is a known location in modern Oaxaca: Cerro Jasmin. Eight Wind's site shown in Codex Selden (5-III) and Bodley (5–6) (Jansen and Jimenez 2005:37a) was known as Suchixtlan in Postclassic times, and the currently unknown site called "Monkey Hill" in the codices is likely in this same area. Therefore, all three locations are generally synonymous. The Codex Selden tableau names our protagonist "Lord Eight Wind Twenty," and this is also the case in Codex Vienna (35a) when he attends the Tree-Birth ceremony at Apoala.

Reading Orders for Pages 1 and 2

There are two reading orders possible for this two-page introduction. The first of them (see Pohl's introduction to this volume) is by similarity of dates, which orders the tableau as page 1 tableau 1 dated Year 1 Reed 1 Alligator; then the tableau above it, dated 1 Reed 1 Alligator. This scheme then takes the next tableau on page 1, dated Year 7 Flint Day 1 Motion, and relates it to the topmost date on page 2, which is the same. The sequence then progresses to the central date on page 2, which is Year 3 Reed Day 4 Flint. The eye then logically proceeds to the first date on page 3, which is Year 3 Reed Day 6 Dog (Williams 1991:2b). These five dates among four tableaux can be expressed by number in reading order from right to left.

4. 7 Flint 1 Motion	2. 1 Reed 1 Alligator
5. 3 Reed 5 Motion	3. 7 Flint 1 Motion
	1. 1 Reed 1 Alligator

However, there is a chronological sequence to the dates that proposes a more sophisticated reading order less obvious to casual inspection, and I prefer this system. It follows a year-progression in the Mixtec calendar, cycle 2, and the European calendar dates are included to render this progression obvious (table 3.1). Expressed by chronological progression of years, this reading order is:

3. 7 Flint 1 Motion   5. 1 Reed 1 Alligator
2. 3 Reed 4 Motion   4. 7 Flint 1 Motion
                         1. 1 Reed 1 Alligator

This second reading sequence is roughly circular or oval, beginning at the lower right of page 1 and ending at the upper right of that same page.

At first glance, this circular reading scheme seems unusual, but a similar pattern appears on page 19 in the second saga, and the final page of Zouche-Nuttall obverse has an identical pattern—beginning at the lower right and ending at the upper right. It is a way of setting a text sequence apart from what precedes and/or follows it. For this reason, we can see that pages 1 and 2 constitute Lord Eight Wind's introduction and summarize a complete calendar cycle. Then the war story is told on pages 3 and 4, and Eight Wind's biography is resumed on page 5.

In summary, the day 12 Alligator occurs once (day 200) in solar year 1 Reed, as does day Eight Wind (day 242), so Lord Eight Wind was born on the 242nd day in that year. These two pages provide a glimpse of the first fifty-two years of his life. He was born supernaturally from Toto Cuee Cave in AD 935; in his twenty-eighth year he was at Yucuñudahui; seventeen years later, at age forty-five, he went to Apoala; and seven years after that, at age fifty-two, he began his rule at Suchixtlan.

Who Was Lord Eight Wind?

Lord Eight Wind's identity and qualities provoke the reader's curiosity and are proper subjects of investigation, enlarged and explained subsequently as the scribes reveal him to us. The first two pages of Codex Zouche-Nuttall obverse do state interesting and important things about Eight Wind during the first part of his life, when he functioned as a *santo* with the supernatural abilities of a yaha yahui priest.

Lord Eight Wind's association with the pivotal lineage site of Apoala is prominent in two ways. First, we see his institution of the fire-drilling ordering ritual at Yucuñudahui. A similar ceremony is also an Apoala ritual (Furst 1978a:17b) pictured in Codex Vienna, page 18, Year 3 Reed Day 2 Grass to

Year 7 Flint Day 1 Flower. The years in both codices are the same, but not the days; therefore, they are rituals specific to each location, and the metaphorical content carried in the 260-day sacred calendar differs between the two sites. Second, on page 1 in the Codex Zouche-Nuttall Apoala tableau, Eight Wind emerges from a cave in the river at Apoala. This is very likely a direct reference to Apoala as the co-source of this ritual. This tableau visually links to Codex Zouche-Nuttall page 18b, which shows a sacred fire-drilling bundle emerging from a cave in the river at Apoala. Thus Lord Eight Wind's tableau at Apoala on Zouche-Nuttall page 1 may be read as an ideological statement indicating that both he and the fire-drilling bundle, with its associated ritual, are the same intrinsically as the one in Codex Vienna, but specifically tied to Yucuñudahui.

Another quality of Lord Eight Wind concerns his association with sacred plants used in ordering rituals. He raises a bundle of three plants over areas to be ordered in the Codex Vienna ceremonial scenes portraying these rituals (Vienna 22-1; Furst 1978a:229–256). Three plants are associated with Lord Eight Wind in the Zouche-Nuttall page 2 ordering ritual. One grows from the hill behind him and is the same as that portrayed in Codex Vienna, one is in his crown, and another grows from the hill before him. Yet another, fourth, sacred plant associated with ordering rituals is the maguey, which is displayed as part of Eight Wind's costume and seems to grow from his throat (ZN page 2). In the final tableau on page 1, at Monkey Hill, Lord Eight Wind literally speaks or sings one of the sacred plants and another seems to grow from his body. I infer that Lord Eight Wind is the bundle of sacred plants, or that he embodies them intrinsically.[1] We will see in Codex Zouche-Nuttall page 5 tableau 1 that the chief ordering ritual ceremonialist of Codex Vienna, Lord Two Dog, appears in a ceremony honoring Lord Eight Wind, thus showing Eight Wind in a superior position to one of the Apoala "gods," Two Dog.

A third consideration regarding Lord Eight Wind's metaphysical nature is his similarity to a prominent god, Lord Nine Wind Quetzalcoatl. While this will be examined more completely elsewhere, it is worth noting here that these two individuals shared the dignity of dual birth. That is to say, Lord Eight Wind was born from the earth and subsequently became one of

1. Mayan kings dressed and represented themselves as maize plants, literally becoming the maize god.

the tree-born nobles at Apoala (Vienna 35). Codex Bodley (40-I) tells us that Lord Nine Wind Quetzalcoatl was born either from or on the earth at Temzacal, and Codex Vienna (48c) illustrates that he was subsequently born from a stone knife in the sky. The chronological events in the careers of these two men (or demigod and god) are also interrelated and will be examined in a later chapter.

There is no doubt about it: this two-page introduction and synopsis of Lord Eight Wind's first fifty-two years is a wonder story. As an individual with supernatural abilities, he is intimately associated with caves and is able to move through the earth with apparent ease. His abilities at Yucuñudahui are recognized, and utilized by the holy place in the northern Mixteca—Apoala. Eight Wind enacts the ceremony for sanctifying the landscape there and generally, establishing though his own power and authority the all-important landscape resource, Rain God Hill (Yucuñudahui). This activity implies that Eight Wind has an intimacy with Dzaui, the rain god himself. When it is time to sanctify and unify the rain god's landscape, Lord Eight Wind emerges from the earth there and embodies the sacred plants necessary to envivify the place for the benefit of his people. Dzaui is seldom personified as a complete anthropomorph in Mixtec manuscripts, but the god is seen in human form twice in Codex Zouche-Nuttall's first eight pages. In one of these scenes he transforms Lord Eight Wind prior to the assumption of his career as lineage founder—a lineage which, by the way, endured for very nearly five hundred years and is well documented in Codex Selden.

Lord Eight Wind's later life as a "natural" human being—his rule and lineage founding at Monkey Hill/Suchixtlan/Cerro Jasmin—is the subject of his continuing biography, which resumes on page 5. However, shortly after his arrival at Yucuñudahui in AD 963, the epic War from Heaven began, and that is the subject of pages 3 and 4.

7 The War from Heaven, Part One

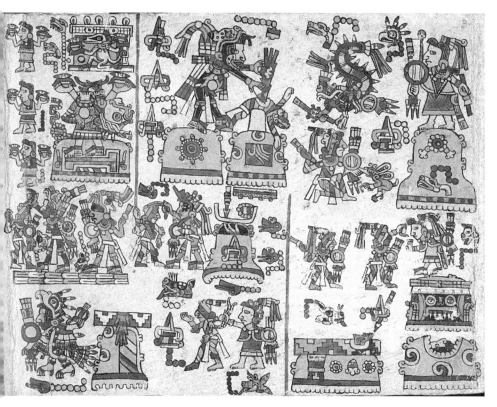

Figure 7.1. Codex Zouche-Nuttall page 3 (British Museum folio no. 3), the War from Heaven, part 1. (© Trustees of the British Museum, The British Museum Company, Ltd.)

Codex Zouche-Nuttall Page 3: War with the Stone Men and the Battle for Yucuñudahui

Page 3 (figure 7.1) has six tableaux and two sequential year dates. The first tableau occurs in Year 3 Reed (AD 963) Day 6 Dog, the next four occur in Year 5 House (AD 965) on various days, and the last is an undated, chronologically ambiguous ceremony related to the last two tableaux on page 4. The day sequences for the Year 5 House events are not in chronological order but are listed in a proposed order in appendix II.

Tableau 3 displays three year dates spanning the remainder of the war, from Year 5 House (AD 965), to Year 12 Flint (AD 972), and Year 5(6) Reed (AD 979). This is appropriate because the chief actor is Lord Seven Motion, who also participates in the War with the Striped Men on page 4. Therefore he is a dominant actor. His tableau and tableau 2 are larger than the others on page 3 and have a visual precedence not related to order of presentation.

The first tableau tells us that the war began at Yucuñudahui in Year 3 Reed on Day 6 Dog, or 132 days after Lord Eight Wind arrived there, as indicated on page 2 for Year 3 Reed Day 4 Flint. There are two days 6 Dog (#30 and #290) in Year 3 Reed, and only one day 4 Flint (#158), so it is possible that the war began 108 days before Lord Eight Wind arrived at Yucuñudahui.

A curious pair of related pictograms begins tableau 1. An unnamed male, assumed to be Lord Eight Wind because of his characteristic face paint (yellow mask, red mouth area), is shown going into a cave at one place and observing the war at Yucuñudahui from a cave opening at another place. Since Lord Eight Wind is seen previously as one who travels through caves, and since his granddaughter, Lady Six Monkey of Jaltepec, is seen doing the same thing (Codex Selden 6-III), Lord Eight Wind can be identified by a preponderance of narrative continuity rather than by an inscribed name. On the two pages devoted to the War from Heaven in this first saga (it is also told in this codex in saga 2, pages 20b–c and 21a) Lord Eight Wind is not a combatant (Furst 1978b:6b–7b); in fact, the text implies that he avoided the war entirely. He is invisible because he is a part of the landscape.

Tableau 1. This tableau has two parts. The first, described above, shows Lord Eight Wind "going underground." The second has the date, Year 3 Reed Day 6 Dog, and shows Lady Eight Monkey at Yucuñudahui captured by one of two attacking Stone Men. Lady Eight Monkey appears again in the terminal scene of page 4.

Tableau 2. In year 5 House Day 7 Snake (AD 965), Lady Six Eagle, the god Lord Seven Snake, and an insect signifying the polity of Sayultepec defend Yucuita against the Stone Men. The war has spread! Size makes this a dominant tableau.

Tableau 3. This second dominant tableau displays Lord Seven Motion and three year signs in a district consisting of two hills. He sacrifices a Stone

Man. As mentioned previously, the years are 5 House, 12 Flint, and 5(6) Reed.

Tableau 4. This tableau is chronologically complex because it has four day signs. The day sign associated by size with the year sign for 5 House is 4 Dog. Two day signs associated with the Lord Seven Wind captures are the first Day 4 Wind and Day 8 Wind. The next Day 4 Wind is directly above Lady Eight Deer's capture. Lord Seven Wind and Lady Eight Deer both capture Stone Men. Also, the Year 5 House Day 4 Dog is drawn close to this and the following tableau.

Tableau 5. The Year 5 House is assumed. Lord Seven Wind appears clothed in full eagle attire at an unknown place, as though perambulating. It may be that his full-body eagle costume tells us that he has transformed into his spirit animal, functioning as a yaha yahui priest. Because of this and his face paint, this male identified as Seven Wind more closely resembles our protagonist, Lord Eight Wind. Directly above him Lords Seven and Six Dog capture a Stone Man.

Tableau 6. There is no associated date for this depiction of a maguey goddess ceremony. Although Furst (1978a:233) notes these ceremonies, she does not discuss them in reference to this Zouche-Nuttall tableau; therefore, the complex associations involved with the maguey goddess displayed in this context merit discussion.

The tableau exists in three parts. On the viewer's right are two places, one above the other; the day name 11 Alligator is associated with them in this tableau and connects to the final tableau of page 4 (figure 8.1). The uppermost place is a building in which an opossum holds two cups overflowing with red liquid and topped by sacrificial flint knives. A decapitated female is directly below the opossum house, standing on a ballcourt at a hill and holding the same overflowing cups and flint knives. This same ballcourt appears in the final part of the last tableau on page 4.

On the hilltop, next to the decapitated female, is a round, woven, green grass mat of the kind associated with bird decapitation sacrifice. A sinuous ropelike object with six numeral circles issues from the mat. The third part of this tableau is figured at the viewer's left and consists of three females equally spaced from top to bottom of the scene and named Eleven Snake, Seven, and Five ("Snake" is assumed as day names for these two women).

The full-to-overflowing cups of blood may signify the blood of the goddess since pulche is made from the heart of the very plant she represents:

the maguey (Vienna 25, institution of the pulche ritual). In fact, pulche and blood are synonymous, and pulche may even represent the human body (Monaghan 1990:567).

Maguey, maguey ceremonies, the maguey goddess, and personified maguey with associated personnel are frequently displayed in Codex Vienna (table 7.1). In those scenes featuring the decapitated goddess and opossum, both hold cups overflowing with red liquid and topped by sacrificial flint knives, as in this Zouche-Nuttall tableau, but the female named Eleven Snake does not appear. In this respect the Zouche-Nuttall page 3 tableau is unique.

All of the Vienna scenes listed above are ceremonial in nature. Lady Eleven Snake on Vienna page 33d is in conference with several other gods headed by the brother gods, Lords Four and Seven Snake. Other personnel of interest to us are mentioned in this scene (Vienna pages 33–32), including Lord Two Dog (ZN page 4, tableau 6), Lords Four Motion and Seven Flower (ZN 4, tableau 4), Lord Seven Wind (ZN 3, tableau 5, shown in full eagle attire), and Lady Eight Deer (ZN 3, tableau 4).

Eleven Snake appears with Lady Eight Deer again on Vienna page 25d, which illustrates an ear perforation ceremony with many participants, including Lord Two Dog and Lords Four Motion and Seven Flower. On page 25a the maguey plants and goddess head-in-vat are associated with Lord Two Dog. Page 22a associates the decapitated goddess, opossum, and maguey plants with Lord Two Dog, and page 20a associates them with Lord Four Motion. The scene on 13a associates them with Lord Eleven Alligator, whose

Table 7.1. Depictions of Maguey in Codex Vienna

Vienna Page	Maguey Topic
33d	Lady Eleven Snake
25d	Lady Eleven Snake with decapitated goddess head on her back
25a	Maguey plants and head in pulche vat
22a	Decapitated goddess plus opossum, maguey plants
20a	Decapitated goddess plus opossum, maguey plants
13a	Decapitated goddess, opossum, maguey plants
3	Lady Eleven Snake

name qualifies a place in this tableau as well as in the final tableau on page 4. On page 18a the maguey plants are associated with Lord Seven Flower. In short, in virtually every appearance of the decapitated maguey goddess and opossum, the Lady Eleven Snake in Codex Vienna has associated personnel found in Codex Zouche-Nuttall on pages 3 and, significantly, 4.

Yucuñudahui, Lord Eight Wind, and the Stone Men

These first three Zouche-Nuttall pages reveal a society in dramatic, conflictive change from the Late Classic era, to the Epiclassic period, to early Postclassic times. Yucuñudahui, the location of Lord Eight Wind's ceremony on ZN page 2, is also the territory of the original inhabitants of the Mixteca: the Ñuu, or Stone Men. Significantly, Lord Eight Wind is an earth-born noble. Antonio de los Reyes (1976 [1593]:i–ii) recorded from folklore that the Mixtec conquered the original inhabitants, indigenes called Tey Ñuu who came from the center of the earth. This is one subject of Codex Zouche-Nuttall pages 3 and 4, as well as the Tree Birth ceremony told by Codex Vindobonensis Mexicanus I obverse (36–35a).

These people, called simply "Ñuu," are well represented in Mixtec art and myth, and are identified as Stone Men. In codices they wear colored diagonal bands of body paint resembling the exposed strata of colored rock, and they often have prominent fanged teeth and large, round eyes. Small, legless, spirit-like creatures that emerge from the earth and go back into it are associated with Stone Men and called Ñuu as well. John Monaghan (1990) writes that the rain god, Dzahui, was their chief lord. Mary Elizabeth Smith (1973, cited in Byland and Pohl 1994:11) suggests that the Reyes myth was a direct reference to the War from Heaven, and my interpretation of the final tableau of ZN page 4 supports her conclusion. We have noted that Codex Zouche-Nuttall tells us the war itself began at Yucuñudahui (Rain God Hill) shortly after Lord Eight Wind arrived there in AD 963.

The Zouche-Nuttall manuscript begins with an account of this struggle between the Mixtecs and the original inhabitants of the northern Nochixtlan Valley. It also tells us that one of the Stone Men nobles, Lord Five Flower, participated with Lord Eight Wind in the ordering ceremony at Yucuñudahui and survived the war itself, and that the conquering Mixtecs made their peace with him and his rain god lord (ZN page 4, tableau 6). Thus, the Mixtecs themselves became People of the Rain, and their territory the Land of the Rain God (Jansen and Jimenez 2005:12b–13a).

The Stone Men thus avoided extermination, and this is why we see them honorably remembered in later text with the Mixtecs, notably on page 23a, where Lord Ten House and Lady One Grass, who founded the first dynasty of Tilantongo, ruled at Stone Man River. Still later, when Lord Eight Deer Jaguar Claw usurps rulership at Tilantongo and establishes his state with 112 nobles and their districts in the Mixteca, a Stone Man named Lord Ten Alligator is among them (ZN page 66b).

Lord Eight Wind's relationship to Yucuñudahui and the Stone Men is also highlighted. Page 2 shows Eight Wind peacefully interacting with Stone Men at Yucuñudahui and indicates that he was there for seventeen years, leaving for Apoala one year after the war and just before the institution of the Tree Born lineage there. Page 4 indicates a peaceful resolution between the Stone Men and the new Apoala lords of the Mixteca. Jill Furst (1978b:7b) writes that Lord Eight Wind "is therefore described as an original Mixtec who may be entitled to his territories by right of first possession. It also suggests that Eight Wind is on the losing side of the war between the stone men and the victorious Mixtec-speakers, and yet manages to keep his lands. Perhaps he is a noble ambassador between the conflicting parties. The first seven pages of Zouche-Nuttall repeatedly make the point that Eight Wind is earth-born."

Codex Vienna records three conferences immediately attending the Apoala Tree Birth ceremony (pages 37a–35a). Lord Eight Wind has "Twenty" added to his name and is seen in the third conference held between the Ladies Five and Seven Flint, the Lords Five and Seven Vulture, Lord One Flower and Lady Seven Flower, and the Lords Seven and Eight Flower, Five and Nine Wind, Seven Deer, and the Lords Seven Vulture #2 and Four Reed. Significantly, a qualifying Ñuu spirit (Stone Man) figure appears in the section displaying Lords Eight Wind Twenty, Seven Vulture #2, and Four Reed in Year 13 Rabbit Day 2 Deer. This conference with Eight Wind and his delegation, qualified by the Ñuu figure, is likely the Stone Man delegation or, at least, the Yucuñudahui contingent.

The War from Heaven, Part Two

Figure 8.1. Codex Zouche-Nuttall page 4 (British Museum folio no. 4), the War from Heaven, page 2. (© Trustees of the British Museum, The British Museum Company, Ltd.)

Page 4, War with the Striped Men and Subsequent Events

This page is visually and chronologically complex, with six tableaux and four year dates, one of which (10[9]) House) is reconstructed. These years are: 12 Flint (AD 972), 13 Rabbit (AD 986), 6 Rabbit (AD 966), and 10(9) House (AD 969). Three tableaux are concerned with war events, one with a retrospective event, and the final two with events after the war.

Tableau 1. The event depicted in the upper right corner of page 4 occurred in Year 12 Flint (AD 972), with a one-day interval from days 7 Alligator to 8 Wind. There is no ambiguity about this interval since both numbered days occur only once in vague solar Year 12 Flint. This year was first seen on page 3, tableau 3, associated with Lord Seven Motion's sacrifice of Stone Men.

The antagonists are three identically costumed males painted with red and white stripes who emerge from a cave opening in the sky and descend to earth. The sky itself is a place sign and has the day names of two divinities within it: Two Alligator and Seven Flower. The striped men have no day names but are given meteorological qualities. The first one (to the reader's left) makes a loud sound and is thus associated with thunder. He also holds a heavy object about to be thrown. The second striped man, in the center, is lightning, and he holds a long object curled at either end and festooned with stars, indicating it is bright. The third man, on the right, is rain, for he holds a gout of water. All three are armed with war instruments: darts and shields. In the animistic religion of the Zapotecs, natural forces such as lightning and its companions of cloud, rain, wind, and hail were personified, as were earthquake and thunder, called "lightning's earthquake" (Marcus and Flannery 1996:19). This Codex Zouche-Nuttall scene reflects such personification of natural forces, as does Rain God Hill (Yucuñudahui) on previous pages.

Tableau 2. This scene, directly below the first, shows Lord Four Snake (the deity-brother of Lord Seven Snake who first appeared on page 3, tableau 2, defending Yucuita) and an unnamed Lord Seven Motion capturing two of the striped men. These two captives are without meteorological attributes. Lord Four Snake stands on a square containing the year sign for 10 House, which is corrected here to be 9 House (AD 969), three years before tableau 1. This is one of four connected squares, each with illustrations within: the next square to the right contains a day sign for "flower," the next for "grass," and the last an unnumbered year sign for House.

Tableau 3. This scene is brief: Lord Four Snake (brother of Seven Snake) sacrifices an eagle named One Jaguar in Year 12 Flint on Day 12 Motion (AD 972). The deity name Two Alligator, which first appeared in the sky in tableau 1 on this page, is repeated here at the same level with Lord Four Snake's name. This is not a bird-decapitation sacrifice, but rather a heart excision sacrifice, with the eagle lying upon a hill toponym. Birds for sacrifice are not usually named and, typically, they are decapitated and not subjects of heart excision.

Tableau 4. This retrospective scene shows the mummy-bundling of two supernatural lords in Year 6 Rabbit Day 2 Motion (AD 966). A bird sacrifice accompanies this ceremonial bundling of Lords Seven Flower (whose name appeared in the sky in tableau 1 on this page) and Four Motion. Both lords are associated with the maguey goddess and various ceremonies in Codex Vienna, as mentioned in the previous chapter. Two unnamed secondary actors directly above the bundled lords are singing, and both hold trilobed wands of the kind seen on page 1. The day sign 9 Motion is between them. This Year 6 Rabbit tableau introduces events in the next tableau (see appendices II and III). Both days (2 Motion and 9 Motion) occur twice in Year 6 Rabbit 2 Motion on days 62 and 322, and 9 Motion on days 82 and 342, so there are always twenty days between them.

Tableau 5. This tableau is displayed across the top of page 4 from right to left and spans text columns B and C. It shows three unnamed lords and Lord One Wind facing left and processing to a Stone Man named Five Flower, who faces right. Five Flower appears on page 2 as a ceremonial participant at Lord Eight Wind's ordering ceremony for Yucuñudahui. According to visual presentation, Lord Five Flower is one of three individuals but separate from them: the Lord Ten Death and the rain god, Dzaui, are directly below him and facing right. These latter two lords are in conference with others: Lord Ten Death with Lady Eight Monkey (who was captured at Yucuñudahui on page 3, tableau 1) and the rain god, Dzaui, with Lord Two Dog. This is one of the few instances where the rain god is personified; another occurs on ZN page 5. Lord Ten Death is presenting Lady Eight Monkey with a kind of baton, and Dzaui, who has been noted as the chief patron of the race of Stone Men, is speaking with Lord Two Dog. A round grass mat for the bird sacrifice is shown between Dzaui and Lord Two Dog. The date is Year 13 Rabbit Day 2 Deer (AD 986).

This tableau is introduced by tableau 4 and connected to the one that follows in this page's last column of text. The ceremony depicted is a bird-decapitation sacrifice combined with the subsequent conference.

Tableau 6. The events of this tableau also occurred in Year 13 Rabbit Day 2 Deer, but at two places: the Ballcourt of Death (last seen on page 3, tableau 6) and Eleven Alligator place (also on page 3, tableau 6, at the maguey goddess and opossum ceremony). This tableau is a séance wherein Lady Eight Monkey and an unnamed woman are seated at Eleven Alligator place. Lady Eight Monkey faces the previously mummified and bundled Lords Seven Flower and Four Motion, now shown alive and seated in the Ballcourt of Death. Directly above the unnamed woman (who faces away from Eight Monkey) is the day sign 7 Wind. A cup filled with red liquid and surmounted by an indistinguishable object is connected to the round scene directly above Eight Monkey's head. A large bird hovers above both women.

Regarding the day signs 2 Deer and 7 Wind (assuming that the latter is a day sign, and not Lady Eight Monkey's companion's name), they both appear only once in Year 13 Rabbit. Day 7 Wind is first (#47), and 2 Deer is second (#172), with an interval of 125 days between them. So, by chronological progression the tableaux from four to six are ordered: tableau 4, bundling of two lords (AD 966); tableau 6, on Day 7 Motion, the séance with the two bundled lords (AD 986); tableau 5, the conference with Lord Five Flower, Dzaui, Lord Ten Death, Lord Two Dog, and Lady Eight Monkey.

The séance tableau is drawn in a slightly smaller scale; however, the date of this tableau, Year 13 Rabbit Day 2 Deer, is critical because it directly corresponds to events in Codex Vienna (35–37) involving Lord Eight Wind (Vienna 35a) and the founding of the Tree-Born lineage at Apoala. The Stone Man conflict, which began at Yucuñudahui, ended at the same time the War from Heaven did (AD 979), and, according to Codex Vienna, a new lineage system was instituted subsequently. The terminal scenes of both page 3 (the Maguey/Pulche Goddess ceremony) and page 4 (the séance and the conference with the rain god Dzaui and Lord Two Dog) are related and terminate the war sequences of each page as a kind of visual literary device that relates the Apoala events to those in the northern Nochixtlan Valley after the War from Heaven.

Another critical point about this final page 4 tableau and the one preceding it is that they bring together both a prominent lord of the Stone Men (Five Flower) and his deity, the rain god Dzaui, both displayed in peaceful circumstances. Since the War from Heaven began at Yucuñudahui, Rain God Hill, the scribes now relate a peaceful conclusion achieved between the nobles of Apoala, the Stone Men, and their deified town of Yucuñudahui.

As mentioned, this Zouche-Nuttall tableau depicts a conference and resembles similar gatherings seen in Codex Vienna, specifically conferences after the Apoala Tree-Birth ceremony (Vienna 37–35). Subsequent to the Tree-Birth ceremony, there are three conferences in Year 13 Rabbit Day 2 Dog. The first (and closest to the ceremony) occurs on pages 37b–36b. In it, twelve lords—among them Lords Ten Death (also on ZN page 4, tableau

5), Ten Dog, and Ten Jaguar—speak to ten nobles, among them Lady Eight Monkey (who also appears on ZN pages 3 and 4).

The second conference, on Vienna pages 36b–c, involves Lords Nine Wind Quetzalcoatl and four other lords who are speaking to six lords, among whom is Eleven Alligator (Eight Wind's companion on ZN pages 1 and 2). In the third conference (Vienna 36b–35a), the Ladies Seven and Five Flint and the Lords Five and Seven Vulture speak to ten lords, among whom are Lord Seven Flower (also on ZN page 4) and our protagonist Lord Eight Wind Twenty (ZN pages 1–8).

After the establishment of the Apoala lineage (Vienna 35–34d), a fourth conference occurs. The brother gods, Lords Four and Seven Snake (both seen on ZN pages 3 and 4), speak to twenty-six nobles prior to the beginning of the Vienna ordering rituals. The ones who also appear in the Zouche-Nuttall pages examined so far include Lords Two Dog, Four Motion, Seven Flower, and Seven Motion, Lady Eleven Snake (also in the maguey ceremony, ZN page 3), Lord Seven Wind (ZN page 3, tableau 5), Lady Six Eagle (ZN page 3, at Yucuita), and Lady Eight Deer (ZN page 3, tableau 4).

After the Apoala Tree-Birth ceremony but prior to the Vienna ordering rituals, several individuals present at the various conferences at Apoala are major actors in the events on ZN pages 3 and 4, With the exception of Lord Five Flower, the Stone Men, Dzaui the rain god, the maguey ceremony Ladies Six and Five (Snake?), Lords Seven and Five Dog, the five striped men, the two unnamed actors at the mummy-bundling ceremony, Lord One Wind, and three unnamed ceremonialists processing to Lord Five Flower, all of the other actors on ZN pages 3 and 4 are in pivotal Apoala events in Codex Vienna.

Yucuñudahui

Obviously, Apoala played a major role in the War from Heaven, before and after the Tree-Birth ceremony. Lord Eight Wind Eagle Flints (Twenty) is a fulcrum of these events, chiefly because of his activities at Yucuñudahui (Rain God Hill). Yucuñudahui is among the first places mentioned in Codex Vienna (47b) as the site of the first earthly activities of Lord Nine Wind Quetzalcoatl after being born from a sacrificial stone knife in the sky. According to Codex Vienna, it is one of the places in a district where Nine Wind Quetzalcoatl holds sky and water above the earth. This makes a conclusive statement about the importance of Rain God Hill and establishes an ideological link between the two deities Dzaui (the rain god) and Nine Wind Quetzal-coatl, who conducted important conferences listed in Codex Vienna, and Lord Eight Wind, who conducted important ceremonies in Zouche-Nuttall. The ideological link between Nine Wind Quetzalcoatl and Lord Eight Wind Eagle Flints (Twenty) appears in text subsequently, especially as regards their interlaced chronologies—the first recorded in Codex Vienna, and the second (for Eight Wind) recorded in Codex Zouche-Nuttall.

Chronology for Pages 3 and 4

Since this interpretation is driven by chronological sequences, it is produc-tive to integrate both sets of pages (1 and 2, and 3 and 4) in table 8.1 by pro-gression of years.

Discussion: The War from Heaven

Alfonso Caso (1960:58a) remarks that the War from Heaven "which ended the dynasty of [Wasp Hill] is extraordinarily important in the history of the Mixtec region, for it was this development which permitted Tilantongo to establish itself as the metropolis of the Northern Mixteca." (Caso referred to Wasp Hill, its modern designation, as "Hill that Opens-Bee." I have modern-ized it here because scholars writing after Caso refer to the site as "Hill of the Wasp," and I, as "Wasp Hill.") This event—or, more accurately, events—are indeed extraordinarily important for they are twice told in two codices, Zouche-Nuttall pages 3–4 and 20b–21a, and Codex Bodley pages 3–4 and 34–36. As seen in the forgoing description and analysis, the ZN pages pro-vide the most detail for us by dividing the war into two accounts from two political regions of the Nochixtlan Valley: the north, pages 3 and 4, and the south, pages 20b–21a (Pohl 1994:53).

It also indicates that two wars were fought as one, sequentially: first with the original inhabitants of the Mixteca, the Stone Men, and another with the Striped Men. This latter group is unnamed as to individuals, and there is no other course left but to associate them as allies with the Wasp Hill dynasty and Zapotec influences. In both Zouche-Nuttall appearances these mysteri-ous beings have meteorological attributes and, as mentioned, no calendric names.

While the ZN pages 20b–21a account informs us that this was a dynastic conflict against Wasp Hill, Codex Bodley provides the most detail about the extermination of this political lineage, naming perhaps thirteen royal per-

Table 8.1. Chronology of Codex Zouche-Nuttall Obverse Pages 1–4

Page/Tableau Event	Mixtec Date	European	Date AD
1/1. ♂ 12 Alligator birth	1 Reed, 12 Alligator		935
1/1. ♂ 8 Wind birth	1 Reed, Eight Wind		935
		+28 years	
2/2. At Yucuñudahui	3 Reed 4 Flint		963
3/1. War/Yucuñudahui	3 Reed 6 Dog		963
		+2 years	
3. War/Stone Men	5 House		965
3/3. ♂ 7 Motion sacrifice	5 House		965
		+1 year	
4/4. ♂ 4 Motion and ♂ 7 Flower	6 Rabbit		966
		+3 years	
4/2. Capture of Striped Men	10(9) House		969
		+3 years	
4/1. Striped Men from sky	12 Flint		972
4/3. Eagle sacrifice	12 Flint		972
3/3. ♂ 7 Motion sacrifice	12 Flint		972
		+7 years	
3/3. ♂ 7 Motion sacrifice	5(6) Reed		979
		+1 year	
1/3. ♂ 8 Wind at Apoala	7 Flint 1 Motion		980
		+6 years	
3/6. Maguey Goddess ceremony	13 Rabbit 2 Deer		986
4/6. Séance ♂ 4 Motion, etc.	13 Rabbit 2 Deer		986
4/6. Rain God ceremony	13 Rabbit 2 Deer		986

sonages who were executed (as does ZN page 20a–b). Codex Bodley portrays the oracle of the dead, Lady Nine Grass of Chalcatongo, as the chief executioner of Wasp Hill royalty, but she is shown only in the second account in Codex Zouche-Nuttall, which displays her as a combatant and as executing Lord Nine Wind Curly Hair. This activity highlights Lady Nine Grass's role in determining lineage alliance and validity, as will be seen later in text during the lineage war between Tilantongo and Hua Chino.

According to the Zouche-Nuttall chronology, the war lasted for sixteen years. It had many anabases, skirmishes, and battles. The next year after the 13 Rabbit 2 Deer conference (AD 986), which ends ZN page 4, is 1 Reed 1 Alligator (AD 987). A full-length red line divides pages 4 and 5, signifying the end of this section of the narrative. Lord Eight Wind is seen on page 1, tableau 4 at Suchixtlan on 1 Reed 1 Alligator, the date that begins the resumption of his biography on page 5.

Lord Eight Wind's Family

Figure 9.1. Codex Zouche-Nuttall page 5 (British Museum folio no. 5). (© Trustees of the British Museum, The British Museum Company, Ltd.)

Page 5, Continuation of Lord Eight Wind's Biography

Page 5 (figure 9.1) of Codex Zouche-Nuttall resumes the biography of Lord Eight Wind, now at the beginning of Mixtec Year Cycle 3. There are four tableaux and seven dates, for a span of forty years (table 9.1).

Tableau 1. In Year 1 Reed (the literal date of AD 987, but metaphorically meaning "beginnings" [Furst 1978a:91]) Lord Eight Wind emerges from a cave opening in the temple at a place qualified by a small yellow man seated below and in front of the temple. This occurs in Lord Eight Wind's fifty-second year of life and is preparatory to his lineage founding and rule at Monkey Hill/Suchixtlan/Cerro Jasmin.

Also pictured are four ceremonial assistants with implements. Lord Six Death pours tobacco and holds a sacrificial bird; Lord Six Water blows a conch shell trumpet; Lord Seven Monkey bears a torch; and Lord Two Dog holds a trilobed wand. When last seen on page 4, tableau 5, Lord Two Dog was conferencing with Dzaui, the rain god. He is also a primary actor and associate with the god Nine Wind Quetzalcoatl in Codex Vienna obverse. This event precedes a Rain God ceremony many years later, depicted in tableau 2 and spanning two columns of pictogram text (4a–b).

Tableau 2. In Year 5(6) Flint (AD 1004) on Day 7 Flower, Lord Eight Wind emerges from a cave opening in a masonry enclosure before an effigy of the rain god. He is sixty-nine years old. A bird-decapitation ceremony is conducted above on a feather carpet surmounted by a half-round, green grass mat and white-bound bundle. Two unnamed males participate: one bears a spear and incense burner, and the other wears a two-faced mask and carries a torch. The second part of this tableau shows the results of the ceremony: the rain god appears from above and pours water over Lord Eight Wind, who subsequently marries and founds his lineage at Monkey Hill.

Although bathing rituals frequently precede marriages (Codex Selden 7-I; Codex ZN page 19) they usually include both marriage partners. This ritual is different because, although it precedes a marriage, no marriage partner is illustrated. Therefore this ceremony is particular to Lord Eight Wind. Byland and Pohl (1994:121) remark that this ceremony transforms Lord Eight Wind into a fully human person, authorized to marry and found lineages. The event clearly marks Eight Wind's transition from the first part of his life (ZN pages 1 and 2) to the second. From this point on, Lord Eight Wind no longer appears from cave portals to the underworld. This makes sense because in the first part of Lord Eight Wind's life, he was a great wizard, priest/shaman, or santo, but in the second part (told here) he is a "normal" human being, concerned with marriage and lineage founding.

Tableau 3. Reading from right to left, the first pictogram is the toponym for Monkey Hill. To the left, seated on a yellow mat, are Lord Eight Wind, now seventy-three, and his first wife, Lady Ten Deer. They founded the female line for the second dynasty of Jaltepec (Selden 5-III). A vessel footed with snakeheads and containing frothy liquid and flowers stands between them. Three dates are displayed: Year 9(10) House Day 1 Eagle (AD 1007, the end of the Rain God ceremony), Year 9 Flint Day 6 Flower (AD 1008, the date of this marriage), and Year 2 Reed Day 2 Reed (Eight Wind's death). This tableau continues on page 6a, which displays Lord Eight Wind's second and third wives: the Ladies Five Grass and Ten Eagle.

The third part of page 5 tableau 3 shows the children of Lord Eight Wind and Lady Ten Deer displayed in the register above them: Lord Thirteen Grass, born in Year 2 Rabbit (on Day 13 Grass, AD 1014); the twin Lords Three Lizard; Lady Two Snake; and Lady Six Reed. One of the twin Lords Three Lizard will play an important role in the later disastrous attack by Tilantongo (under its boy-king Two Rain) against Jaltepec.

Lord Eight Wind's death at age ninety-two in Year 2 Reed is implied. The year and day sign appears directly over his head, and the year qualifier "reed" or "dart" points directly to him. Reed date pointers are rare but do occur, as on page 20c of this manuscript, where they indicate the sequence of two day dates and events (specifically the deaths of two chief actors) associated with each day. This scene on page 20c is also an abbreviated, composite reading, or text; however, in this Mixtec notational form, complicated data is reduced to its simplest elements, intended to be understood by the reciting bards. Once one begins to interpret a pars pro toto text, the data unfolds. Further, Lord Eight Wind is not shown as a mummy, as is typical in other codices for death events, because available space demands visual abbreviation. When he does appear again on ZN page 7, he is shown seated in a temple and conversing with his great-great-grandson, the six-year-old king of Tilantongo, Lord Two Rain. If Eight Wind were alive for this conversation, he would be 146 years old. Therefore, his death at age ninety-two is here shown in abbreviated form to save space. I infer from these data that Lord Eight Wind's chronology fits within the possible span of a human life. Ronald Spores (1974:303) writes that for Mixtec succession, old age is an esteemed factor. Some perhaps think it odd (or impossible) that a man so elderly would or could found a family. In answer to this: (1) the Mixtecs were not us; and (2) in our era the examples of the actors Tony Randall and Anthony Quinn come to mind. Also, for the unimpeachably dubious, paternity is easy to fake.

Table 9.1. Zouche-Nuttall Obverse Page 5 Chronology

Page/Tableau/Event	Mixtec Date	European Date AD
5/1. Yellow Man Hill	1 Reed 1 Alligator	987
5/2. Rain God ceremonies	6(5) Flint 7 Flower	1004
5/2. End Rain God ceremonies	9(10) House 1 Eagle	1007
5/3. ♂ Eight Wind's first marriage	9 Flint 6 Flower	1008
6a. Second marriage	11 Rabbit 3 Eagle	1010
6a. Third marriage	12 Reed 9 Deer	1011
5/3. ♂ Thirteen Grass's birth	2 Rabbit 13 Grass	1014
3/3. Unexplained	9 House 1 Eagle	1020
3/3. ♂ Eight Wind's death	2 Reed 2 Reed	1027

Lord Eight Wind's Family

As patriarch, Lord Eight Wind founded two (there were more) lines of descent through his daughters, who were ultimately in conflict. The beginning and resolution of this conflict are the subject of pages 7d and 8b. One line of descent founded the first dynasty of Tilantongo, which failed in the time of Lord Two Rain Twenty Jaguars (Eight Wind's great-great-grandson), and the second founded the dynasty of Jaltepec, which continued through his granddaughter Lady Six Monkey's son Lord Four Rain until the Spanish entrada in AD 1521 (table 9.2).

In Year 9 Flint (AD 1008), Lord Eight Wind married Lady Ten Deer, as depicted on Codex ZN page 5. Their daughter, Lady Two Snake (page 5c), married Lord Ten Flower of Tilantongo (ZN page 23b; Bodley 5-V). Their son was Lord Twelve Lizard Arrow Legs, who inherited the mat (throne) of Tilantongo. Lady Two Snake's sister, Lady Nine Wind of Jaltepec, married Lord Ten Eagle, the brother of Lord Ten Lizard Arrow Legs (Selden 5-IV). The following diagram (table 9.2) displays this descent through Eight Wind's daughters.

The chronologies of these births and marriages are interesting. The births of Lord Eight Wind's female children are undated. However, Eight Wind and Lady Ten Deer married in Year 9 Flint (AD 1008). Assuming their first daughter's birth to be one year after their marriage, Lady Two Snake was only five years old when she was betrothed or married to Lord Ten Flower in Year 1 House (AD 1013) (ZN page 23 and Bodley 5-V). Lady Two Snake and Lord Ten Flower's first son, Twelve Lizard Arrow Legs, was born in Year

Table 9.2. Lord Eight Wind's Daughters and the First and Second Dynasties of Tilantongo

---

THE FIRST DYNASTY OF TILANTONGO

♂ 8 Wind of Suchixtlan + ♀ 10 Deer

*

*

♀ 2 Snake + ♂ 10 Flower of Tilantongo

*

*

♂ 12 Lizard Arrow Legs and ♂ 10 Eagle . . . .

*

*

♂ 12 Lizard Arrow Legs + ♀ 4 Flint and ♀ 4 Alligator

*

*

♂ 5 Motion + ♀ 2 Grass

*

*

♂ 2 Rain, last king of first dynasty

THE SECOND DYNASTY OF JALTEPEC

♂ 8 Wind of Suchixtlan + ♀ 10 Deer

*

*

♀ 9 Wind of Jaltepec + ♂ 10 Eagle of Tilantongo . . . .

*

*

♀ 6 Monkey and ♀ 4 Death

*

*

♀ 6 Monkey + ♂ 11 Wind of Hua Chino

*

*

♂ 4 Wind and ♂ 1 Alligator

5 Reed (AD 1043) (ZN page 23b), which is also the date of his marriage to the Ladies Four Death and Four Alligator (Byland and Pohl 1994:240). On the other hand, if his birthday is one year after his parents' marriage in AD 1013 (Year 2 Rabbit, or, AD 1014), then he marries the ladies at age twenty-nine in Year 5 Reed (AD 1043). However, this would mean his mother was no more than six years old at the time of his birth. The birth of the second son, Ten Eagle, is undated.

Lady Nine Wind (Lady Two Snake's sister) of Jaltepec married Lord Ten Eagle of Tilantongo in Year 3 House (AD 1040) (Selden 5-III). If she were born the year after her sister, Lady Two Snake, in Year 11 Rabbit (AD 1010), then she would have been thirty-one years old at the time she became regent of Jaltepec by marrying Lord Ten Eagle.

Given these dates, the only understandable part of this sibling chronology is the birth and marriage of Lady Nine Wind of Jaltepec. The other elements involving her sister, Lady Two Snake of Suchixtlan, are irresolvable.

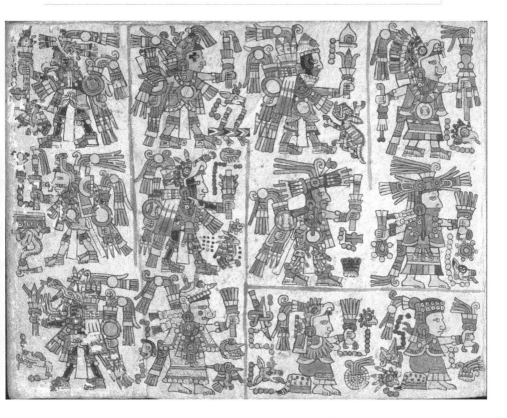

Figure 10.1. Codex Zouche-Nuttall page 6 (British Museum folio no. 6). (© Trustees of the British Museum, The British Museum Company, Ltd.)

Page 6: Two Processions of Nobles and Divine Ancestors

As mentioned in the previous chapter, Codex Zouche-Nuttall obverse page 6a illustrates Lord Eight Wind's second and third wives. The dates of these marriages as they appear in the codex have been incorporated into my reconstructed chronology. Page 6b is a separate entity, and no other chronological markers appear in the manuscript text until pages 7d and 8.

Page 6b–d presents a series of individuals facing right, against the reading order and toward Lord Eight Wind's children illustrated in the last tableau on page 5. The seven individuals, from right to left, are: the Ladies Nine Eagle and Twelve Dog; then, in the next column, the Lords Six Motion and Five House; and in the next column, Lords Five Deer, Twelve Alligator, and Lady Nine Monkey. Many have personal names attached and carry ceremonial instruments. Of those in this array, Lord Twelve Alligator was born from the great tree at Apoala (Vienna 37c). The last column of pictogram text (6e), to the reader's left, begins a series of individuals facing left, toward the reading order and away from Eight Wind's offspring.

The processing individuals (6b–d) are mysterious; however, they do serve an interpretative function by their position—that is, they face against the reading order and toward Eight Wind's children. This position contra read-

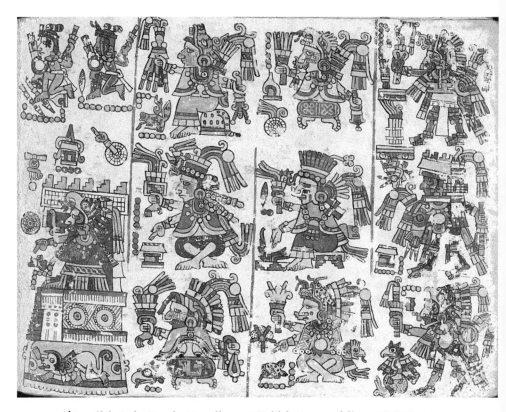

Figure 10.2. Codex Zouche-Nuttall page 7 (British Museum folio no. 7). (© Trustees of the British Museum, The British Museum Company, Ltd.)

ing order serves as a visual "stop" and divides page 6a–c from the tableaux that follow it; that is, pages 6e–8. A similar technique is used on ZN reverse page 42, which is the parentage statement for Lord Eight Deer and his half-brother Lord Twelve Motion. The children that follow them face contra reading order, and this directional shift is a visual clue that separates scenes without providing a full stop, as would a dividing red line.

Page 7

The individuals in reading-order direction continue onto page 7, columns a–c. Counting the three on page 6, there are twelve in all. On page 6 are Lords Four Snake, Seven Flower (Vienna 33b), and Seven Motion (Vienna 33d). On page 7 are Lords Thirteen Reed, Nine House, and Five Motion; in the next column, from bottom to top, are the Ladies Nine Jaguar, Two Flint, and Six House; and in the last column, from top to bottom, Ladies Ten Deer, Nine House, and Three Eagle.

The tableaux of these mysterious individuals (who may in some instances be deceased, mummified ancestors) comprise a transition from the time of Lord Eight Wind and his family into the future. We know this because the final scene on page 7 displays a special event in which Lord Eight Wind reappears many years after his death. Page 7d illustrates him seated in the temple at Monkey Hill. He is very elderly, as indicated by the snaggle-tooth at the corner of his mouth. According to the date displayed (Year 4 House Day 1 Rain, AD 1081), he would be 146 years old. He is deceased yet shown alive and speaking with his six-year-old great-great-grandson, Lord Two Rain Twenty Jaguars (shown across the page-fold on 8a), the last king of the first dynasty of Tilantongo.

Mixtecs preserved their dead ancestors as mummies and stored the mummy-bundles in caves. Thus they could have festivals with them and consult them via certain priests or by the oracle of death, Lady Nine Grass at Chalcatongo. This prominence of the Mixtec Cult of the Dead was recorded by the early Spanish, notably de Burgoa, who compared Zapotec and Mixtec burial customs (1934 [1674], II:64). These early references specifically refer to Chalcatongo Temple and its oracle, Lady Nine Grass. Burgoa noted that the Mixtec kings were buried at a specific place, which he called "the Cave of Chalcatongo." This custom of regarding the dead as having special abilities important for the living can also be related to European Catholic societies and the Medieval/Renaissance custom of establishing shrines of spiritual power that were special tombs for saints. An especially important and impressive one can still be seen at the Basilica of Saint Ambrose in Milan, Italy, which displays the skeletal relics of Saint Ambrose the Great (died ca. AD 400) and the martyred twins, saints Gervasius and Protasius, to constant public veneration. It is a common practice for people to pilgrimage to the saints at Milan for spiritual consultation as well as consolation.

Mixtec encounters with the dead shown alive also occur in Codex Alfonso Caso (Colombino-Becker I) when the warlord of Tilantongo, Eight Deer Jaguar Claw, enters the realm of the sun god and overcomes defending warriors who were previously sacrificed by heart excision (Troike 1974:267; Codex Colombino-Becker I, 2–3-III). ZN page 4 also displays two deceased, previously mummified individuals as alive during a consultation with living persons.

The ZN page 7 tableau with Lord Eight Wind's mummy is a consultation invoked by his great-great-grandson Lord Two Rain Twenty Jaguars in Year 4 House Day 1 Rain. Six-year-old Two Rain is shown on page 8a (figure 10.3) attired as a priest and bowing to his great-ancestor, seen across the page-fold on page 7d. This begins a series of events in Mixtec history that prove ruinous for Tilantongo.

Page 8a, second figure up from the bottom right, shows the boy-king, Lord Two Rain, venerating his deceased ancestor, Lord Eight Wind of Monkey Hill, shown across the page-fold in the last column of text on page 7. Page 8b shows the adult Lord Two Rain seated in a temple and surrounded by warriors. Two of these warriors appear at the top of page 7d above Lord Eight Wind in the Monkey Hill Temple, and their presence in that position demonstrates that these two tableaux are continuous despite a separation in time. It may be that the two warriors in the top register of page 7 refer to Tilantongo's attack on Jaltepec, when Lord Two Rain was only six years old, and not to the later event, some four years after his death. The date on page 8b is Year 10 Flint (AD 1100), Days 1 Eagle and 2 Flint (an interval of 280 days). Year 10 Flint occurs four years after Lord Two Rain's death in AD 996. Therefore, he, too, is a mummy shown as alive and communicating with the living. This event connects in chronology with an event in the career of Lord Eight Deer Jaguar Claw of Tilantongo (figure 10.4). A cognate scene appears on pages 82–84 of this codex reverse and establishes that, indeed, Lord Two Rain as seen here is a mummy. Considering this, page 8 (the last page of saga 1) ends on a high note, without resolution, and can only be resolved by integrating it with relevant codex tableaux on Zouche-Nuttall reverse. This is the

Figure 10.3. Codex Zouche-Nuttall page 8 (British Museum folio no. 8). Six-year-old Lord Two Rain is the second figure up from the bottom right. The older, post-mortem Lord Two Rain is the central figure seated in the hilltop temple at mid-page. (© Trustees of the British Museum, The British Museum Company, Ltd.)

reason the transitional tableaux of processing individuals on pages 6 and 7 move us into the future, into the time of Lord Eight Deer of Tilantongo.

The Parliament of Mummies, the Marriage Alliance War, and Lord Eight Deer's Resolution

The history encapsulated by this final tableau details a complex series of historical events. They involve Mixtec marriage alliances, the oracle of the dead at Chalcatongo, Lord Eight Wind's descendant Lord Two Rain of Tilantongo, and a political conflict resolved later during the lifetime of Lord Eight Deer, who usurped the throne of Tilantongo after Two Rain's death. This complex story is best told by the codices themselves, and we will use three of them to do it briefly: the present manuscript, Zouche-Nuttall, both sides; Codex Selden, a document of the royal families of Jaltepec; and Codex Bodley.

In Year 4 House on Day 1 Rain (AD 1081), the boy-king of Tilantongo, Lord Two Rain, attired as a priest (ZN page 8a), conferred with his ancestor, the deceased Lord Eight Wind of Monkey Hill (ZN page 7d). According to Codex Selden (6-II), three days after this consultation, one of Lord Eight Wind's twin sons, the elderly Three Lizard, acted on behalf of boy Two Rain of Tilantongo; attacked Tilantongo's marriage alliance partner, Jaltepec; and lost the war and his life, after which Two Rain sought refuge in a cave-shrine.

This event fractures the marriage alliance between Tilantongo and Jaltepec, and later there is a conference with Lady Nine Grass at Chalcatongo (ZN page 44). She confirms not only the severance of the previous alliance between Tilantongo and Jaltepec, but reassigns it between Jaltepec (in the person of Lady Six Monkey, Lord Eight Wind's granddaughter) and Tilantongo's rival, Hua Chino, in the person of a suitor, Lord Eleven Wind (Selden 6-IV).

Lord Two Rain, the defeated king of Tilantongo, lived until AD 1096. According to Codex Zouche-Nuttall reverse, Lord Eight Deer used this time to enterprise himself successfully by gaining a reputation as ruler of Tututepec and developing skills as a warlord and politician (including formulating an alliance with the Tolteca-Chichimeca). After Two Rain commits suicide under mysterious circumstances (Codex Bodley 5-I), Eight Deer becomes ruler at Tilantongo and avenges the insult to his town by destroying Hua Chino and its rulers, Lord Eleven Wind and Lady Six Monkey of Jaltepec (ZN pages 81–84; Bodley 34–35; Codex Alfonso Caso 36–37). Lord Eight Deer also sacrifices Eleven Wind's sons by a previous marriage, but spares his two children from Lady Six Monkey, Lords Four Wind and One Alligator.

This is the ultimate meaning of the mummy scenes on the final two pages of the first saga of Zouche-Nuttall's obverse. It connects the previous Lord Eight Wind founding events—events which profoundly influenced the entire subsequent history of the Mixteca and the Stone Men—to events that happened in the future, in the time of the all-famous Lord Eight Deer of Tilantongo. These two men were the greatest social "reformers" in Mixtec history, but the connection between Zouche-Nuttall obverse and reverse events requires further elaboration, which would have been inserted by the original performers of the drama.

The year of Lord Two Rain's mummy event on ZN page 8 is 10 Flint (AD 1100) Days 1 Eagle to 2 Flint, with the latter (2 Flint) qualifying the mummy event itself. We know this to be so because Day 2 Flint is recorded on that page near a ballcourt at the place where Lord Two Rain is displayed (a ballcourt consultation with the dead also appears on page 4 tableau 6). Day 1 Eagle is prominently displayed "floating" near the year indicator near the middle of the page. This same date (Year 10 Flint Day 2 Flint) appears on Zouche-Nuttall reverse, pages 80–82, prior to Lord Eight Deer's attack on Hua Chino. Page 82 depicts Eight Deer consulting with an unnamed mummy-bundle on Day 2 Flint at a site drawn as a decorated snake—that is, the place in Codex Bodley (5-I) where Lord Two Rain's mummy was interred after his mysterious death four years previously. After this consultation, Lord Eight Deer attacks Hua Chino in the following year, 11 House (AD 1101). The interval of 280 days written on ZN page 8 is from Day 1 Eagle to Day 2 Flint, and that is likely the period in which Lord Eight Deer collected his army, a few chiefs of whom are shown displayed and surrounding Lord Two Rain's living mummy as he gesticulates with his right hand. This emblem of communication—his right hand pointing—also contains a reference to the receptor of his communication; namely, a single jaguar claw, which is Lord Eight Deer's personal name. On Codex Zouche-Nuttall reverse, Lord Eight Deer points to Lord Two Rain's mummy; on the codex obverse Lord Two Rain's mummy points and has an emblem of Eight Deer's personal name on the sleeve of his pointing hand, indicating they were communicating with each other. And, last, the 280-day interval is why the siege of Hua Chino began in the following year, 11 House (AD 1101).

It is clear, therefore, that the reverse side Zouche-Nuttall scene shows Lord Two Rain as an actual mummy and the object of Lord Eight Deer's ceremony preparatory to besieging Hua Chino. The display recorded on obverse pages 7 and 8 shows Two Rain and his ancestor Eight Wind alive post-mortem and communicating with the living. The first consultation starts a marriage alliance war, and the second resolves it, or nearly so. The history continues and has an unexpected outcome—but that story is not within the purview of this book. Interestingly, after consulting with Lord Two Rain's mummy on ZN page 82a, Lord Eight Deer burns it (82b). Thereafter Eight Deer, now a Mixtec-Toltec lord, becomes founder of the second dynasty of Tilantongo.

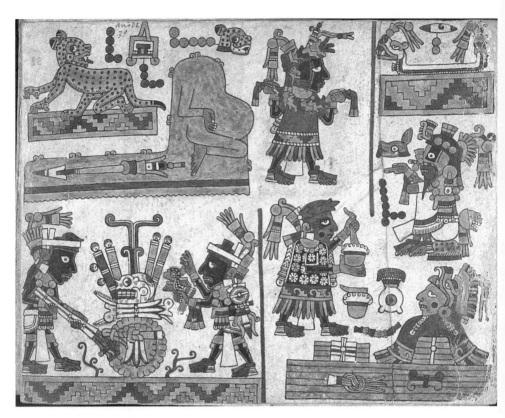

Figure 10.4. Codex Zouche-Nuttall page 82 (British Museum folio no. 88). Lord Eight Deer consults with Lord Two Rain's mummy and then burns it. (© Trustees of the British Museum, The British Museum Company, Ltd.)

Perspective

Obviously, the later scribes who wrote Zouche-Nuttall obverse connected it with Lord Eight Deer events on the older Zouche-Nuttall reverse. They did so to provide clarification by identifying the unnamed mummy that was the subject of Lord Eight Deer's communication ceremony. They also connected the important founder, Lord Eight Wind, with the equally important and famous usurper, Lord Eight Deer.

Why did Eight Deer burn Two Rain's mummy? Perhaps, since the oracle of the dead (whose job it was to consult with mummies) had caused so much trouble by severing the marriage alliance between Tilantongo and Jaltepec, Eight Deer wanted to make sure no one else could talk to it—and he wanted to remove Two Rain from the company of ancestors. Zouche-Nuttall reverse implies that after the oracle's action, Eight Deer rose to power and suppressed it, so, perhaps, Eight Deer was striking a blow to transfer power from the Chalcatongo oracle to priestly Mixtec kings. These priests also had the authority to consult with the dead, as Eight Deer's talk with Two Rain's mummy demonstrates.

This analysis of only the first eight pages of Zouche-Nuttall's reverse is a chronological one. The idea is to define indigenous Mixtec history as they wrote it by translating their calendar to our European calendar. At this point, it is possible to list all twenty-six dates on the first eight codex pages with the people and events they qualify (table 10.1). Perhaps it seems spare when written this way, but it is not—especially when we remember that these pictogram manuscripts encoded narratives that came to life through elaborated performance. These histories (mainly the histories of ceremonies), sung on special occasions, were acted, at least in part. Therefore, these histories were always alive and contemporary on demand. I remarked previously that in this Native American culture there was no division between the "physical" and "metaphysical." To dress and act as a certain being was to be that being, and it is likely the same applied to enacting historical events as well. They were enacted and therefore always contemporary. This is not a concept alien to us. Our modern religious ceremonies are "timeless" and enact eternal events so as to always keep them in the present.

The History in Zouche-Nuttall Pages 1–8

Throughout the twenty-six dates recorded on the first eight pages of Codex Zouche-Nuttall obverse, 165 years of history unfold, from the Epiclassic era to the Early Postclassic period (table 10.1). Lord Eight Wind's biography encompasses a possible human lifespan, and his life and history as detailed on the codex obverse are connected to those that transpired in the time of Lord Eight Deer the Jaguar Claw of Tilantongo, whose life and history are detailed on the codex reverse. The scribes who painted the first side of Codex Zouche-Nuttall had a vested interest in connecting what was for them older epic history with more recent epic history, and doing that provided a detailed saga of the founding of their people's culture. Therefore, this analysis elucidates the purpose of Codex ZN pages 1–8.

This pre-Hispanic history of the Mixtec people of Oaxaca is as astonishing, dramatic, colorful, insightful, and valuable as any we have from an-

Table 10.1. Complete Chronology of Codex Zouche-Nuttall Obverse Pages 1–8

Page/Tableau	Event	Mixtec Date	European	Date AD
1/1.	♂ Eight Wind's birth	1 Reed 8 Wind		935
2/2.	♂ Eight Wind at Yucuñudahui	3 Reed 4 Flint		963
3/1.	War at Yucuñudahui	3 Reed 6 Dog		963
3.	War with Stone Men	5 House		965
3/3.	♂ Seven Motion sacrifice of Stone Men	5 House		965
4/4.	Mummy bundling	6 Rabbit		966
4/2.	Capture of Striped Men	10(9) House		969
4/1.	Striped Men from the sky	12 Flint		972
3/3.	♂ Seven Motion sacrifice of Stone Men	12 Flint		972
4/3.	Eagle sacrifice	12 Flint		972
3/3.	♂ Seven Motion sacrifice of Stone Men End of war	5(6) Reed		979
1/3.	♂ Eight Wind at Apoala	7 Flint 1 Motion		980
3/6.	Maguey Goddess ceremony			
4/6.	Séance, conference	13 Rabbit 2 Deer		986
1/4.	♂ Eight Wind at Suchixtlan	1 Reed 1 Alligator		987
5/1.	♂ Eight Wind at Yellow Man Hill	1 Reed 1 Alligator		987
5/2.	Rain God ceremonies	6(5) Flint 7 Flower		1004
5/3.	End Rain God ceremonies	9(10) House 1 Eagle		1009
5/2.	End Rain God ceremonies	9(10) House 1 Eagle		1007
5/3.	♂ Eight Wind's first marriage	9 Flint 6 Flower		1008
6a/3.	Second marriage	11 Rabbit 3 Eagle		1010
6a/3.	Third marriage	12 Reed 9 Deer		1011
5/3.	Birth of ♂ Thirteen Grass	2 Rabbit 13 Grass		1014
5/3.	♂ Eight Wind dies	2 Reed 2 Reed		1027
7d–8a.	Eight Wind's mummy	4 House 1 Rain		1081
8b.	Two Rain's mummy	10 Flint 2 Flint		1100

cient Greece, Rome, or Medieval Europe. Great men and women, with interested motives, interacted forcefully and dramatically with people and places—physical and metaphysical, familial and political—to weave the elaborate tapestry of their enduring culture. As did the non-Mixtec cultures mentioned, these great men and women seized their moments with forceful intelligence and insight. They created the kingdoms of their Mixteca. These royal people stand now as "types" of ancient Oaxaca, itself a unique culture area amid the rich, intellectually nourishing splendors of ancient Mesoamerica. Although comprising only eight pages of a much longer text, the beginning of Codex Zouche-Nuttall and its story of Lord Eight Wind of Suchixtlan inspires the anthropologist, ethnographer, and historian with many feelings. Perhaps chief among them is gratitude for the privilege of knowing the cultural poetry and heroic deeds of great men and women who lived long ago, and whose descendants are alive today in the Mixteca.

PART THREE

11 Rituals of Order
Codices Zouche-Nuttall and Vienna

In their codices, the Mixtec scribes define the history of Lord Eight Wind of Suchixtlan, his person, and his Mixtec descendants. The histories of other great Mixtec leaders are part of that historical panoply. The first goal of this book, the elucidation of Eight Wind's history, is accomplished. However, to gain further insights into the man himself, it is necessary to compare the sister manuscripts, codices Zouche-Nuttall obverse and Vienna obverse, since he appears in both.

The first point of comparison between codices ZN obverse pages 1–8 (specifically page 2) and Vienna concerns pages 22–11 in the latter. These Vienna passages are qualified by Furst (1978:229) as "the Nine Rites" (table 11.1). These rituals for ordering the Mixtec world occupy the last twenty-two pages of Codex Vienna. Furst notes they are similar in structure and content, and follow a basic pattern that includes seven elements, listed on pages Vienna 22a–5: (1) an initial date, (2) a cradleboard, (3) a major deity or deities as subjects of the dedication ceremonies, (4) objects pertaining to architecture and measuring, (5) a second date different from the first, (6) a fire-drilling or the apparatus for it, (7) and place signs that include both man-made constructions and natural features.

The first seven rites on Vienna pages 22a to 11b have three components not mentioned above: (1) one to four sets of ritual objects, (2) a bird sacrifice, and (3) a ceremony whereby three plants bound together by white paper or cloth are raised before the place signs. In these first seven rites the bird sacrifice, fire drilling, and ceremony of three bound plants occur together (Furst 1978a:231). Furst (1978a:229) notes that the rite displayed on page 10 includes these seven basic elements as well as the three bound plants, but page 5 is only the minimal basic structure, including fire-drilling apparatus. I note a further distinction among these rites; namely, some are short-term and others long-term when comparison is made between their first and sec-

Table 11.1. Codex Vienna Ordering Rituals

Pages 22–21
Year 13 Rabbit Day 2 Deer
Year 5 House Day 5 Snake . . . . 31 years
Pages 20–19
Year 8 House Day 4 Rain
Year 13 Rabbit Day 7 Lizard . . . . 5 years
Pages 18–17a
Year 3 Reed Day 2 Grass
Year 7 Flint Day 1 Flower . . . . 17 years
Pages 17b–15a
Year 10 Flint Day 1 Eagle
Year 5 House Day 13 Wind . . . . 21 years
Pages 15b–14
Year 9 Rabbit Day 1 Lizard
Year 1 Reed Day 1 Alligator . . . . 5 years
Pages 13–12a
Year 7 Reed Day 4 Alligator
Year 7 Reed Day 4 Deer . . . . 26 days
Pages 12b–11
Year 5 Flint Day 5 Flint
Year 5 Flint Day 7 Vulture . . . . 148 days
Pages 10–9
Year 7 Reed Day 4 Motion
Year 7 Reed Day 6 Eagle . . . . 58 days
[Note: A third date, 1 Reed 1 Alligator, occurs on page 10.]
Page 5
Year 5 House Day 7 Snake
Year 5 House Day 9 Snake . . . . 60 days

ond inclusive year dates. Also there is a correspondence in first and second dates between one of the Vienna rituals (pages 18–17a) and the Lord Eight Wind fire-drilling ritual at Yucuñudahui as written on ZN page 2.

The ZN page 2 ritual at Yucuñudahui has the same years and thus the same interval as the Vienna ritual recorded on pages 18–17a. The entire page is devoted to a single complex ceremony, and because it has the most space allotted to it, I conclude that it is the peak event recorded on the codex's first two pages. It lists some of the same elements as the ordering rituals described by Furst for pages 22a to 11b; specifically, (1) an initial date, (2) a major deity or deities to whom the dedication is made, (3) a second date different from the first, (4) fire-drilling apparatus, (5) a list of place signs consisting of both natural and man-made features, and (6) secondary actors employed as ceremonial assistants. In addition to these ritual elements, the Zouche-Nuttall narrative also includes a bird sacrifice and the three bound plants ceremony, although here displayed differently than portrayed on the Vienna pages. The Zouche-Nuttall ritual also differs from that in Vienna by day dates and toponyms; that is, they do not occur in the same place and, though in the same years, not on the same days.

The three bound plants found in Codex Vienna are also seen on ZN page 2: one growing from Rain God Hill directly behind the emerging figure of Lord Eight Wind, another in his eagle crown, and the third growing from Rain God Hill at his feet. The first of these is exactly the same plant displayed in the Codex Vienna tableau, except in Zouche-Nuttall they are unbound and growing unplucked from both Rain God Hill and, apparently, from Lord Eight Wind. As mentioned previously, the implication given by the Codex Zouche-Nuttall is that Rain God Hill is the source of these particular plants. Although these three plants are seen frequently associated with ordering rituals in Vienna, their meaning remains elusive, as Furst notes in her excellent dissertation (1978). The data recorded on ZN page 2 is both evocative and suggestive.

As I have mentioned, Lord Eight Wind Eagle Flints is another manifestation of the three bound plants and also has strong associations with the fire-drilling bundle and apparatus. Further, his identification with both ordering of places and lineage-founding indicates an implied meaning for these ritual plants, which the gods at Apoala raise over places founded and ordered. That is to say, in Codex Vienna, the three bound plants are raised over or before places to be ordered; in the Zouche-Nuttall tableau Lord Eight Wind himself is raised over Yucuñudahui at its fire-drilling ritual. The god in Codex Vienna, Lord Two Dog, conducts ordering rituals and appears in other ritual contexts. Codex ZN page 5 shows Two Dog as one of four secondary actors functioning as ceremonialists conducting a ritual in honor of Lord Eight Wind (Furst 1978a:162). Significantly, neither codex shows Lord Eight Wind conducting a ritual in honor of anyone else except the rain god. By this I understand that he is the precedent figure in his own domain and stands in dignity above the gods of Apoala, excepting only Lord Nine Wind Quetzalcoatl. This is an important point. The comparison of Eight and Nine Wind is, so far, chronological and concerns circumstances of their dual births.

In addition, the Vienna rites on pages 22a–21, 20–19, 18a–17a, and 13a–12a illustrate the decapitated maguey/pulche goddess or maguey plants themselves as elements of ordering rituals. The Zouche-Nuttall tableau on page 2 shows the maguey plant growing from Lord Eight Wind's throat as a part of his accoutrements. In effect, then, Yucuñudahui is the source of the three ceremonial plants, and Lord Eight Wind a seminal figure for them and for the all-important maguey itself. Also, on Codex ZN page 1, tableau 4 Lord Eight Wind speaks or sings a type of plant used for ceremonial wands, and yet another grows from his body. As to ideology contained in these scenes, then, Lord Eight Wind and Yucuñudahui are both sources of these plants.

The ZN page 2 tableau indicates that the deity to whom the fire-drilling ordering ceremony is dedicated is the rain god, as personified by his toponym. This deity/toponym is also seen on Vienna page 48 as the site where the god Lord Nine Wind Quetzalcoatl holds up sky and water. Therefore Yucuñudahui seems to preexist the later ordering rituals shown in Codex Vienna. Subsequently, Yucuñudahui is seen on Vienna page 38b (Year 8 Flint Day 8 Grass) just prior to the Tree-Birth ceremony in which Lord Eight Wind participates. This is eighteen years before the Tree-Birth ceremony at Apoala (Year 13 Rabbit Day 2 Deer) and five years after the date recorded for Lord Eight Wind's arrival there.

Yucuñudahui is then shown on Vienna page 10, where Lord Nine Wind Quetzalcoatl drills for fire and deity Lord Two Dog raises the bound plants over a vast, two-page schematic map of the Mixteca. Otherwise, the rain god as an individual does not appear in Codex Vienna obverse, although he does so on ZN pages 4 and 5. Codex Vienna suggests that the rain god is personally manifested as a place that preexisted the ordering rituals and is first in that ritual, which ultimately unified the whole Mixteca. Inasmuch as the rain god is known as the deity of the original inhabitants of the Mixteca, the Stone Men, and the Mixtecs themselves became known as People of the Rain, this preeminence of place for Yucuñudahui seems appropriate.

This precedence of place may also apply to the person of Lord Eight Wind as implied in our recovered chronology. Is his ordering ritual on ZN page 2 a tenth ordering rite, separate from those in Codex Vienna, or a rite conducted simultaneously with that in Vienna? Or is it the prototypal ordering rite initiated for Yucuñudahui, which Lord Eight Wind then took to Apoala, where it was utilized by the gods in various ordering ceremonial contexts (Powell n.d.)? The codex chronology suggests the latter—and even more.

The attendants for Lord Eight Wind at Apoala (ZN page 1, tableau 3) and then at Suchixtlan in tableau 4 suggest ordering rituals at those places also, but conflated to the simplest representations for the sake of available space (pars pro toto). As I have shown in the proposed chronology, Lord Eight Wind arrived at Apoala some years before the Tree-Birth ceremony. Soon after the conclusion of the War from Heaven, he was present at that ceremony and assumed his dual dignity as both earth-born and tree-born noble; he then founded his lineage at Monkey Hill/Suchixtlan/Cerro Jasmin.

The scribes suggest that Lord Eight Wind's greatness is more than that of a lineage patriarch: he also participated in some way in the War from Heaven, perhaps precipitating it by his arrival at Yucuñudahui, and that war spread and ultimately destroyed the old lineage at Wasp Hill. Then he was a seminal figure instituting a new lineage order and the ritual ordering system for a new lineage franchise of tree-born nobles at Apoala. Perhaps this is the reason why, if he was an original resident and ruler at Yucuñudahui, he survived the war and did so well for himself.

The ideology of birthing nobles from trees caught on, apparently, because codices Selden and Bodley mention it also. Of interest is the fact that Codex Selden states that the first dynasty to rule Jaltepec was earth-born and tree-born, yet it failed for unstated reasons. The second dynasty of Jaltepec, which succeeded, was that of Lord Eight Wind and Lady Ten Deer of Suchixtlan.

Yet another ritual seen in Vienna on page 24 implies a correspondence with a Zouche-Nuttall tableau. ZN page 1, tableau 3 shows Lord Eight Wind at Apoala. He emerges from a cave in one of two rivers—a river and cave that also produce the fire-drilling bundle. A cave at Apoala is also associated with, or produces, a sacred plant, as shown on Vienna page 24b. Among other things, the magic mushroom ceremony begins with Lord Nine Wind Quetzalcoatl before an effigy of the rain god. At the conclusion of the ceremony, Lord Seven Motion of the Two Faces enters a cave in a river at Apoala (as did Eight Wind), and then, standing at that same cave, displays a sacred three-leaved plant to Lord Seven Motion (the sacrificer of Stone Men in ZN page 3, tableau 3, and capturer of Striped Men in ZN page 4, tableau 2). The plant in Vienna resembles the one spoken by Lord Eight Wind at Suchixtlan (ZN page 1, tableau 4). After all, Lord Eight Wind frequently emerges from caves, and travel beneath or through the earth was not considered unusual for him.

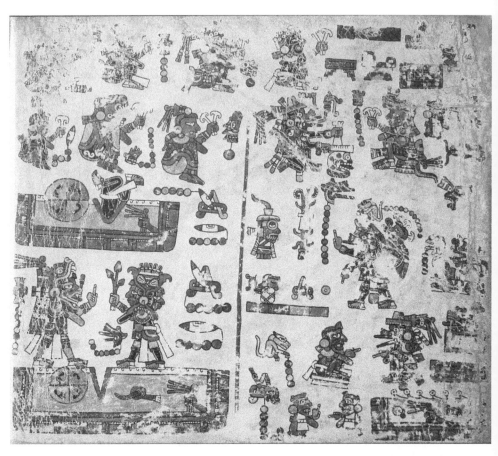

Figure 11.1. Codex Vindobonensis Mexicanus I (Vienna) page 24. The sacred plants are pictured in the second column (reading right to left). ADEVA, Graz, Austria. (© Akademische Druck- u Verlagsanstalt, Graz, Austria)

The Two Codices as Maps

These sister manuscripts portray individuals, temporal indicators, and geographical places (both natural and man-made) as integrated units. A typical tableau presentation consists of four elements: place, date, actor(s), and action(s). In Codex Vienna there are often more places than temporal indicators or actors. In effect, Codex Vienna is one long map ranging from sky to earth and divided into several sections representing individual places, districts, actors in those places, and regions. Codex Zouche-Nuttall employs similar visual devices, has many more actors, and occasionally represents entire regions as unified map-tableaux, as in double-page 19, page 22, and page 36. The introduction page for the third saga (ZN page 36) is a single-page toponym for Apoala, showing the two lineage rivers, valley walls, a waterfall, Serpent's Mouth Cave, and lineage persons associated with the two rivers. The effect of this union of place, person, and time is to firmly associate the elite with their hereditary territories and rights to rule to them.

My interest focuses on the specific Epiclassic era site of Yucuñudahui since it is prominent as the major toponym on Zouche-Nuttall's first two pages. It appears three times in Codex Vienna on pages 47b, 45d, and in the regional map on pages 10–9, where it is included as first in the ordering ritual conducted by Lord Two Dog for an entire landscape composed of twelve hills and a number of buildings, valleys, and lakes.

This latter map representation and ordering ritual by Lord Two Dog differs in scope from the ritual conducted by Lord Eight Wind at Yucuñudahui and its immediate precincts. Two Dog conducts the former for a larger area that includes Yucuñudahui as first among many. As mentioned previously, ZN page 5, tableau 1 shows Lord Two Dog participating in a ritual at Yellow Man Hill honoring Eight Wind, formerly of Yucuñudahui.

Yucuñudahui, Lord Nine Wind Quetzalcoatl, and Lord Eight Wind

Codex Vienna places Yucuñudahui in a unique context that serves to underscore it as literally the first ordered area in Codex Zouche-Nuttall. After an ordering or creation event that occurs in the sky (Vienna pages 52–48b), and after the birth and empowerment of Lord Nine Wind Quetzalcoatl in the sky and his subsequent descent (Vienna 48c), Yucuñudahui is seen as the place where Lord Nine Wind Quetzalcoatl holds up water and the sky in Year 10 House on Day Two Rain. Suggestively, Lord Eight Wind's ordering ritual for Yucuñudahui has Year 3 Reed for its initial date and Year 7 Flint as final date, a seventeen-year interval. Year 7 Reed, associated in Vienna with Yucuñudahui itself, occurs four years after 3 Reed. Year 10 House occurs five years before 3 Reed. This provokes thought about an interesting sequence of events regarding these two heroes, Eight Wind and Nine Wind (tables 11.1 and 11.2). Although they are not recorded in the codices as interacting directly, they are shown in Vienna as being at the Tree-Birth ceremony at the same time, Year 13 Rabbit Day 2 Deer. Nine Wind is seen on Vienna 36b, and Eight Wind on Vienna 35a. Both were also at Yucuñudahui.

Remembering that pictograms only show parts of any particular ritual, a twenty-eight year series of rituals is demonstrated involving the god Lord Nine Wind Quetzalcoatl and the patriarch Lord Eight Wind of Suchixtlan. Yucuñudahui and the individuals associated with it serve as connecting elements between these two codices, and the chronologies reinforce these documents, the individuals, and their actions. The Apoala event at which both were present is an evocative point in their chronology. One hallmark, then, of the first eight pages of Codex Zouche-Nuttall is that it mixes and matches actors and actions with some from Codex Vienna. The chronology in table 10.1 functions as a kind of concordance to enhance Zouche-Nuttall's representation of Lord Eight Wind, just as connecting his biography with that of the later Lord Eight Deer of Tilantongo on Zouche-Nuttall reverse does.

The Zouche-Nuttall narrative creates a unified history and ideology with its own obverse/reverse narratives and also with those in Codex Vienna. Whether or not correlation of dates in Codex Vienna with European calendar dates is possible can be debated, but one such correspondence has been demonstrated reasonably, and I intend to investigate whether other correspondences exist. For those who interpret events in Codex Vienna's first pages as the beginning or creation of the world long ago, correspondence with European calendar sequences will seem inappropriate. Yet, as noted previously, there is nothing in the codices to suggest that the Mixtecs were interested in vast cycles of time, as would be implied by cycles of creation in either the Mayan religious system or that of the Aztecs. Hamann (2002) has

Table 11.2. Nine Wind and Eight Wind at Yucuñudahui

Codex/Page	Event	Mixtec Date
Vienna 47b	♂ Nine Wind holds sky, water at Yucuñudahui	10 House 7 Rain
		+5 years
Nuttall 2	♂ Eight Wind at Yucuñudahui	3 Reed 4 Flint
		+4 Years
Vienna 47b	Yucuñudahui itself	7 Reed 7 Reed
		+13 years
Nuttall 2	End of ordering ritual; Eight Wind goes to Apoala one year after the war ends.	7 Flint 1 Motion
		+6 years
Vienna 37b	Eight Wind and Nine Wind at Apoala	13 Rabbit 2 Deer

noted ethnographic evidence regarding previous cycles of creation, but this happened after the Mixtecs were conquered by the Aztecs.

Codex Vienna begins its events in the sky (or on it, if sky and earth were not separated at that time), but in both manuscripts, several events begin in the sky and then individuals descend to earth. The most prominent to do so is Lord Nine Wind Quetzalcoatl, and it is possible that the Vienna representation of his descent constitutes a paradigm for subsequent individuals doing the same, notably on Codex ZN obverse pages 18, 19, and 22. Codex Vienna describes the celestial creation of certain unique stones, the birth of Lord Nine Wind Quetzalcoatl from a stone knife, his descent to earth, and his holding up water and sky at Yucuñudahui (Furst 1978a:109) (figure 11.2).

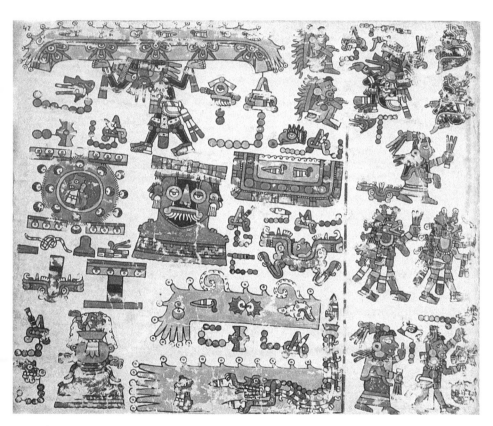

Figure 11.2. Codex Vindobonensis Mexicanus I (Vienna) page 47. Lord Nine Wind Quetzalcoatl lifts water and sky above the earth at the Place Where the Sky Was. Yucuñudahui is the central toponym. (© Akademische Druck- u Verlagsanstalt, Graz, Austria)

The Codex Zouche-Nuttall scribes integrated these chronological events according to their own traditions, but with subtlety, each series of tableaux presupposing unstated prior events or excluding events between tableaux known to those who painted and recited them. From the point of view of occulted information, the Vienna and Zouche-Nuttall narratives are not mutually exclusive, but mutually inclusive and integrated, although differing by details chosen for inclusion or omission by the various authors of each document. One codex recites certain parts of an event, and the other recites those or other parts of events particular to its concerns. The relationship between them is not impaired by this political selection of historical poetry.

Since Zouche-Nuttall is a historical manuscript with verifiable dates, we should not be surprised that historicity transfers to Codex Vienna as well. As seen previously regarding the events of Year 13 Rabbit Day 2 Deer recorded in both codices and connected by the historical person of Lord Eight Wind Eagle Flints, Vienna has historicity. These sister documents need not have been painted at the same time by the same artists from the same place. They illustrate a common ideological history from mutually shared traditions that were important in the Epiclassic era and assumed greater value as time passed. They can illustrate different parts or facets of those traditions with the whole efficiently implied.

The scribes who painted Zouche-Nuttall obverse did so with the intention of unifying their ancient Epiclassic history and its ideology from the northern Nochixtlan Valley with critical events at Apoala, and also with those in the time of Lord Eight Deer at Tilantongo, in the southern Nochixtlan Valley. These royal anonymous princes had an eye to the future and exploited their prestigious past with admirable skill.

As we have seen, the Mixtec scribes took great care to unify their pictogram historical texts by combining events in different eras and the individuals associated with them. Lord Eight Wind Eagle Flints, the subject of ZN pages 1–8, is joined by mystical and historical events with Lord Eight Deer Jaguar Claw of Tilantongo and, through association with him, Lady Six Monkey of Jaltepec/Hua Chino, and the ill-fated young king of Tilantongo, Lord Two Rain. In effect, the history of one, Eight Wind, is the history of all the rest, in one unified series of sequences. Codex Zouche-Nuttall obverse is more recent than the biography of Lord Eight Deer Jaguar Claw on the reverse side; therefore, the scribes joined the history of the former hero with that of the latter by studied intention. Why? As illustrated previously, these two lords were possibly the greatest social reformers in the Mixteca. Having examined Lord Eight Wind's history thoroughly, we now proceed with that of Lord Eight Deer of Tilantongo.

The Problem of the Two Dead Lords

Codex Zouche-Nuttall reverse was painted, according to best guess, in thirteenth-century Oaxaca, and the obverse perhaps as late as the early to middle fifteenth century. The obverse is complete, but the reverse is unfinished. Various commentators have remarked that the obverse is obscure. The older reverse side is the sequential, chronologically progressive political biography of the great culture hero Lord Eight Deer Jaguar Claw of Tilantongo. Recent studies illuminate this biography, but some obscurities remain. The younger obverse document is episodic, presenting at least three sagas separated by genealogical data. The poorly understood obverse fits commentators' characterization of the document perfectly.

This chapter examines two essential passages of the codex, one occurring on the ZN obverse pages 7d–8, and the other on reverse pages 80c–82b, depicting events recorded for Lord Eight Deer's mature career as a Mixtec/Toltec *techutli* ruler of Tilantongo. These passages have not previously been linked in the literature. The first for consideration is obverse pages 7d–8, wherein we elucidate further the problem of the two dead lords.

Recapitulation: Summary of Codex Zouche-Nuttall Pages 1–8

These obverse pages present the first of three sagas recorded on this side of the manuscript: the history of the lineage founder, Lord Eight Wind of Monkey Hill (Cerro Jasmin/Suchixtlan). He was born from a cave in 1 Reed 1 Alligator (AD 935 [page 1a]). His history included many events, including the founding of lineages in several places (pages 1–2). In contrast, the War from Heaven (which began in AD 963), and in which he apparently did not participate, is recorded as a secondary story on pages 2b–4. Finally, Lord Eight Wind reigned as king of Monkey Hill/Suchixtlan, where he married Lady Ten Deer of Suchixtlan in AD 1008, when he was seventy-three years old. His second and third wives were Lady Five Grass, whom he married in 1010 AD, and Lady Ten Eagle, whom he wed one year later, when he was seventy-six years old.

One of the important things to note is that Eight Wind's union with Lady Ten Deer produced two separate royal dynasties that later came into conflict: the first dynasty of Tilantongo (ZN page 5c), whose last king was Eight Wind's great-great-grandson Lord Two Rain Twenty Jaguars, and the second dynasty of Jaltepec (Codex Selden page 5-III), whose queen at the time of conflict was Eight Wind's granddaughter, Lady Six Monkey. At the time of conflict, Two Rain was six years old, and Lady Six Monkey was eight years old.

This saga ends abruptly with two events on pages 7c–8, for which, to the casual observer, there is no reason; however, closer examination illuminates the mystery and provides us with important insights into royal politics and religious practice among the Mixtecs of Postclassic Oaxaca.

The first of these two terminal scenes (ZN 7d) shows Lord Eight Wind seated in a temple at Monkey Hill speaking with his great-great-grandson Lord Two Rain Twenty Jaguars, who is illustrated just across the page-fold on page 8. This event is problematical because this interaction occurs in Mixtec Year 4 House (AD 1081), when Eight Wind would have been 146 years old. He is obviously deceased, yet speaking from Monkey Hill to his six-year-old descendant.[1] Many modern students of the codices are undetermined about this, or else vacillate. Was Lord Eight Wind dead at this time, or merely very old? Based on the codex material interpreted in the previous chapters, it seems clear he was dead.

The second, and last, of these terminal scenes (page 8) ends the narrative sequence. The boy-king, Two Rain, speaks to his deceased relative located just across the page-fold, so this is part of the event begun on page 7 and is part of the first scene described. This is a masterstroke of pictorial narrative, explaining as it does past and future events.

This full-page scene occurs in Year 10 Flint (AD 1100), when Two Rain would have been twenty-five years old. He is seated in a temple (as was his ancestor, Lord Eight Wind) and speaking with thirteen assembled warriors, notwithstanding the fact that Two Rain had died mysteriously four years earlier. Thus we have the problem of the two dead lords.

The people of ancient Oaxaca believed that they could interact with the deceased either through the agency of an established oracle (Lady Nine

1. The image of Lord Eight Wind seated in a temple after his death is wonderfully suggestive. Ancestral bundles were sacred, appropriate contents for a temple. Although few survive, one wonders if they were stored in miniature temple structures like those shown for the Inca mummies in Guaman Poma's *Corónica*.

Grass at Chalcatongo) or a *yaha yahui* priest. Byland and Pohl (1994:241) note: "Supernatural encounters with dead ancestors in caves are mentioned in the *Relaciones* of Mitlantongo and Penoles." Indeed, historiographic evidence confirms the existence of a well-developed cult of the dead in pre-Columbian Mixtec times that was centered on mummy bundles of deceased royalty. Therefore, since both parties shown (Eight Wind and Two Rain) are deceased, we conclude that these post-mortem conferences are between the two lords' respective mummy bundles and the living.

The Mixtec Cult of the Dead and Royal Politics

In post-Conquest times, Fray Franciso de Burgoa (1934 [1674], cited in Byland and Pohl 1994:199), described three prominent Oaxaca oracles that were consulted in important matters of state. The one that interests us here is that of the goddess of the underworld, Lady Nine Grass, whose oracular priest presided at the temple in Chalcatongo. In a cave near Chalcatongo the mummy bundles of deceased royalty were consulted by an oracular priest attired as Lady Nine Grass when called upon to do so. This was an important resource for Mixtec royalty when it came to resolving disputes.

These mummy bundles were housed ceremonially in caves in various places throughout the Mixteca. Remains of these cave shrines (now mostly destroyed) have been found in several locations other than Chalcatongo. One such investigation is described by Byland and Pohl (1994:87) in Cavua Colorado, located in a canyon wall directly below the ancient town of Hua Chino.

With this basic information in mind, we can infer with certainty that the two consultations with deceased kings illustrated for our attention concern the resolution of thorny questions important in the context of the Mixtec political and economic systems of their day. In both illustrations, though, it is important to note that the Oracle of Chalcatongo does not appear. These were priestly consultations alone. In the case of the boy-king Two Rain, he is attired in priestly garments during his visit with Eight Wind's mummy, and we know the subject of this consultation was Jaltepec, a close ally of Chalcatongo.

If we look only at the ZN obverse page 8 scene, we find ourselves with a question: who was the priest who consulted with adult Two Rain's mummy? None are mentioned there, only assembled warriors, but that information is, in fact, provided on the codex reverse; therefore, I assert that the obverse data is explanatory to reverse-side events, and the remaining data support this. We are also left to discover the exact nature of the important problem that the Mixtec scribes intended to illuminate.

Problematical Marriage History in the Mixteca

This chapter proposes data interpretations suggesting that the material on the obverse pages 7c–8 explains an important conflict told in the biography of Lord Eight Deer of Tilantongo, related on the final pages of Codex Zouche-Nuttall reverse. Superficially, this is a tale of murder and revenge, but an in-depth analysis of historical background from the codices themselves details political history of major importance to Mixtec elite culture in general and, specifically, to the advancement of the political career of the self-made king, Eight Deer of Tilantongo. In fact, it probably explains *why and how* he became king by his own hand. As our conventional wisdom has it, necessity is the mother of invention—or, in Eight Deer's case, opportunity is the agency of advancement.

The historical facts of this conflict—which can be drawn from codices Selden, Bodley, and Zouche-Nuttall—can be summarized briefly as having to do with established marriage alliances between royal families and the lucrative trade networks attendant upon them.

Lord Two Rain Twenty Jaguars was the last ruler of Lord Eight Wind of Suchixtlan's first dynasty at Tilantongo. Traditional marriage alliance was maintained with the related royal dynasty at nearby Jaltepec. For unknown reasons, the six-year-old Two Rain consulted with his deceased ancestor Lord Eight Wind, after which the boy's uncle Three Lizard (Eight Wind's son) attacked Jaltepec and lost the war. This event likely precipitated the rift between Tilantongo and Jaltepec, with an attendant loss of prestige for Tilantongo.

Lord Eight Deer of Tilantongo, not of royal blood, but the son of the high priest, attended a conference at Chalcatongo two years later, wherein Lady Six Monkey of Jaltepec was given permission by the Chalcatongo oracle, Lady Nine Grass, to marry outside the Tilantongo marriage alliance agreement. Specifically, she was betrothed to a rival of Tilantongo, Lord Eleven Wind of Red and White Bundle. Codex Zouche-Nuttall, a Tilantongo document, shows this conference. So does Codex Selden, a Jaltepec document, although the accounts differ. In the first, Eight Deer and Lady Six Monkey are seen with the goddess-oracle Lady Nine Grass, who consults with the mummy bundle of Lord Three Lizard. Neither Two Rain of Tilantongo nor Eleven Wind of Red and White Bundle are included. Lord Eight Deer (who is twenty years old at the time) sits looking downward. The Selden scene omits Eight Deer and shows Lady Six Monkey and Lord Eleven Wind betrothed, but not married, by the oracle in AD 1083.

Six Monkey and Eleven Wind were not formally married until AD 1090. Six years later (AD 1096), Lord Two Rain died mysteriously and, as we discovered, became a mummy bundle. There was a power vacuum at Tilantongo.

This is the essential imbalance of political power that, it is assumed, resulted in Two Rain's death almost twenty years after he consulted with his deceased great-great-grandfather Eight Wind. This and subsequent events had repercussions. Lord Eight Deer was at Chalcatongo when the conference occurred. His omission from the Codex Selden scene is suggestive, inviting speculation. All we can say about it, however, is that both codices are political documents: one for Tilantongo and the other for Jaltepec.

A chronological summary of these complicated historical events is helpful.

In AD 1081 the six-year-old king Lord Two Rain Twenty Jaguars of Tilantongo consults with the mummy bundle of his great-great-grandfather Lord Eight Wind of Monkey Hill/Suchixtlan/Cerro Jasmin. Three days later, Two Rain's uncle, Lord Three Lizard, acting on his nephew's behalf, attacks Jaltepec but loses the war and is captured. Lord Two Rain hides in a cave and consults an oracle there. This may actually be Two Rain's consultation with his great-great-grandfather's mummy, but abbreviated to save space in the pictogram text.

Two years later, in AD 1083, the conference between the oracle Lady Nine Grass of Chalcatongo and the disputants occurs. The Codex Zouche-Nuttall scene is unresolved but suggests the beginning of Lord Eight Deer's mature career. The Codex Selden scene, however, shows the alliance created by the oracle between Jaltepec and Red and White Bundle (Hua Chino).

In AD 1090, Lady Six Monkey and Lord Eleven Wind are formally married at Red and White Bundle (Selden 8-III).

In AD 1096, Lord Two Rain, the last and heirless king of the first dynasty of Tilantongo, dies mysteriously. Codex Bodley (5-I) suggests that he commits ceremonial suicide.

With the Tilantongo dynasty defunct, teenage Lord Eight Deer—not a noble but the son of Tilantongo's high priest, the chief of the Council of Four—begins his career.

Where Is Lord Eight Deer?

Codex Zouche-Nuttall reverse is explicit regarding the career of Lord Eight Deer of Tilantongo after the disappointing conference at Chalcatongo. He immediately makes an offering to the sun in a Sun-Tree ceremony (ZN page 44c) and becomes Warlord of Tututepec, a town on the southwestern coast of Oaxaca, on the Gulf of Tehuantepec. The codex details his expansion of power beginning in AD 1083—the same year, but after the unfortunate conference at Chalcatongo. Having enterprised himself with boldness by force of arms, he conquered everything worthwhile or else subdued towns and polities by threat.

In the catalogue of polities subdued or controlled by Eight Deer, Chalcatongo is listed (page 50b), but the oracle Lady Nine Grass is not mentioned. The codex specifically displays Tututepec above Chalcatongo, despite the fact that they are widely separated geographically. Then Eight Deer travels outside his territory to Coixtlahuaca/Tulancingo, allies with the Tolteca/Chichimeca ruler there (Lord Four Jaguar), and receives the nose-perforation ornament of a *techutli* (lineage founder) in AD 1097—just one year after Lord Two Rain of Tilantongo dies. Lord Eight Deer thus acquires a prerogative of kingship: he is now a lineage founder.

Ever one to keep goals in sight and stay keenly aware of the interregnum at Tilantongo, with no lineage candidate to fill it, Lord Eight Deer conquers his way back to his hometown and assumes control. A rule in codex-painting must be noted here: the more pages devoted to an event, the more important that event is. Lord Eight Deer Jaguar Claw and his older half-brother, Lord Twelve Motion, convene a conference with 112 lords in AD 1098, an event that occupies fourteen and a quarter pages of Codex Zouche-Nuttall's reverse forty-two pages. All displayed polities are under his control, including Chalcatongo. Again, the oracle Lady Nine Grass is absent: in her place before her temple there is a Lord One Death sun god substitute. Jaltepec and Red and White Bundle are not listed.

Lord Eight Deer, accompanied by his half-brother Twelve Motion and his ally Lord Four Jaguar, then conquers the Place Where the Sky Is Held Up (ZN page 75), enters the realm of the sun god (the oracle at Achiutla), establishes an alliance with that oracle, and returns to earth (pages 75–80b).

Lord Eight Deer and the Mummy Bundle of Lord Two Rain

The next series of events occurs within one solar year (10 Flint), and the scribes were careful to record them by days in that year. A sequence of days is now listed, arranged chronologically in progressive order to illustrate succinctly the actions that connect the codex reverse narrative with the elaborations provided on that same manuscript's obverse page 8. Although some day names and numbers occur twice in that year, the methodology employed to distinguish between them is simple: because the crucial day for the precipitating event occurs only once, the other days recorded must be in compliance with it.

The precipitating event that permits Lord Eight Deer to rectify the marriage misalliance that happened years before is stark: his older half-brother and confederate in arms, Lord Twelve Motion, is assassinated: his heart is excised while he takes a sweat bath. The chronological sequence is as follows:

1. Day 41, 11 Death, assassination of Lord Twelve Motion (page 81a).
   + 3 days
2. Day 44, 1 Water, baking Lord Twelve Motion's mummy in hot sand (page 81b).
   + 8 days
3. Day 52, 9 Motion, completion of the mummification (page 81b).
   + 18 days
4. Day 70, 1 Eagle, gathering of warriors for the consultation with Lord Two Rain's mummy (page 8b).
   + 20 days
5. Day 90, 8 Eagle. Unexplained (page 80d).
   + 13 days
6. Day 103, 8 Rabbit. Unexplained (page 80d).
   + 12 days
7. Day 115, 7 Flower. Funeral ceremonies for Lord Twelve Motion (page 81c–d).
   + 138 days
8. Day 253, 2 Flint. Lord Eight Wind consults with Lord Two Rain's mummy at the warrior's gathering (pages 8b and 82a).

The last day, 2 Flint, is crucial to connecting obverse page 8 to reverse page 82a. It is found on page 8, just below the temple effigy containing Lord

Two Rain's mummy and just above the ballcourt shown at the foot of the hill. The codex obverse page 8 shows the warriors collected there for a period of 183 days, which is probably the interval it took for Lord Eight Deer to raise an army against Red and White Bundle. The following year Lord Eight Deer destroys Red and White Bundle, sacrifices Lady Six Monkey of Jaltepec and her husband Lord Eleven Wind, and executes Lord Eleven Wind's two sons by a previous marriage, but spares the boy Lord Four Wind, who is the child of Six Monkey and Eleven Wind.

Of the thirteen warriors named on ZN obverse page 8, nine are named on the reverse conference with 112 lords (table 12.1). Identification is by day name, not accoutrements, because the scenes depict different events interpreted by scribes in different eras.

The Historical Drama Concluded

This chapter offers convincing evidence, not supposition, that at least one seminal passage of Codex Zouche-Nuttall obverse explains crucial events in the life of Lord Eight Deer of Tilantongo as recorded in the first-painted reverse of that same codex: namely, ZN obverse page 8, which not only termi-

Table 12.1. Thirteen Warriors Named on Zouche-Nuttall Obverse Page 8 and Reverse Pages

ZN Obverse Page 8	Reverse
Seven Lizard	56a
Three Alligator	64b
Five/Six Rain	86b
Nine Rabbit	57d
Five Lizard	66b
Two Monkey	...
Seven Motion	64a
Ten Eagle	59c
Ten Wind	57b
Three Water	...
Nine Deer	...
One Alligator	55a
Nine Alligator	...

nates a general biography of the lineage founder, Lord Eight Wind of Monkey Hill, but also displays the complex nature of elite politics and cultural events in Postclassic Oaxaca among the Mixtec people.

This interpretation of an often misinterpreted set of passages on both sides of Codex Zouche-Nuttall involves more than a correct identification of mummy bundles. One often reads in commentaries that the mummy consulted by Lord Eight Deer on the codex reverse is that of his assassinated half-brother, Lord Twelve Motion, but as shown, this is not the case. Further data extrapolated from this historical biography of Lord Eight Deer reveals that he was motivated by political events that occurred during the boyhood of the last king of Tilantongo. We also see that he extended his "correction" of events to include an established and well-respected oracle, that of Lady Nine Grass at Chalcatongo. After the conference with Eight Deer and Lady Six Monkey at Chalcatongo, she disappears from Codex Zouche-Nuttall, only to appear in later history in Codex Bodley consulting with the man who would replace Eight Deer: Lord Four Wind, whom Eight Deer spared from death when he destroyed Red and White Bundle. However, the Bodley narrative does not record her as being at Chalcatongo. Alfonso Caso, in his 1960 commentary on Codex Bodley, is unable to identify her location. Eight Deer remembered that the oracle was complicit in permitting a new marriage alliance and, as Codex Zouche-Nuttall is at pains to state, allied himself with the Sun God oracle at Achiutla. Eight Deer was a *yaha yahui* priest and could consult the dead (Lord Two Rain) without the intervention of an oracle he had no reason to trust. Yet, as noted in previous chapters, this policy was begun in the regency of young Two Rain when he consulted the mummy of his ancestor Lord Eight Wind.

Perhaps this earlier consultation influenced the Chalcatongo oracle's decision to vitiate the marriage alliance between Tilantongo and Jaltepec, but we will never know. Codex Selden's history of the second dynasty of Jaltepec (Lady Six Monkey's town of origin) does state an astonishing fact: women ruled there, and the town had a close alliance with Chalcatongo and its oracle. Codex Selden suggests that perhaps Jaltepec was a dependency of Chalcatongo. However, for his own reasons, Lord Eight Deer understood that the Chalcatongo oracle was not all-powerful, but subject to the convenience of a standing army. Lord Eight Deer's agenda was busy, his goals complex, and his methods efficient and well planned.

Regarding Mixtec history, Byland and Pohl (1994:228) note that "the elite members of Mixtec society thus had the ability to manipulate history to their own advantage. Through the collusion of separate supernatural authorities the most influential noble families could fix their own version of the foundational history."

Lord Eight Deer, and those who came after, surely did so, and in the process he bent the supernatural authorities to his own will to preserve the dignity and hereditary rights and policies of his native Tilantongo. Those who succeeded him and dominated Mixtec history were not only his own descendants. They were also from the Lord Eight Wind female Jaltepec/Hua Chino lineage through Lord Four Wind and his younger brother One Alligator. Speculation has it that Four Wind engineered Eight Deer's assassination (Troike 1974) when Eight Deer was fifty-two years old, in AD 1115. Both brothers—Four Wind and One Alligator—married Eight Deer's daughters, the princesses of Tilantongo.

13   The Epiclassic Mixtec Ceremonial Complex

The obverse of Codex Zouche-Nuttall—throughout all forty-one pages—is primarily a document recording ceremonies, the histories of these ceremonies, and, therefore, almost certainly, the ideology which these ceremonies validate. For purposes of definition, and considering the similarity of the ZN rituals with those recorded in Codex Vienna, I call the implied ideology the Epiclassic Mixtec ceremonial complex. All three narratives, which I have termed "sagas," are in fact ritual histories. All involve lineage, ordering rituals, and the Cult of the Dead.

All of the pictogram tableaux recorded on ZN pages 1–8, including the capture events in the War from Heaven (pages 3–4), are ceremonies. The locus of this ceremonial complex is found at Apoala, and the relationship and exchange of ceremonial components between Apoala and Yucuñudahui are emphasized by the codex scribes. According to the narrative testimony examined in previous chapters, this ceremonial complex—which includes the Mixtec system of oracles—remained a stabilizing feature of Mixtec culture. The reverse of Codex Zouche-Nuttall, which details the political history of Lord Eight Deer Jaguar Claw of Tilantongo, indicates that this warlord attempted cultural changes during his lifetime. Codex Bodley records that subsequent to Eight Deer's assassination in AD 1115, most of the changes he attempted to make, primarily those involving the oracle of the dead at Chalcatongo, did not continue after death.

Shifts in Epiclassic Settlement Patterns and Ideologies

Careful archaeological work in the Nochixtlan Valley (Spores 1969:560c) indicates previous settlements from about AD 300 gradually phased out during the Classic and Late Classic periods. This process began in the era we have identified as Epiclassic—a period between the Late Classic and the Postclassic periods. Some settlements, however, persisted and flourished, especially Yucuita and, very notably, Yucuñudahui. Other civic centers or towns developed and/or expanded at this time, including Cerro Jasmin (Suchixtlan, Monkey Hill) and Jaltepec. Furthermore, in the Epiclassic and Early Post-classic periods—at a time Spores (1969:561c–562a) refers to as the Natividad phase beginning ca. AD 1000—the number and population of civic centers in this area continued to increase until the Spanish *entrada* in 1521. In fact, a long ridge from Yanhuitlan to Sayultepec and Etlantongo shows evidence of nearly continuous occupation in the Natividad phase.

Codices Zouche-Nuttall and Vienna pictorially record Epiclassic ideological changes. The second saga (ZN obverse pages 14–22) concerns itself with (1) the founding of the Wasp Hill ruling lineage prior to Lord Eight Wind, (2) the extermination of that lineage in the War from Heaven, and (3) the founding of the first lineage at Tilantongo. It almost certainly depicts the founding of four great temples, or ceremonial centers. Pages 14–19 are replete with sky images and descents of various persons from the sky—essentially representing interactions between earth, sky, and water landscapes. Pages 14–22 display thirteen sky and water images, five of them with cave openings, and three of those have individuals associated with them. The first saga (ZN pages 1–8) has only one tableau where landscape water is featured, and a second one where water is poured from a jar. Representations of sky appear only once in the War from Heaven sequence, on page 4 where Striped Men from the Sky are captured. Otherwise, pages 1–8 have twenty-five cave/earth images.

Codex Vienna begins paradigms of order in the sky, and many things happen there, but paramount among them is the birth of Lord Nine Wind Quetzalcoatl—an event upon which all subsequent events in Vienna depend. In other codices, Lord Nine Wind is a prominent ceremonial figure and battles against both Stone Men and the Striped Men from the Sky in the War from Heaven. During this war, another individual named Nine Wind fights against Lady Nine Grass, the oracle of Chalcatongo, in the southern Nochixtlan Valley (ZN pages 20b–21a).

The ideological shift implied by various portrayals of Nine Wind is dramatic: the previous and subsequently exterminated Wasp Hill lineage/ideology is replaced with the establishment of a different set, with the emphasis shifting to sky elements at Apoala in Codex Vienna. In Zouche-Nuttall's first saga Lord Eight Wind is prominently associated with caves. He appears from a cave in water only once (page 1); all other appearances are either in earth caves or temple caves. In Eight Wind's case, caves imply movement from one place or element to another. Remembering that ZN pages 1–8 have just one scene with prominent water (page 5) and one with landscape water (page 1), and only one scene representing sky (page 4), the preponderance of earth images and the absence of sky and water iconography are striking.

Remembering also that the first saga has strong connections with Apoala and Lord Eight Wind's emergence from a cave there, the third saga (ZN pages 36–41) begins in Apoala with a cave event. This saga has no sky images whatever, and water appears as the two Apoala lineage rivers and a waterfall on page 36.

The data recorded in the first pages of Codex Zouche-Nuttall obverse indicate that the protagonist, Lord Eight Wind, was a prime mover in an era of sweeping, dramatic, and conflictive social change. He either forged links with the new lineage order emerging at Apoala or was an intrinsic part of its formation. Subsequent data in this and other codices indicate the extreme importance of his lineage and the organization associated with it.

Although Lord Eight Wind is not displayed as a direct participant in the crucial War from Heaven, the Zouche-Nuttall manuscript indicates that he was involved with its conflict with the Stone Men, and that he was a seminal figure in the organization and subsequent institution of a new order of rule by the miraculous tree-born nobles from Apoala. After his political career ended, he married three women late in life and began a large, enduring family. In the later war of extermination conducted by Tilantongo against the Jaltepec/Hua Chino marriage alliance, the two conflicting royal parties (Tilantongo's first dynasty and Jaltepec's second dynasty) were descended from Lord Eight Wind through his daughters. The exterminated lineage at Hua Chino was not (Caso 1964:54a).

Regarding this intra/extra-familial fight, Eight Wind's power and influence did not end with his death at age ninety-two. Communication with his mummy was instrumental in beginning the marriage alliance war between his descendants. The codex scribes even provide us with a visual connection to events on the manuscript reverse that transpired in the time of Lord Eight Deer Jaguar Claw. It is reasonable to conclude that a function for Zouche-Nuttall's first saga is to connect formational events in the Early Epiclassic era ordering of the new Mixtec society to its later history through the power and prestige of a dominant patriarch.

Lord Eight Wind was indeed a great patriarch. His influence continued both mystically and physically as his lineage grew, diversified, and extended itself through time. One can assert that descent from Eight Wind through his daughters validated some royal descents in the female line. The three sagas of Zouche-Nuttall obverse all involve lineage establishment, and all are connected by lineage histories. That is why Jansen and Jimenez (2005:14b) propose that the manuscript should be called "Codex Tonindeye," the Book of Lineage History.

These narratives tell us that early Mixtec history was tripartite in the minds of the scribes: the first saga (pages 1–8) presents the beginnings of Mixtec history, with a new lineage formation at Apoala. Saga 2 (pages 14–22) is a Mixtec history based around a previous lineage subsequently removed from power and the founding of ceremonial centers. The third saga (pages 36–41) is Mixtec history descended entirely from Apoala lineage validation.

In order to give us the complicated historical and ideological information encoded in Codex Zouche-Nuttall's first eight pages, the scribes enhanced the project by using interesting, creative formats. One such format allows certain pages to be "eclipsed," or hidden, by folding preceding and succeeding pages to cover them, and still another involves integration of the chronology with that in Codex Vienna.

The text also displays a kind of literary duality. Each two pages comprise a data set. Pages 1 and 2 are Eight Wind's introduction as a santo or supernatural being who participates in creating the ideology for Mixtec people to be called "People of the Rain," and the Mixteca itself the "Land of the Rain God." Pages 3 and 4 tell of the War from Heaven, itself in two parts: the campaign against the Stone Men and the battle against the Striped Men from the Sky. Pages 5 and 6 are the history of Lord Eight Wind's lineage founding and the patron deities attendant upon them. Pages 7 and 8 are a transition to the future era of Lord Eight Deer of Tilantongo. These last two pages depict two metaphysical events that may be seminal to the Oaxaca cult of the dead—namely, conferences with the mummy bundles of two deceased kings.

Also, pages 3 and 4 each terminate with a section from a ceremony known to be associated with Apoala; that is, each page has a terminal text comprising part of a whole, so that the ceremony itself is displayed in two parts. Even the protagonist of this story, Lord Eight Wind, is associated with the deity Lord Nine Wind Quetzalcoatl by sharing the dignity of double birth. In this later association there are two sequential interconnecting chronologies, as has been shown. Lord Eight Wind himself had two lives: one supernatural, during his first fifty-two years, and the second natural, during his final forty years. This latter "life" is enriched by a third quality, however: his life beyond the grave, whereby he continued to influence the political history of his descendants.

Codex Zouche-Nuttall itself is not a singular artifact. It is closely associated with its "sister," Codex Vienna. This dual association has been recognized from the time Zelia Nuttall first examined them and even before, during the time of the Aztecs. Both artifacts were presented by Emperor Montezuma II as part of the treasure he gave to Hernán Cortés (Nuttall 1902:9a–11b). The codices traveled to Europe together and were separated only after arriving in that strange land. Although they remain physically separated, the investigations of scholars have recognized them to be part of a historical and ideological unity representing in bold and beautiful artistic statements the greatness of the Mixtec people who wrote them more than seven hundred years ago.

In this present era we acknowledge that these ancient manuscripts were not written specifically for us to read. Nevertheless, they are time machines that provide windows through which we can see the world of a great indigenous people who pursued the dynamics of their existence without European influence. Theirs was a world of animated power which astonishes us even now—perhaps because it is literally focused in might and authority upon great houses of nobles who controlled their keeps wisely and at no great distance from one another.

This historical panorama is also tinged with an enduring sorrow, because when Europeans finally arrived in Oaxaca in 1521, the new cultural paradigm imposed on Native Americans swept away preexisting societies, creating people without history. The Mixtec codices—fragile manuscripts painted in bright colors on leather pages covered with thin gesso—are the remaining true testimonies of that history. I would like to think this the reason that the doomed Emperor Montezuma II included them as treasure to be sent to the great royal houses of alien Europe. For the most part, the gold and jewels that the Spanish so esteemed have either vanished or are forgotten now that the flurry of excitement surrounding them has been quelled by the passing of five centuries. At this time, in more considered and reflective, and perhaps more appreciative, moments, we can see and know the true treasure that grew and blossomed among the indigenous peoples of

New World Oaxaca because we are now learning to read their few surviving books, the *tonindeye*: their family histories, and accounts of the deeds of their great kings and queens. In these books, which stand among the great literatures of the world, one can recognize that the political and ideological culture of ancient Oaxaca was brought to life by the deeds of their great lords and ladies.

APPENDIX I Biographical Sketches of Major Personnel from the Codices

Lord Eight Deer the Usurper, Lord Two Rain the King, and Lady Six Monkey of Jaltepec

Because this book is primarily concerned with the chronological interpretation of events in the life of Lord Eight Wind of Suchixtlan, it is helpful to clarify those major historical personages with whom he interacted, or whose later lives he influenced, some of whom were his descendants. This book is about Mixtec manuscripts and the people who wrote them. It is thus reasonable to let the books themselves speak to us, insofar as is possible.

The following data are from the Mixtec codices themselves, generally in the sequence presented in those documents, with modern calendar equivalent dates added to allow us to make historical sense of them from our perspective. Commentary is minimal for the most part, but sometimes I cannot restrain myself. Perhaps interested persons, whether general reader or scholar, will be moved to acquire photographic copies of the codices for private study and, yes, enjoyment. Many are available on the Internet, particularly at the FAMSI Web site, and excellent photo facsimiles can be obtained from the Akademische Druck- u., Verlagsanstalt, Graz, Austria. Whether one reads them or not, they remain great visual art, with vivid imagery that can be appreciated by the historian, art historian, artist, anthropologist, archaeologist, and the merely curious. After all, Dover Press kept Zelia Nuttall's artist-copied edition of the codex named for her and Lord Zouche in print for years not because anyone was actually reading it, but because it is great art.

Of the following biographies, the only extensive one is that of Lord Eight Deer Jaguar Claw, the Usurper of Tilantongo. Although not of direct royal descent, he became the most powerful ruler in the land. Instead of being destroyed and written out of the pages of Mixtec history, he is remembered with pride. He was glorious, ambitious, intelligent, insightful, culturally reforming (apparently he committed the cultural heresy of banishing the all-powerful Oracle of the Dead at Chalcatongo), conniving, treacherous, unstoppable, the founder of Tilantongo's second dynasty—in short, a politician worthy of Julius Caesar, and a military leader worthy of Napoleon.

After his assassination in AD 1115, his descendants (he had several wives) were welcomed because everyone wanted to be related to Eight Deer the Great. Even those who had every reason to hate him married his daughters (Selden 8-IV, 9-I). Although mentioned in every major Mixtec codex, Lord Eight Deer's biography is the exclusive subject of Codex Zouche-Nuttall reverse and comprises at least half of the Codex Alfonso Caso fragments. The biography provides us not only with Eight Deer's mighty deeds, but also insight into the Mixtecs' use of their indigenous calendar. Each part of Eight Deer's life in Codex Zouche-Nuttall appears with dates in the 365-day solar year. Whereas the War from Heaven events, which transpired in the time of the precedent Lord Eight Wind Twenty of Suchixtlan, are mysterious and even vague, resisting interpretation, many of those in Lord Eight Deer Jaguar Claw's biography are not. Many days recorded in the 260-day sacred calendar for Eight Deer events are obvious calendric sequences. An example of this occurs on ZN page 75, where Eight Deer and his heroic companions travel across the water to conquer the Place Where the Sky Is Held Up; in other words, Eight Deer and his companions enter the sky where Lord Nine Wind Quetzalcoatl first lifted it above the earth. The three day dates are sequential, and our conclusion is obvious: the journey across the water, or the battle to conquer the place, took three days. Besides providing a complete schematic outline of the Eight Deer biography on ZN pages 42–84, every day recorded therein is considered in the appendix, and the sequences marked.

Lord Two Rain Twenty Jaguars, the last king of Tilantongo's first royal dynasty, is the man whom Eight Deer replaced. He was born Seven Reed, had his name changed to the more auspicious one of Two Rain (to no avail), sponsored a disastrous war against Tilantongo's lineage ally Jaltepec at age six, and died (some say by "assisted" suicide) at age twenty-one. He was unmarried and left no descendants; however, he did leave something very useful—an empty throne. The enterprising Eight Deer Jaguar Claw used that vacancy as his road to ultimate power and everlasting fame.

Lady Six Monkey, the Warrior Princess of Jaltepec and the queen of Hua Chino (Red and White Bundle), also survives as a compelling historical personage. Her biography in Codex Selden is a detailed one. After the six-year-old Lord Two Rain Twenty Jaguars of Tilantongo sponsored an attack against her town of Jaltepec, she sought redress from the oracle of Chalcatongo, severed the marriage alliance with Tilantongo with the oracle's connivance, and married Lord Eleven Wind, the king of Tilantongo's rival polity, Hua Chino. She gave him two illustrious sons, the princes Four Wind and One Alligator. Eight Deer Jaguar Claw executed her and her husband in AD 1101–1102, when he settled the war begun years before by Lord Two Rain Tilantongo. Their son, Four Wind, is the suspected assassin of Lord Eight Deer Jaguar Claw, and surely the man who replaced him. His brother, One Alligator, ruled his mother's polity, Jaltepec, and both brothers married Eight Deer's daughters, the princesses of Tilantongo. Four Wind (the great-grandson of our protagonist Lord Eight Wind of Suchixtlan) married several wives, lived into his seventies, and produced a line of descent still ruling when Pedro de Alvarado marched into Oaxaca in AD 1521. The Lienzo de Zacatepec mentions Lord Four Wind from the "long ago time" as a founder of the Zacatepec dynasty.

Lady Six Monkey's document is Codex Selden, the *tonindeye* of Jaltepec. It is interesting not only for content. A palimpsest written over an older manuscript, and unfolding through twenty pages from bottom to top, it is from the early Spanish Colonial era. Considering the animosity between Tilantongo and Jaltepec, it is not surprising to discover Lord Eight Deer mentioned in it only as the father of the two Tilantongo princesses married by Six Monkey's sons, the princes Four Wind and One Alligator. Virtually every other major Mixtec manuscript features Eight Deer with prominence: Vindobonensis Mexicanus I reverse records Eight Deer's expanded lineage, Zouche-Nuttall reverse (outlined below) is Eight Deer's political biography (and he is mentioned on the obverse as well), and he also appears in Bodley obverse and reverse, and the Codex Alfonso Caso (Colombino-Becker I fragments).

Abbreviations used in the following schematics are:

ZN	Zouche-Nuttall
Sel	Selden
Bod	Bodley
Becker-I	Alfonso Caso (listed only as its fragment in the Vienna Library)
con	Conquest

These schematics and small essays are: (1) a historical concordance of the three heroes, (2) the biography of Lord Eight Deer Jaguar Claw, (3) the biography of Lord Two Rain Twenty Jaguars of Tilantongo, (4) and the biography of Lady Six Monkey of Jaltepec/Hua Chino. Finally, appendices II and III deal with chronological sequences in the 260-day calendar as tables.

I. Historical Concordance of the Three Heroes

(For the sake of space, numerals in personal names are expressed as such.)

AD 1008. Lord 8 Wind of Suchixtlan + Lady 10 Deer. Their two daughters are the Princesses 2 Snake and 9 Wind.

♀2 Snake + ♂10 Flower Tilantongo. Their sons are ♂12 Lizard Tilantongo and ♂10 Eagle Tilantongo.

AD 1041. ♂10 Eagle + ♀9 Wind Jaltepec. Their daughter is ♀6 Monkey, born AD 1073.

AD 1043. ♂12 Lizard Tilantongo + ♀4 Flint and ♀4 Alligator. A son of the marriage is ♂5 Motion, who marries ♀2 Grass. Their son ♂2 Rain is born AD 1075.

AD 1063. Birth of ♂8 Deer Jaguar Claw the Usurper.

AD 1073. Birth of ♀6 Monkey Jaltepec.

AD 1075. Birth of ♂2 Rain Tilantongo.

AD 1081. ♂2 Rain conferences with ♂8 Wind Suchixtlan's mummy. ♂2 Rain attacks Jaltepec.

AD 1083. The meeting at Chalcatongo: ♂8 Deer, ♀6 Monkey Jaltepec, ♂11 Wind Hua Chino.

AD 1083. ♂8 Deer at Tututepec.

AD 1091. ♀6 Monkey Jaltepec + ♂11 Wind Hua Chino.

AD 1092. Birth of ♂4 Wind Hua Chino.

AD 1095. Birth of ♂1 Alligator Hua Chino.

AD 1096. ♂2 Rain Tilantongo dies/suicides.

AD 1100. ♂8 Deer conferences with ♂2 Rain's mummy.

AD 1101. ♂8 Deer destroys Hua Chino, executes ♀6 Monkey and ♂11 Wind, but spares their sons 4 Wind and 1 Alligator.

AD 1102. ♂8 Deer executes ♂11 Wind Hua Chino's sons 10 Dog and 6 House.

AD 1102. ♂1 Alligator rules Jaltepec.

AD 1103. ♂8 Deer marries ♀13 Snake Hua Chino.

AD 1105. ♂8 Deer marries ♀6 Eagle Chalcatongo.

AD 1115. ♂8 Deer is sacrificed.

Lord Eight Deer the Usurper

This begins the biography of Lord 8 Deer Jaguar Claw, the king of Tilantongo, as told by the Mixtec codices Zouche-Nuttall reverse, Bodley, Selden, and the Alfonso Caso fragments (Colombino-Becker I).

Codex/Page	Date(s)	Event(s)

FOURTH CALENDAR CYCLE, AD 1039–1093

[Parentage Statement: Lord 5 Alligator's First Family]

ZN 42a	6 Flint 7 Eagle	♂ 5 Alligator marries
	AD 1043	♀ 9 Eagle at the Temple of
		Heaven in Tilantongo.
		Their children are:
ZN 42b	7 House 12 Motion	♂ 12 Motion,
	AD 1045	
ZN 42b–c		♂ 3 Water and ♀ 6 Lizard.

[Parentage Statement: Lord 5 Alligator's Second Family]

ZN 42c	10 House 6 Deer	♂ 5 Alligator marries
	AD 1061	♀ 11 Water. Their children are:
ZN 43a	12 Reed 8 Deer	♂ 8 Deer Jaguar Claw,
	AD 1063	
ZN 43a		♂ 9 Flower,
ZN 43b		♀ 9 Monkey.

[Lord 8 Deer's Early Career]

ZN 43b–c	7 Reed 10 Vulture	♂ 8 Deer, age 8,
	AD 1071	conquers 4 sites,
ZN 44a		conquers 2 sites.
Bod 9-V	3 Flint 5 Rain	♂ 8 Deer in cave.
	AD 1080	He is 17 years old.
Bod 10-IV	4 House	♂ 8 Deer and ♂ 1 Motion
	AD 1081	ballcourt and conquest.
		He is 18 years old.
ZN 44a–b	6 Reed 6 Snake	♂ 8 Deer, ♀ 6 Monkey
	AD 1083	at Chalcatongo.
		He is 20 years old.
Bod 9-IV 6 Reed		♂ 8 Deer at Chalcatongo.
ZN 44c		Same date, 8 Deer conducts a
		Sun-in-Tree (Holy Tree) ceremony.

FIFTH CALENDAR CYCLE, AD 1091–1142

[Lord 8 Deer's Mature Career]

	+ 8 years	

Codex/Page	Date(s)	Event(s)
ZN 44c	1 Reed 6 Water **AD 1091** +4 years	♂8 Deer conquers one place. He is 28 years old.
ZN 44c	5 Reed 2 Water **AD 1095**	♂8 Deer conquers one place. He is 32 years old.
ZN 44c	same date	♂8 Deer and ♂12 Motion conduct an animal sacrifice/grass mat ceremony, the god ♂13 Reed in the sky.
ZN 45a–b	same year, days	♂8 Deer conquers 2 Flower, 13 Motion, three places.

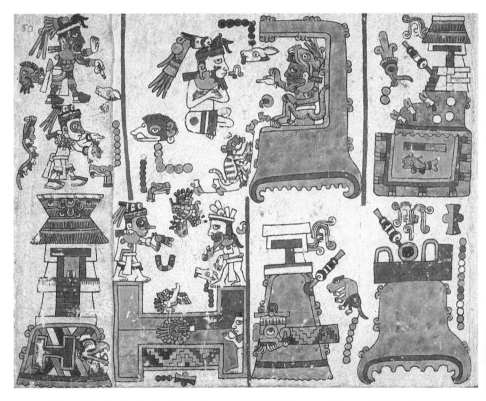

Figure AI.1. Codex Zouche-Nuttall page 45 (British Museum folio no. 50). Lord Eight Deer at Tututepec. From right to left: Column a, two conquests; Column b, a conquest, then Eight Deer's cave empowerment ceremony; Column c, a ballcourt ceremony; Column d, sacrifice at Star Temple, Tututepec. (© Trustees of the British Museum, The British Museum Company, Ltd.)

Codex/Page	Date(s)	Event(s)
ZN 45b–c	Year 5 Reed	♂8 Deer at
	Day 3 Motion	Tututepec. ♂7 Vulture, ♂7 Snake.
		Human sacrifice
ZN 45d	same year	at Tututepec Temple.
		♂7 Snake and ♂1 Deer.
ZN 46a	same year	♂9 Wind Quetzalcoatl.

[Lord 8 Deer's first major campaign as ruler of Tututepec]

Codex/Page	Date(s)	Event(s)
ZN 46a–d	Year 5 Reed	Conquests and ceremonies.
	Day 13 Rain	Conquest, Red Ocelot Hill
	Day 4 Reed	Conquest, Flute Tree Hill
	Day 5 Wind	Conquest, Jaguar Hill
	Day 1 Alligator	Conquest, Fire Snake Hill
	Day 7 Flower	Conquest, Blue Bird Hill
	Day 12 Rain	Conquest, Spine/Ribs Hill
		Conquest, Smoke Plain
ZN 47a–c	Day 5 Wind	Offerings, Head Town
	Day 5 Eagle	Offerings, Maguey Town
	Day 9 Motion	Offerings, Split Town
ZN 47b–d	Day 9 Deer	Offerings, Cormorant Town
	Day 6 Flower	Offerings, Cormorant Town
	Day 7 Alligator	Offerings, Cormorant Town
	Day 13 House	Conquest, Venus Staff Hill
	Day 7 Flower	Conquest, Star River
ZN 48a	Day 7 Motion	Conquest, Stone Hill
	Day 10 Grass	Conquest, Blue Snake Hill
ZN 48b–d	6 Flint 11 Death	Conquest, Black Bird Hill
	day 201	8 Deer is 33 years old.
	AD 1096	

[This is the year Lord Two Rain of Tilantongo dies.]

Codex/Page	Date(s)	Event(s)
	Day 3 Deer	Conquest, White Olla Hill
	Day 10 Rabbit	Conquest, Jade Mask Hill
	Day 12 Dog	Conquest, 2 Trees Hill
	Day 3 Jaguar	Conquest, Odd Hill
	Day 4 Flower	Conquest, White Fire Hill
ZN 49a–d	Day 4 Flower?	Conquest, White Hill
	Day 4 Flower?	Conquest, Temple Hill

Codex/Page	Date(s)	Event(s)
	Day 9 Flower	Conquest, White Water Hill
	Day 6 Lizard	Conquest, Lake and River
	Day 10 Snake	Conquest, Nuu in Cave
		Conquest, Paddle Tree Hill
	Day 7 Flint	Conquest, 5 Beans Town
		Conquest, Black Frieze
	Day 11 Wind	Conquest, Nuu Lake and River
	(Day unpainted)	

[First subjugation of Chalcatongo to Tututepec]

ZN 49d		♂8 Deer Jaguar Claw
ZN 50a–b	Day 1 Alligator	receives tribute from the priests at Chalcatongo sans oracle.
ZN 50b–c	Day 4 Flint	♂8 Deer at Tututepec.

[In Year 6 Flint the days 1 Alligator and 4 Flint occur once, with 4 Flint twenty-three days *before* 1 Alligator. The implications are that Chalcatongo acknowledges 8 Deer as ruler of Tututepec, which is shown here directly above Chalcatongo.]

ZN 50c–d	Day 9 Deer	Tecutli Lord Hill
		Jaguar Hill
ZN 50d–51a	7 House 9 Snake	♂8 Deer conference
	AD 1097	♀9 Reed Oracle at Blood Rivers Hill. He is 34 years old.

Note: The following sequence of events leading up to Lord 8 Deer's alliance (nose-piercing) with the Tolteca/Chichimeca Lord 4 Jaguar is conflated. In Codex Alfonso Caso at least two prior embassages sent by 8 Deer to 4 Jaguar are rejected. The final embassage is accepted, and 8 Deer becomes a Tolteca/Chichimeca *techutli* lord. An alliance with Lord 4 Jaguar is implicit because they subsequently participate in a series of conquests, including the famous Battle in the Sky beginning on Codex ZN page 75.

ZN 51a–d		♂8 Deer and ♂12 Motion peregrinate through Grass Knot and Mat

Codex/Page	Date(s)	Event(s)
		Plain, White Pot River, Snail Hill,
		Alligator Tree Hill,
	Day 11 Rain	Circle Hill
		♂8 Deer at Tilantongo and
ZN 52a	Day 12 Flower	Earthquake Hill,
ZN 52a–b		♂8 Deer at Rain God Effigy
		Hill and ♂9 Flower
		+ Venus Staff perambulates.
ZN 52b–c	7 House 13 Alligator	♂8 Deer and ♂4 Jaguar
	AD 1097	Bundle ceremony.
ZN 52c–d	Day 1 Wind	♂8 Deer nose-piercing.
ZN 52d–53a	Day 7 Jaguar	♂1 Snake and ♂8 Snake,
		♂8 Deer and ♂4 Jaguar
		Bird Sacrifice ceremony.
ZN 53a–c	Day 7 Jaguar	Conquest, Eagle Plain
	Day 8 Water	Conquest, Eagle Hill
	Day 7 Flower	Conquest, Smoke Hill
	Day 9 Alligator	Conquest, Spikes Hill
	Day 4 Flint	Conquest, Big Square Rock Hill
ZN 53d	Day 1 Alligator	♂8 Deer at Tilantongo in Lord 9 Wind
		Quetzalcoatl/Venus Staff ceremony.

[The following passage includes the second subjugation of Chalcatongo by 8 Deer.]

Codex/Page	Date(s)	Event(s)
ZN 54–68a	Various days	♂8 Deer and ♂12 Motion
		conference with 112 lords.
		This includes the installation of
		sun god oracle ♂1 Death
		at Chalcatongo (55c–d).
ZN 68b	8 Rabbit 4 Wind	Tilantongo
	AD 1098	8 Deer is 35 years old.
ZN 68c–69a		Peregrination from Tilantongo by
		♂8 Deer, ♂12 Motion, ♂2 Monkey,
		♂8 Death, ♂9 Deer.

Codex/Page	Date(s)	Event(s)
ZN 69a–b	8 Rabbit 10 Rabbit	Ceremonies: Jaguar and Eagle Stone Combat, *Yaha Yahui* Priest, Coyote and Human Sacrifice by ♂9 Flower.
ZN 69b–d		Eight Places: Bundle Hut,
	Day 11 Water	Insect Valley, Walking Man Hill, Three Darts Hill, Cormorant Market, Sky Pillar Valley, Head on Rack Hill,
	Day 2 Reed	Flower Tree Plain.
ZN 70a–b	Day 9 Alligator	8 Deer receives bird sacrifice from two males representing three places.
ZN 70b–c	Day 9 Snake	At Tilantongo, ♂8 Deer and ♂4 Jaguar in ceremonial combat.
ZN 70c–d	Day 2 Rain	♂8 Deer and ♂4 Jaguar Bird Sacrifice ceremony.
ZN 70d–71a	Day 12 Vulture	Unnamed male ceremony at two places.
ZN 71a–d	Day 8 Eagle	Conquest, Feather Hill Town
	Day 12 Eagle	Conquest, Eagle Beak Hill Town
	Day ?	Conquest, Fat Tree Hill Town
	Day 11 Snake	Conquest, Seated Man and 2 Flowers Hill Town
	Day ?	Conquest, 7 Stars Hill Town
	Day 13 Rain	Conquest, 2 Birds Hill Town
	Day 7 Grass	Conquest, 4 Spiky Things Town
	Day 3 Alligator	Conquest, 3 Gator Hill
	Day 5 Rain	Conquest, Quetzal Capture Hill
	Day 1 Jaguar	Conquest, Coyote Town
ZN 72a–d	Day ?	Conquest, 4 Shells Town
	Day 2 Eagle	Conquest, 3 Dancing Guys Town
	Day 7 Jaguar	Conquest, White Bird Hill
	Day 12 Grass	Conquest, 2 Turquoise Axes Town
	Day 4 Monkey	Smoking Necklace Hill
	Day 11 Dog	Dzaui Pectoral Hill
	Day 12 Deer	Mean, Ugly Woman Town

Codex/Page	Date(s)	Event(s)
	Day 1 Rabbit	Water Temple Hill Town,
	Day 2 Water	Circle Corn Hill
	Day 3 Dog	Cut Down Tree Hill
	Day ?	Coyote Hill Town
	Day 6 Reed	Stone Jaguar Hill
ZN 73a–d	Day 8 Eagle	Conquest, Eagle Town Hill
	Day 9 Vulture	Conquest, Jaguar Town
	Day 10 Motion	Fangs Hill Town
	Day 11 Flint	Rolling Stone Town
	Day 1 Rain	Blue Bird Town
	Day 5 Lizard	Smoking Hill
	Day 4 Monkey	Dancing Singing Man Hill
	Day 10 Flower	Conquest, Coyote Trees
	Day 10 Deer	Conquest, Slope Hill Town
	Day 3 Vulture	Conquest, 2 Trees Hill Town
	Day 4 Motion	Conquest, 2 Trees Collar Town
	Day ?	Conquest, Blanket Hill Town
		More conquests:
ZN 74a–c	Day 7 Flower	Humming Bird Hill,
	Day ?	Blue Sacrificial Stone Town
	Day 2 Dog	Temple Lake
	Day 12 Grass	Really Fancy Hill Town
	Day 11 Monkey	Snake Town
	Day 2 Monkey	3 Necklace Ball Court
	Day 9 Jaguar	Lady Stirring Pot Lake
	Day ?	Weeping Man Plain
	Day 4 Deer	Smoking Town River
ZN 74d	Day ?	Not conquered.
		Cormorant Town.
		At Woodpecker Hill:
		♂ 9 Water, the Guide.

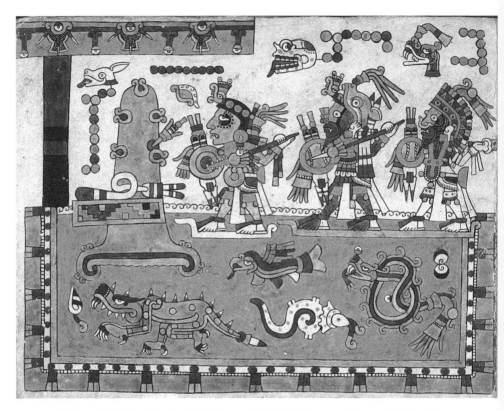

Figure AI.2. Codex Zouche-Nuttall page 75 (British Museum folio no. 80), introduction to the Battle in the Sky. (© Trustees of the British Museum, The British Museum Company, Ltd.)

Codex/Page	Date(s)	Event(s)
ZN 75	Days 10 Snake, ♂ 9 Water, ♂ 8 Deer, 11 Death, 12 Deer	♂ 4 Jaguar boat to the Place Where the Sky Is Held Up and conquer it.

[The Battle in the Sky, pages 76–78a; page 76 is a double page.]

Codex/Page	Date(s)	Event(s)
ZN 76a–d	Day 11 Motion	One place conquered.
	Day 13 Eagle	One place conquered.
	Day 12 Water	Two places conquered.
	Day 8 Death	
	Day 7 Flower	Star River conquered.
	9 Reed 4 Alligator	War Axe River conquered.
	AD 1099	Nuu Sun conquered.
		8 Deer is 36 years old.
	Day 12 Death	♂8 Deer conquers Fire Serpent Hill; his brother 9 Flower dies.
	Day 9 Death	♂8 Dear defeats the sacrificed warriors of the sun:
ZN 76a–d		♂2 Flower, ♂13 Rain, ♂10 Jaguar, ♂13 Motion, ♂7 Flower, ♂4 Motion, ♂9 Wind, ♂13 Rabbit, ♂12 Death, ♂13 Death, ♂12 Water,
ZN 77a–c		♂3 Snake, ♂11 Snake, ♂9 Snake flees, the conquest of four places:
	Day 11 Reed	Singing Man Hill, Nuu Woman Hill,
	Day 11 Rabbit	Loincloth Stone Hill, Blue Temple Hill.
ZN 77c–d		♂8 Deer, ♂4 Jaguar, ♂12 Motion battle the
ZN 78a		warrior creatures of the sun.
ZN 78b–c	Day 7 Motion	♂8 Deer and ♂4 Jaguar meet the sun god at his temple and give him gifts.
ZN 78c	Day 7 Dog	♂8 Deer and ♂4 Jaguar drill for fire.
ZN 79a	Day 9 Grass	Fire Serpent Hill.
ZN 79a–b	Day 11 Grass	The sun god Lord 1 Death shows
ZN 79b–c		♂8 Deer and ♂4 Jaguar the temple above the sky with exit portal.

Codex/Page	Date(s)	Event(s)
ZN 79c–d	Day 3 Monkey	The sun god gives ♂8 Deer a belt with gold bells while ♂4 Jaguar watches.
ZN 80a–b	Day 9 Motion	♂8 Deer, ♂4 Jaguar, ♂9 Water boat home.
	Day 6 Jaguar	♂8 Deer and a Striped Man in a ballcourt parlay; they exchange gifts.
ZN 80b	10 Flint 8 Eagle	Feather Town Hill.
	8 Rabbit	Smoking Necklace Mt.
	AD 1100	8 Deer is 37 years old.

[**This is the year shown on the obverse of Codex Zouche-Nuttall, page 8. The calendar sequence is as follows: Day 11 Death is #41, Day 9 Motion is #52, Day 1 Eagle is #70, Day 7 Flower is #115, Day 2 Flint is #213. The span for this assassination/mummy consultation is 172 days in year AD 1100/10 Flint.**]

Codex/Page	Date(s)	Event(s)
ZN 81a	Day 11 Death	♂12 Motion (8 Deer's half-brother) is assassinated in a sweat bath.
	+11 days	
ZN 81b	Day 9 Motion. . .	Eleven days in which ♂12 Motion's mummy is prepared, then. . .
ZN obverse, 8	+18 days	
	Day 1 Eagle	♂8 Deer collects troops.
	+63 days	
ZN 80b–c	Day 7 Flower . . .	♂12 Motion's funeral obsequies.
	+138 days	
ZN 82a–b	Day 2 Flint	♂8 Deer consults ♂2 Rain's mummy.
ZN obverse, 8	Days 1 Eagle to 2 Flint	♂8 Deer consults ♂2 Rain's mummy.
ZN 82c	10(11) House	♂8 Deer burns ♂2 Rain's mummy at
	6 Jaguar	Jaguar Town near Pregnant Woman
	AD 1101	Arrow Hill. 8 Deer is 38 years old.
ZN 83a–b	11 House	The Siege of Hua Chino.
	12 Monkey	♂8 Deer captures boy 4 Wind.
ZN 83b–c	12 Rabbit 6 Snake	At the ballcourt at Eagle Hill ♂8 Deer
	AD 1102	sacrifices the children by a previous marriage of Hua Chino's king, 11 Wind: ♂10 Dog by gladiatorial ceremony and

Codex/Page	Date(s)	Event(s)
ZN 84a		♂6 House by scaffold sacrifice.
		8 Deer is 39 years old.
ZN 84a–b	Day 2 Vulture	A 9 Wind bird-decapitation
		sacrifice and mummy burning.
Sel 9-I	12 Rabbit	♂1 Alligator of Hua Chino (4 Wind's
	AD 1102	brother) becomes ruler of Jaltepec.
Bod 11-I	13 Reed	♂8 Deer marries ♀13 Snake of Hua
	AD 1103	Chino, ♂10 Dog and ♂6 House's
		sister (and 8 Deer's niece). 8 Deer is 40
		years old. He founds the second dynasty
		of Tilantongo.
Bod 12-I	2 House	♂8 Deer weds ♀5(6) Eagle of Chalcatongo.
	AD 1105	He is 42 years old.
Bod 14-V–IV	12 Reed	♂8 Deer is sacrificed. He is 52 years old.
	AD 1115	His daughters, the princesses of
		Tilantongo, marry Lord 1 Alligator of
Sel 9-II	AD 1122	Jaltepec and Lord 4 Wind of Flint Town.
Bod 29-IV	AD 1125	
Sel 8-IV		

Lord Two Rain Twenty Jaguars, the Last King of the First Dynasty of Tilantongo

Codex/Pages	Date(s)	Event(s)
Fourth Calendar Cycle, AD 1039–1090		
ZN 24	11 Reed 9 Reed	Birth of 2 Rain, but on Day 9 Reed;
	AD 1075	his name is changed. His parents are
		♂5 Flower and ♀2 Grass.
ZN 8	4 House 1 Rain	2 Rain (at age 6 years) speaks with his
		deceased great-great-grandfather,
		♂8 Wind of Suchixtlan.
	+3 days	
Sel 6-II	4 House 4 Lizard	8 Wind of Cerro Jasmin
	AD 1081	elderly son 3 Lizard (one of twins) attacks
		Jaltepec. 2 Rain the boy-king hides in a
		cave.

Figure AI.3. Codex Selden 3135 (A.2), page 6. (Sociedad Mexicana de Antropología, Mexico, 1964)

Codex/Pages	Date(s)	Event(s)
ZN 44a–b	6 Reed 6 Snake	The meeting at Chalcatongo.
Sel 6-IV	5(6) Reed 6 Snake	The oracle of the dead, ♀9 Grass, severs
	AD 1083	the marriage alliance between
		Tilantongo (8 Deer in ZN 44) and Jaltepec
		(♀6 Monkey in ZN and Selden) and

Codex/Pages	Date(s)	Event(s)

reassigns it to Hua Chino, also called Red and White Bundle Town, ruled by ♂11 Wind (Selden 6, register IV at the top). The deceased elderly warrior, ♂3 Lizard, is seen in the ZN tableau. ♂2 Rain is 8 years old.

[Fifth Calendar Cycle, AD 1091–1142]

Bod 5-I	6 Flint 7 Motion	♂2 Rain's death/assisted suicide.
	AD 1096	He is 21 years old.
ZN 8, 82	10 Flint 2 Flint	♂8 Deer of Tilantongo consults
	AD 1100	with ♂2 Rain's mummy, then burns it.
	10(11) House 6 Jaguar	
	AD 1101	

Lady Six Monkey, the Warrior Princess of Jaltepec, Queen of Hua Chino

Codex Selden is the primary document for Lady Six Monkey's biography, but she also appears in Bodley, Zouche-Nuttall, and Alfonso Caso. In my classes, I refer to Codex Selden as a glorious fascination. Page 5-III illustrates the founding of the second dynasty at Jaltepec by a woman named Nine Wind. She is the daughter of Lord Eight Wind and Lady Ten Deer of Suchixtlan. Lady Nine Wind is actually shown conducting a royal bundle ceremony before the temple at Jaltepec—usually a male ruler's prerogative. She then marries a relative from Tilantongo, a royal prince named Lord Ten Eagle, who was the son of Lord Ten Flower and Lady Two Snake. The first three children of this marriage, all sons, are sacrificed at Chalcatongo, but the fourth child, Lady Six Monkey, lives. She is apparently under the tutelage of an oracular priest named Lord Ten Lizard, who is, presumably, a functionary of Chalcatongo. This priest is her guide in important events, especially those leading up to Lady Six Monkey's betrothal to the lord of Hua Chino, Eleven Wind.

The bundle ceremony by Six Monkey's mother, Lady Nine Wind, is interesting because it gives the reader the impression that it rectifies or revalidates an earlier ceremony conducted at the end of the first Jaltepec dynasty. The first dynasty of Jaltepec failed for unspecified reasons soon after that bundle event. A king of Jaltepec's first dynasty, Lord Ten Reed, was involved in a series of bundle events prior to his dynasty's failure. Codex

Selden (3-I–IV) shows two priests named Ten Lizard and Three Flower making two bundles suffixed with the bar numbers for "twenty." Then, also in the presence of Lord Ten Reed, a priest named Ten Flint conducts a bundle ceremony. In the final two registers of Selden page 3, Lord Ten Reed either makes a bundle or opens it. Although Alfonso Caso interprets the contents as gifts for royals, they appear to be specifically bundle-related and are twenty objects in number, presented in strict order in groups of two: twelve in the first group, eight in the second. Lord Ten Reed's son Three Rain conducts a bundle event just before the record of his dynasty ends.

These objects in Ten Reed's bundle are: a copper axe, a stone-blade axe, two ropes, a cup of blood, a cup holding a heart, a red circular object, a white circular object, an incense bag, a cup holding an unidentified substance, and a kind of eagle-down purse attached to head and arm. Then, in the second group, an eagle head, a red and white eagle head, two jaguars on scaffolds, a regular eagle on a scaffold, a red and white eagle on a scaffold, a spear and shield with *ñuu* head, and then the bundle itself with *ñuu* head atop it. The white figures outlined in red give the impression of spirits or ghosts.

Fourteen places with seventeen rulers follow this bundle event. Lord Ten Reed rules at two places, which are not Jaltepec; then he conducts a ceremony before an unidentified temple and marries Lady Two Snake (the daughter of Lord Five Flower and Lady Five Flower). This union produces a son instead of a daughter. His name is Lord Three Rain. He conducts a bundle ceremony before the temple at Jaltepec and then marries Lady Seven Death, daughter of Lord One Snake and Lady Eight Flint. At this point, the first dynasty of Jaltepec ends.

As mentioned, the second dynasty of Jaltepec's first ruler is a woman named Nine Wind. Her marriage with Lord Ten Eagle of Tilantongo produces at first three sons, who are sacrificial victims at Chalcatongo. Only their fourth child, Lady Six Monkey, lives. From the time of her parents, there is emphasis on Jaltepec's relationship/alliance with Chalcatongo and its female oracle of the dead.

The bold implication of the data is that the first dynasty of Jaltepec failed because its final ruler was male. The second dynasty of Jaltepec continued by sacrificing preceding male children in favor of a royal female named Six Monkey.

The following is a summary of the events told in Codex Selden pages 1 through 9-II. It covers both the first and second dynasties of Jaltepec because data revealed in the first are relevant to Lady Six Monkey's biography.

Second Mixtec Year Cycle, AD 935–986

Page 1-I. Year 4 or 5 Reed Day 2 House. Year 4 Reed would be AD 951, year 5 Reed AD 939. Year 6 Reed would be AD 979. The page is damaged, and reading of the inscribed date is insecure, so there is a twenty-eight-year margin of error because of image erosion.

In the sky: the gods 1 Motion and 1 Death. A reed dart opens a hill, and from it is born Lord 11 Water. He goes to a place called Effigy Head in a Cave and marries Lady 7 Eagle there.

Page 1-II. Their child is Lady 10 Eagle, who marries Lord 4 Eagle. His parents are Lord 10 House and Lady 1 Grass from Serpent River. The child of this marriage between 10 Eagle and 4 Eagle is Lady 8 Rabbit.

Page 1-III. Two elderly priests, Lords 10 Lizard and 10 Flint Earth Monster Mouth, confer at a lake in which there is a bird's head, a reed bundle, and a copper axe. These two priests then consult with the lineage couple of Apoala: Lady 9 Alligator and her husband, Lord 5 Wind from the Sky.

Page 2-I. Year 10 Reed Day 2 Grass. AD 983? This column of pictogram text presents a complicated tableau. Presided over by the two priests, Lords 10 Lizard and 10 Flint, the Birth Tree at Apoala produces Lord 2 Grass, who is the intended husband of Lady 8 Rabbit (1-II). Six other males are born from the tree: the Lords 1 Eagle River Hair, 3 Water Maguey Hair, 5 Rabbit Vulture Hair, 5 Motion Eagle Hair, 5 Lizard Rain God, and 5 Eagle Rain God. Three connected objects qualify these births. Reading from top to bottom, they are: a bird in a bowl, a turtle-serpent in a bowl, and a personified flint knife with rope held by a hand.

Page 2-II. Year 10 Reed Day 4 Deer. AD 983? This year is the same as previously inscribed on page 2-I; however, the days have changed. The interval between Day 2 Grass and Day 4 Deer is fifteen days. Therefore, fifteen days transpires between the two events. The second event is the marriage of Lord 2 Grass to Lady 8 Rabbit, the child of Lord 4 Eagle and Lady 10 Eagle, previously mentioned.

Page 3-I. The child of this marriage is Lord 10 Reed Eagle Blood.

Year 2 Flint Day 3 Rain, AD 988: In this year, two priests named 10 Snake and 3 Flower make a bundle each. There are four black bars signifying the number 20 beneath the second bundle.

Page 3-II. The third priest, 10 Flint Earth Monster Mouth, offers a tobacco-pouring ceremony before six objects. Reading from right to left, these objects are:

a ñuu bundle,

a kind of bundle composed of three objects, spotted like jaguar skin, sitting in a cup horizontally divided by two reeds attached to the three objects by a rope,

a rectangle of seven planks,

a rectangle of five tree trunks,

a grass-like serpent,

and a large cauldron container filled with hot red rocks.

This is presided over by Lord 10 Reed, seated at the foot of a temple.

Page 3-III–4-III. Year 5 Reed Day 6 Death. AD 991. Lord 10 Reed before twenty connected objects divided into two groups. This bundle-related ceremony is witnessed or attended by several lords from different places.

Page 4-III. Year 9 House Day 7 Eagle. AD 1021. Lord 10 Reed conducts a ceremony before a temple.

Page 5-I. Year 12 Flint Day 7 Deer. AD 1024. Lord 10 Reed marries Lady 2 Lizard Star Foot. She is the daughter of Lord 5 Flower and Lady 5 Flower of Flower Tree Hill.

Page 5-II. The child of this marriage is Lord 3 Rain. He offers incense before the bundle at Jaltepec Temple. Lord 3 Rain marries Lady 7 Death, the child of Lord 1 Snake and Lady 9 Flint of Star River Hill. The first dynasty of Jaltepec ends here.

The Second Dynasty of Jaltepec

Page 5-III. Lord 8 Wind Twenty and Lady 10 Deer of Suchixtlan. Their daughter is Lady 9 Wind, who offers incense before the bundle at Jaltepec Temple.

Fourth Mixtec Year Cycle, AD 1039–1090

Page 5-IV. Year 3 House Day 10 Deer. AD 1041. Lady 9 Wind marries Lord 10 Eagle of Tilantongo. He is the child of Lord 10 Deer and Lady 10 Flower. Their first son, Lord 1 Reed Ball Court, dies by sacrifice at Chalcatongo.

[Lord 8 Deer of Tilantongo is born in AD 1063.]

Page 6-I. Their second child, Lord 12 Water, dies by sacrifice at Chalcatongo. Their third child, Lord 3 Water, dies by sacrifice at Chalcatongo. Year 9 House Day 8 Vulture. AD 1073. Their fourth child, Lady 6 Monkey, confers with a priest named 10 Lizard at Chalcatongo. Male children having been sacrificed at Chalcatongo, female rule continues at Jaltepec in the person of 6 Monkey. The political relationship between Jaltepec and Chalcatongo is also the subject of these tableaux.

[Lord 2 Rain of Tilantongo is born in AD 1075.]

Page 6-II. Year 4 House Day 4 Wind. AD 1081. Tilantongo attacks Jaltepec during the reign of the boy-king 2 Rain. The leader of the Tilantongo forces, Lord 3 Lizard, suffers defeat, and thus Tilantongo loses the war. Lord 2 Rain consults a ritual object in a cave.

Page 6-III. Year 5(6) Reed Day 6 Snake. AD 1083. Priest 10 Lizard and Lady 6 Monkey consult Lord 6 Vulture. Lady 6 Monkey journeys underground.

Page 6-IV. She emerges at Chalcatongo, where she and Lord 11 Wind of Hua Chino consult with the oracle Lady 9 Grass. Six ritual objects are shown in the remainder of this register.

Page 7-I. Six more ritual objects are listed, including an ornamented chile pepper. Year 10 Reed Day 10 Wind. AD 1087. Seven people, two of them women, dance around an ancestor bundle. Year 12 House Day 7 Flower. AD 1089. The nuptial bath of Lady 6 Monkey and Lord 11 Wind.

Page 7-II. Nine gifts (seven garments and two fans) are listed in order. Year 13 Rabbit Day 9 Snake. AD 1090. The priest 10 Lizard presents gifts to Lords 2 Flower and 3 Alligator.

Page 7-III. Led by Lord 3 Alligator, Lord 2 Flower bears Lady 6 Monkey on a journey. On the way, they are insulted by Lords 6 Lizard and 2 Alligator.

Page 7-IV. Lady 6 Monkey consults with the oracle of Chalcatongo, Lady 9 Grass, who presents her with the implements of war and soldiers.

Page 8-I. Lady 6 Monkey attacks and captures Lord 6 Lizard and Lord 2 Alligator at Wasp Hill. She sacrifices Lord 2 Alligator before the temple at Jaltepec.

Page 8-II. Carried by Lord 2 Flower, Lady 6 Monkey journeys to Hua Chino. Lord 3 Alligator leads her other captive, Lord 6 Lizard, to that place. She sacrifices 6 Lizard before the temple.

Page 8-III. Before Lord 2 Flower, Lady 6 Monkey receives a new garment, and thus a new name: War Garment. Lady 6 Monkey and Lord 11 Wind rule Hua Chino.

At this point, Codex Selden fails to mention the fact that Lord 8 Deer of Tilantongo subsequently executes 6 Monkey and 11 Wind in AD 1101–1102.

The following is a schematic of Codex Selden's biography of Lady 6 Monkey.

Codex/Pages	*Date(s)*	*Event(s)*
[Fourth Mixtec Year Cycle, AD 1039–1090]		
Sel 6-I	9 House 6 Monkey **AD 1073**	Birth of ♀6 Monkey of Jaltepec.
[Lord 8 Deer is born in AD 1063, and Lord 2 Rain in AD 1075.]		

Sel 6-IV	6 Reed 6 Snake	Conference at Chalcatongo.
	AD 1083	♀6 Monkey betrothed to ♂11 Wind of Hua Chino (Red and White Bundle Town).
Sel 7-I10	Reed 10 Wind	Wedding bath of ♀6 Monkey
	AD 1087	and ♂11 Wind.
Sel 7-II	13 Rabbit 9 Snake	♀6 Monkey travels to Red and White
	AD 1090	Bundle and is insulted by ♂6 Lizard and ♂2 Alligator of Sun Hill and Salyutepec, respectively. She seeks aid from the oracle of Chalcatongo, conducts a military campaign against the offending kings, and captures them.
Sel 8-II	13 Rabbit 3	♀6 Monkey sacrifices ♂2 Alligator at
	Grass/4 Reed	Jaltepec, ♂6 Lizard at Hua Chino.
[Six Monkey's name is changed to "War Garment."]		
Sel 8-III	13 Rabbit 6 Eagle	♀6 Monkey and ♂11 Wind:
Bod 34-II	13 Rabbit 11 Deer	rulers of Hua Chino.

[Fifth Mixtec Year Cycle, AD 1091–1142]

Sel 8-IV	2 Flint 4 Wind	Birth of ♂4 Wind.
Bod 34-III	**AD 1092**	

[Note: The birth years for Lord 1 Alligator differ by one year between codices Bodley and Selden.]

Bod 34-III	4 Rabbit 1 Alligator	Birth of ♂1 Alligator.
	AD 1094	
Sel 8-III	5 Reed 1 Alligator	Birth of ♂1 Alligator.
	AD 1095	
Bod 34-IV	11 House 12 Monkey	♂8 Deer attacks Hua Chino.
	AD 1101	
Becker-I, 11		He sacrifices ♀6 Monkey and ♂11 Wind.
ZN 83–84	12 Rabbit 6 Snake	He sacrifices ♂11 Wind's sons by a
	AD 1102	previous marriage, 10 Dog and 6 House.

Codex/Pages	Date(s)	Event(s)
Sel 9-I	12 Rabbit 6 Dog	♂1 Alligator rules at Jaltepec.

[Note: Lord Eight Deer is sacrificed in AD 1115.]

Codex/Pages	Date(s)	Event(s)
Bod 31-III	4 Flint 1 Snake AD 1120	♂4 Wind rules Flint Town.
Sel 9-II	6 Rabbit 5 Deer AD 1122	♂1 Alligator marries ♂8 Deer's daughter, ♀6 Wind of Tilantongo.
Bod 29-IV	8 Flint 9 Eagle AD 1125	♂4 Wind marries ♂8 Deer's daughter, ♀10 Flower Tilantongo.

[Note: Byland and Pohl (1994:245) write that with this marriage, "Lord Four Wind consolidates the royal bloodlines of Jaltepec, Red and White Bundle, Cerro Jasmin, Tilantongo, and, ultimately the authority originally vested in Hill of the Wasp," originally destroyed in the War from Heaven.]

The importance of Lady Six Monkey's biography is therefore demonstrated in her son, Lord Four Wind, who by uniting the royal bloodlines of Jaltepec (Lord Eight Wind at Suchixtlan/Cerro Jasmin), Hua Chino (descended from Hill of the Wasp), and Lord Eight Deer at Tilantongo constituted the sine qua non of royal descent in the Mixteca. Adding to this impeccable lineage, Lord Four Wind is shown in Codex Bodley pursued by Lord Eight Deer's Tolteca/ Chichimeca sponsor, Lord Four Jaguar, until he receives the nose piercing and ornament of a Toltec *techutli* and alliance, as did Eight Deer himself. From the birth of Lord Eight Wind in AD 935 until this marriage between Lord Four Wind and Lady Ten Flower Tilantongo, 189 years had elapsed.

APPENDIX II

Notes for Codex Zouche-Nuttall Pages 1–4

Table AII.1. Secondary and Tertiary Actors in Ceremonies Depicted on Codex Zouche-Nuttall Pages 1 and 2

Page	Actor	Action	Secondary (2) and Tertiary (3) Actors
At Toto Cuee Cave			
1	♂ Twelve Alligator	birth ceremony	2
At Suchixtlan			
1	♂ Twelve Alligator	bird sacrifice/ordering	2
1	♂ One Reed	bird sacrifice/ordering	3
1	♂ One Rain	bird sacrifice/ordering	3
1	♂ Eight Vulture	bird sacrifice/ordering	3
1	♂ Ten Lizard	bird sacrifice/ordering	3
At Apoala			
1	♂ Eleven Flower	bird sacrifice/ordering	2
1	♂ Seven Jaguar	bird sacrifice/ordering	3
1	♂ Seven Monkey	bird sacrifice/ordering	3
1	♂ Ten Lizard	bird sacrifice/ordering	3
1	♂ Three Eagle	bird sacrifice/ordering	3
At Yucuñudahui			
2	♂ Twelve Alligator	bird sacrifice/ordering	2
2	♂ Eleven Flower	bird sacrifice/ordering	2
2	♂ Two Lizard	bird sacrifice/ordering	3
2	♂ Five Flower	Stone Man, bird sacrifice/ordering	3
2	♂ Seven Wind	bird sacrifice/ordering	3
2	♂ Four Rain	bird sacrifice/ordering	3
2	♂ Ten Jaguar	bird sacrifice/ordering	3
2	♂ Two Rain	bird sacrifice/ordering	3

The chief figure in charge of, or the recipient of, the ceremonies depicted on ZN pages 1 and 2 is Lord Eight Wind Eagle Flints. In the first, at Toto Cuee Cave, Lord Eleven Alligator is ceremonially present at Lord Eight Wind's birth. The page 1 bird-sacrifice ceremonies show tertiary actors bearing royal garments for Eight Wind (Xicollis); the page 2 ceremony, though also a bird sacrifice, does not.

Table AII.2. Proposed Day-Date Sequence for Year 5 House War Events Depicted on Codex Zouche-Nuttall Page 3

Page	Day/Number(s)	Event
3a	7 Snake, #55 & #315	Stone Men at Yucuita
3b	4 Wind, #52 & #352	Stone Men capture
3b	8 Wind, #212	" " "
3b	4 Wind, #52 & #352	" " "
3b	4 Dog, #260	" " "

The earliest day in this sequence of events in the Stone Men war in Year 5 House is the first occurrence of 4 Wind (#52). The second occurrence of Day 4 Wind is the latest (#352), so it is possible for the other recorded days to fall within that 260-day span from 4 Wind to 4 Wind. The sequence would be:

Day 4 Wind: ♂7 Wind captures a Stone Man.
Day 7 Snake: ♂7 Snake and ♀6 Eagle attack Stone Men.
Day 4 Dog: ♂7 Snake perambulates.
Day 4 Wind: ♀Eight Deer captures a Stone Man.

The difficulty with this purely chronological sequencing is that the Day 4 Dog in Year 5 House is drawn larger than the other days, so it has emphasis. It is also positioned close to Lord Seven Snake's perambulation, so that assignment is made in the sequence. Of the six tableaux shown on page 3, only three have days assigned in Year 5 House, for a total of five days encompassing a 260-day span. Therefore, the page 3 Year 5 House events all occur within that 260-day span of time.

The total length of time for the events on pages 3 and 4 is twenty-three years. The war with the Stone Men begins in Year 3 Reed (#29), and the Year 5 House (#31) events continue it; the war with the Striped Men begins in Year 12 Flint (#38) and ends in Year 6 Reed (#45). The council is held in Year 13 Rabbit (#52).

Table AII.3. Events Depicted on Codex Zouche-Nuttall Pages 3 and 4

Mixtec Year (Number)	AD	Event
3 Reed (#29)	963	War begins
5 House (#31)	965	Stone Men war
12 Flint (#38)	972	Striped Men war
6 Reed (#45)	979	End of war
13 Rabbit (#52)	986	Council at Apoala

Table AII.4. Chronological Schematic for Tableaux on Codex Zouche-Nuttall Pages 3 and 4

	Page 3 Tableau 1
	Year 3 Flint, AD 963
	*
	*
	Page 3 Tableau 2
	Year 5 House, AD 965
	*
	*
*************************	Page 3: Year 5 House
*	Tableau 3
*	*
*	*
*	Page 4 Year 6 Rabbit, AD 966
*	Tableau 4
*	*
*	*
Page 3 Year 12 Flint*********	Page 4 Year 12 Flint AD 972
Tableau 3	Tableaux 1, 2, 3
*	*
*	*
Page 3 Year 5(6) Reed AD 979	*
Tableau 3***************************	
	*
	*
	Page 3 Year 13 Rabbit AD 986
	Tableau 6
	*
	*
	Page 4 Year 13 Rabbit
	Tableau 6

APPENDIX III Codex Zouche-Nuttall
Reverse Day Dates on Pages 46a–48a for Year
5 Reed (AD 1095) and Lord Eight Deer's Campaign
as Lord of Tututepec

The following table shows the order of 260 days and their numbers as
they appear in the Codex Zouche-Nuttall reverse biography of Lord Eight
Deer Jaguar Claw. "As written" days are either out of sequence of calendar
progression or, when recording intervals of passed time, in sequence. Days
out of sequence are as they appear, and then they appear according to their
occurrence in specific *tzolkins* (260-day cycles). More than one 260-day
sacred calendar occurs in a 365-day solar year; therefore, it happens that a
numbered day in the sacred calendar can occur twice in a solar year. When
this happens, the second occurrence is listed in column 2. The Mayan word
tzolkin in these appendices defines the 260-day sacred calendar. The day
numbers refer to their order within the solar year.

Table AIII.1. Order of 260 Days as They Appear in Codex Zouche-Nuttall
Reverse Biography of Lord Eight Deer

Page/Day (as written)	Sacred Calendar No.	Solar Year No.
46a/13 Rain	139	
46b/4 Reed	13	273
46b/5 Wind*	222	
46c/1 Alligator	101 7th tzolkin	
46c/7 Flower*	120	
46d/12 Rain	99	359
47a/5 Wind*	222	
47a/4 Eagle	195	
47b/9 Motion	57	317
47b/9 Rabbit	148	
47c/6 Flower	80	340
47c/7 Alligator	81	341
47d/13 House	243	

47d/7 Flower*	120	
48a/7 Motion	237	
48a/10 Grass	32	293
16 days, 2 repeated, thus 14 days. The calendar sequence of these days follows.		
Tzolkin 6, Year 5 Reed (AD 1095)		
46b/4 Reed	13	273
	+19 days	
48a/10 Grass	32	293
	+25 days	
47b/9 Motion	57	317
	+23 days	
47c/6 Flower	80	340
	+1 day	
47c/7 Alligator	81	341
	+18 days	
46d/12 Rain	99	359
	Tzolkin 7	
	+2 days	
46c/1 Alligator		101
	+19 days	
46c/7 Flower		120
47d/7 Flower		
	+19 days	
48a/13 Rain		139
	+9 days	
47b/9 Rabbit		148
	+47 days	
47a/4 Eagle		195
	+27 days	
46b/5 Wind		222
47a/5 Wind		
	+15 days	
48a/7 Motion		237
	+6 days	
47d/13 House		243
	Total: 230 days	

Array within sixth and seventh tzolkins.		
Page/Day	*No.*	
Tzolkin 7		
46c/1 Alligator	101	
	+19 days	
46c/7 Flower		
47d/7 Flower	120	
	+19 days	
48a/13 Rain	139	
	+9 days	
47b/9 Rabbit	148	
	+47 days	
47a/4 Eagle	195	
	+27 days	
46b/5 Wind		
47a/5 Wind	222	
	+15 days	
48a/7 Motion	237	
	+6 days	
47d/13 House	243	
	+30 days	
46b/4 Reed	273	
	+20 days	
48a/10 Grass	293	
	+24 days	
47b/9 Motion	317	
	+23 days	
46c/6 Flower	340	
	+1 day	
47c/7 Alligator	341	
	+18 days	
46d/12 Rain	359	
	Total: 258 days	
All of these days occur within the seventh tzolkin.		

Table AIII.2. Codex Zouche-Nuttall Reverse Day Dates on Pages 48b–50b for the Year 6 Flint (AD 1096) and Lord Eight Deer's Campaign as Lord of Tututepec

Page/Day	Sacred Calendar No.	Solar Calendar No.
48b/11 Death	201	
48b/3 Deer	102	
48c/10 Rabbit	83	343
48c/12 Dog	85	345
48d/3 Jaguar	89	349
48d/4 Flower	155	
49b/9 Flower	95	355
49b/6 Lizard	79	339
49c/10 Snake	200	
49c/7 Flint	93	353
49d/11 Wind	97	357
50a/1 Alligator	256	
50b-c/4 Flint	233	
50b-c/9 Deer	82	342
14 days, none repeated		

Days, sequenced	Sacred Calendar No.	Solar Calendar No.
49b/6 Lizard	79	339
	+3 days	
50b-c/9 Deer	82	342
	+1 days	
48c/10 Rabbit	83	343
	+2 days	
48c/12 Dog	85	345
	+4 days	
48d/3 Jaguar	89	349
	+4 days	
49c/7 Flint	93	353
	+2 days	
49b/9 Flower	95	355
	+2 days	

49d/11 Wind	97	357
	+5 days	
48b/3 Deer	102	
	+53 days	
48d/4 Flower	155	
	+45 days	
49c/10 Snake	200	
	+1 day	
48b/11 Death	201	
	+32 days	
50b-c/4 Flint	233	
	+23 days	
50a/1 Alligator	256	
	Total: 177 days	

All these day dates occur within the eighth tzolkin, except the last, which begins the ninth tzolkin.

Page	Day	Number in Solar Year
Tzolkin 8, sequenced		
48b	3 Deer	102
		+53 days
48d	4 Flower	155
		+45 days
49c	10 Snake	200
		+1 day
48b	11 Death	201
		+32 days
49b-c	4 Flint	233
		+23 days
Tzolkin 9, sequenced		
50a	1 Alligator	256
		+83 days
49b	6 Lizard	339
		+3 days
50b-c	9 Deer	342
		+1 day
48c	10 Rabbit	343
		+2 days

48c	12 Dog	345
		+4 days
48d	3 Jaguar	349
		+4 days
49c	7 Flint	353
		+2 days
49b	9 Flower	355
		+2 days
49d	11 Wind	357
	Total: 255 days	

Of these day dates, the first five occur within the eighth tzolkin, the last nine within the ninth tzolkin.

Twenty-eight days between two years, with a span of 513 days among the two years AD 1095–1096.

Table AIII.3. Codex Zouche-Nuttall Reverse Day Dates on Pages 53a–68a for Year 7 House (AD 1097) and Lord Eight Deer's Activities as *Techutli*

Dates as they appear in the codex: tzolkins 9 and 10

Page/Day	Sacred Calendar No.	Solar Calendar No.
53a/4 Snake	115* seq.	
53a/7 Rabbit	118* seq.	
53b/8 Water	119* seq.	
53b/7 Flower	170	
53c/9 Alligator	211	
53c/4 Flint	128	
53d/1 Alligator	151, 10th tzolkin	
53d/9 Wind (at Tilantongo, conference)		172
***		
***	***	
53a/7 Rabbit	117	
53b/8 Water	118	
53c/4 Flint	128	
53d/1 Alligator, 10th tzolkin	151	
53b/7 Flower	170	
53d/9 Wind conference	172	
53c/9 Alligator	211	

Table AIII.4. Days in Codex Zouche-Nuttall Reverse for the Year 8 Rabbit (AD 1098) for Lord 8 Deer at Tilantongo and Conquests

Page/Day	Sacred Calendar No.	Solar Calendar No.
Any day after day #45 is the eleventh tzolkin.		
68b/4 Wind	127	
68c/5 House	148	
68c/6 Lizard	129* seq.	
68d/7 Snake	130* seq.	
68d-69a/8 Death	131* seq.	
69a/10 Rabbit	133* seq.	
69b/11 Water	134* seq.	
69d/2 Reed	138* seq.	
70a/9 Alligator	106	
70b/9 Snake	210	
70b–c/2 Motion	242	
70d–71a/12 Vulture	161	
71a/8 Eagle	40, 10th tzolkin	300
71b/12 Eagle	200	
71b/11 Snake	30, 10th tzolkin	290
71c/13 Rain	84	344
71c/7 Grass	117	
71d/5 Rain	24, 10th tzolkin	284
71d/1 Jaguar	59	319
72a/2 Eagle	60	320
72a/7 Jaguar	39, 10th tzolkin	299
72b/12 Death	31 "	291
72b/4 Monkey	36 "	296
72b/11 Dog	95	355
72c/13 Deer	32* seq., 10th tz. 292	
72c/1 Rabbit	33* seq. "	293
72c/2 Water	34* seq. "	294
72d/3 Dog	35* seq. "	295
72d/4 Monkey*	36* seq. "	296
72d/6 Reed	38* seq. "	298
73a/8 Eagle	40* seq. "	300
73a/9 Vulture	41* seq. "	301

73a10 Motion	42* seq. "	302
73b/11 Flint	43* seq. "	303
73b/12 Rain	44* seq. "	304
73b/5 Lizard	89	349
73c/4 Monkey*	36, 10th tzolkin	296
73c/4 Monkey*	36, 10th tzolkin	296
73c/10 Flower		185
73c/10 Deer		172
73d/3 Vulture	61* seq.	321
73d/4 Motion	62* seq.	322
74a/7 Flower	65* seq.	325
74a/2 Dog		255
74a/12 Grass	57	357
74b/11 Monkey	56	356
74b/2 Monkey		216
75c/9 Jaguar	119	
75c/4 Deer	192	
Year 8 Rabbit (AD 1098) Sequenced		
Page/Day	*No.*	*No.*
Tzolkin 10		
71d/5 Rain	24	284
71b/11 Snake	30	290
72b/12 Death	31	291
72c/13 Deer	32	292
72c/1 Rabbit	33	293
72c/2 Water	34	294
72d/3 Dog	35	295
72d/4 Monkey	36	296
73c/4 Monkey	36	296
72d/6 Reed	38	298
72a/7 Jaguar	39	299
73a/8 Eagle	40	300
73a/9 Vulture	41	301
73a/10 Motion	42	302
73b/11 Flint	43	303
73b/12 Rain	44	304

Tzolkin 11		
74b/11 Monkey	56	356
74a/12 Grass	57	357
71d/1 Jaguar	59	319
72a/2 Eagle	60	320
73d/3 Vulture	61	321
73d/4 Motion	62	322
74a/7 Flower	65	325
71c/13 Rain	84	344
73b/5 Lizard	89	349
72b/11 Dog	95	355
70a/9 Alligator	106	
71c/7 Grass	117	
75c/9 Jaguar	119	
68b/4 Wind	127	
68c/6 Lizard	129	
78d/7 Snake	130	
68c–69a/8 Death	131	
69a/10 Rabbit	133	
69b/11 Water	134	
69d/2 Reed	138	
68c/5 House	148	
70d–71a/12 Vulture	161	
73c/10 Deer	172	
73c/10 Flower	185	
75c/4 Deer	192	
71b/12 Eagle	200	
70b/9 Snake	210	
74b/2 Monkey	216	
70b–c/2 Motion	242	
74a/2 Dog	255	
Forty-six days for a span of 231 days.		

Bibliography

Angulo V., Jorge. 1987. "The Chalcatzingo Reliefs: An Iconographic Analysis." In *Ancient Chalcatzingo,* David Grove, editor. University of Texas Press, Austin.

Arana, Evangelina, and Mauricio Swadesh. 1965. *Los Elementos del Mixteco Antigua.* Instituto Nacional Indigenista and Instituto Nacional de Antropología e Historia, México.

Balkansky, Andrew K., et al. 2000. "Archaeological Survey in the Mixteca Alta of Oaxaca, Mexico." *Journal of Field Archaeology,* Vol. 27, No. 4 (Winter), 365–389. Boston University.

Boone, Elizabeth Hill. 2000. *Stories in Red and Black: Pictorial Histories of the Aztecs and Mixtecs.* University of Texas Press, Austin.

———. 2003. "A Web of Understanding: Pictorial Codices and the Shared Intellectual Culture of Late Postclassic Mesoamerica." In *The Postclassic Mesoamerican World,* Michael E. Smith and Frances F. Berdan, editors. University of Utah Press, Salt Lake City.

Boone, Elizabeth Hill, and Walter D. Mignolo, editors. 1994. *Writing Without Words: Alternative Literacies in Mesoamerica and the Andes.* Duke University Press, Durham and London.

Brundage, Burr Cartwright. 1979. *The Fifth Sun: Aztec Gods, Aztec World.* University of Texas Press, Austin.

Burland, C. A. 1957. "Ancient Mexican Documents in Great Britain." *Man,* Vol. 57 (May), 76–77.

Byland, Bruce, and John M. D. Pohl. 1994. *In the Realm of 8 Deer: The Archaeology of the Mixtec Codices.* University of Oklahoma Press, Norman and London.

Carneiro, Robert. 1970. "A Theory of the Origin of the State." *Annual Review of Ecology and Systematics,* Vol. 3, 399–426.

Carrasco, David. 1990. *Religions of Mesoamerica.* Harper and Row, San Francisco.

Caso, Alfonso. 1954. *Interpretación del Códice Gómez de Orozco.* Talleres de Impresión de Estampillas y Valores, Mexico City.

———. 1960. *Interpretation of the Codex Bodley 2858.* Translated by Ruth

Morales and revised by John Paddock. Sociedad Mexicana de Antropología, Mexico City.

———. 1964. *Interpretation of Codex Selden 3135 (A.2)*. Translated by Jacinto Quirarte and revised by John A. Paddock. Sociedad Mexicana de Antropología, Mexico.

———. 1966. *Interpretation of Codex Colombino*. Sociedad Mexicana de Antropología, Mexico.

———. 1971. "Calendrical Systems of Central Mexico." In *Handbook of Middle American Indians*, Vol. 10: *Archaeology of Northern Mesoamerica, Part 1*. University of Texas Press, Austin.

———. 1979[1984]. "Reyes y Reinos de la Mixteca." *Fondo de Cultura Económica*, Vol I, 18.

———. 1998 [1949]. *The Map of Teozacoalco*. Translated by Manuel Aguilar and Claudia Alarcon. Maya Meetings at Texas, Long Workshops, Department of Art and Art History, University of Texas, Austin.

Castellanos, Abraham. 1910. *El Rey: Hombres del Oriente*. A. Carranza e Hijos, Impresores, Mexico.

Cline, Howard F., and Mary W. Cline. 1975. "Ancient and Colonial Zapotec and Mixtec Calendars: A Revisionist View." *The Americas*, Vol. 31, No. 3 (January), 272–288.

Dahlgren de Jordán, Barbro. 1966. *La Mixteca: Su cultura e historia prehispánica*, 2nd Edition. Universidad Nacional Autonomía de México.

de Burgoa, Francisco. 1934 [1674]. "Geografica Descripción, Tomo I." *Talleres Gráficos de la Nación, México*. Estados Unidos Mexicanos, Secretaría de Gobernación.

de los Reyes, Antonio. 1976 [1593]. *Arte in lengua Mixteca . . .* Facsimile of 1593 edition. Publications in Anthropology 14. Vanderbilt University, Nashville.

del Paso y Troncoso, Francisco. 1905. "Papeles de Nueva España." Secunda Serie Geografía y Estadística, Tomo I. Establecimiento Tip. Impresores de la Real Casa, Madrid.

Duran, Fray Diego. 1975 [1580]. *Book of the Gods and Rites: The Ancient Calendar*. Translated and edited by Fernando Horcasitas and Doris Heyden. University of Oklahoma Press, Norman.

Evans, Susan Toby. 2004. *Ancient Mexico and Central America: Archaeology and Culture History*. Thames and Hudson, London.

Fields, Virginia M., and Dorie Reents-Budet, editors. 2006. *Lords of Creation: Origins of Sacred Maya Kingship*. Los Angeles County Museum of Art/Scala Publishers.

Flannery, Kent. 1972. "The Cultural Evolution of Civilization." *Annual Review of Ecology and Systematics,* Vol. 3, 399–426.

Freidel, David, Linda Schele, and Joy Parker. 1993. *Maya Cosmos: Three Thousand Years on the Shaman's Path.* William Morrow and Company, New York.

Furst, Jill Leslie. 1978a. *Codex Vindobonensis Mexicanus I: A Commentary.* Institute for Latin American Studies, State University of New York at Albany, Publication No. 4.

———. 1978b. "The Life and Times of Lord Eight Wind Flinted Eagle: A Commentary on the First Seven Pages of the 'Obverse' of Codex Zouche-Nuttall." In *Alcheringa/Ethnopoetics,* No. 4.2.30.

Garcia, Gregorio. 1729 [1607]. *Origin de los Indios del Nuevo Mundo.* Fondo de Cultura Económica, Mexico, D.F.

Graulich, Michael. 1981. "The Metaphor of the Day in Ancient Mexican Myth and Ritual." *Current Anthropology,* Vol. 22, No. 2 (February), 45–60.

Grove, David G. 1987. "A Catalogue and Description of Chalcatzingo's Monuments." In *Ancient Chalcatzingo,* David Grove, editor. University of Texas Press, Austin.

Hamann, Byron. 2002. "The Social Life of Pre-Sunrise Things." *Current Anthropology,* Vol. 43, No. 3, 351. University of Chicago Press.

Hayden, Doris. 2000. "From Teotihuacan to Tenochtitlan: City Planning, Caves, and Streams of Red and Blue Waters." In *Mesoamerica's Classic Heritage: From Teotihuacan to the Aztecs,* David Carrasco, Lindsay Jones, Scott Sessions, editors. University Press of Colorado, Niwot.

Huntington, Elsworth. 1900. "Electric Phenomena in the Euphrates Valley." *Monthly Weather Review,* Vol. 28, No. 7 (July), 286–287. In *Handbook of Unusual Natural Phenomena,* William Corliss, editor. The Sourcebook Project, Glen Arm, Maryland. 1977 [1900].

Jansen, Maarten. 1988. "Dates, Deities, and Dynasties: Non-Durational Time in Mixtec Historiography." In *Continuity and Identity in Native America: Essays in Honor of Benedikt Hartman,* Maarten Jansen, Peter van der Loo, and Rosewitha Manning, editors. E. J. Brill, New York.

———. 1992. "Mixtec Pictography: Conventions and Contents." In *Supplement to the Handbook of Middle American Indians,* Vol. 5, *Epigraphy,* Victoria Reifler Bricker, general editor. University of Texas Press, Austin.

Jansen, Maarten, and Aurora Perez Jimenez. 2005. *Codex Bodley: Treasures from the Bodleian Library.* The Bodleian Library, University of Oxford.

Jansen, Maarten, and E. R. G. Huisti Tacu. 1983. *Estudio Interpretativo de un Libro Mixteco Antiguo: Codex Vindobonensis Mexicanus I.* Amsterdam.

Joyce, Arthur A., and Marcus Winter. 1996. "Ideology, Power, and Urban Society in Pre-Hispanic Oaxaca." *Current Anthropology,* Vol. 37, No. 2 (February), 33–47. University of Chicago Press.

Joyce, Rosemary A. 2000. *Gender and Power in Prehispanic Mesoamerica.* University of Texas Press, Austin.

Justeson, John S. 1986. "The Origin of Mesoamerican Writing Systems." *World Archaeology,* Vol. 17, No. 3, *Early Writing Systems* (February), 437–458. Taylor and Francis.

Klein, Cecelia F. 1993. "Teocuitlatl, Divine Excrement: The Significance of 'Holy Shit' in Ancient Mexico." *Art Journal,* Vol. 52, No. 3, *Scatological Art* (Autumn), 20–27. College Art Association.

Lejarazu, Manuel A. Hermann. 2007. "Códice Nuttall, Lado 1: La Vida de 8 Venado. Estudio introductorio e interpretación de laminas." In *Arquelogía Mexicana,* No. 23, Edición Especial Códices.

León-Portilla, Miguel. 1969. *Pre-Columbian Literatures of Mexico.* Translated by the author and Grace Lobanov. The Civilization of the American Indian series. University of Oklahoma Press, Norman.

León-Portilla, Miguel, and Earl Shorris, with Sylvia S. Shorris, Ascensión de León-Portilla, and Jorge Klor de Alva. 2001. *In the Language of Kings: An Anthology of Mesoamerican Literature—Pre-Columbian to the Present.* W. W. Norton, New York and London.

Malmstrom, Vincent H. 1973. "Origin of the Mesoamerican 260-Day Calendar." *Science,* New Series, Vol. 181, No. 4103 (September), 939–994. American Association for the Advancement of Science.

Manzanilla, Linda. 2000. "The Construction of the Underworld in Central Mexico." In *Mesoamerica's Classic Heritage: From Teotihuacan to the Aztecs,* David Carrasco, Lindsay Jones, Scott Sessions, editors. University Press of Colorado, Niwot.

Marcus, Joyce. 1976. "The Origins of Mesoamerican Writing." *Annual Review of Anthropology,* Vol. 5, 35–67.

Marcus, Joyce, and Kent V. Flannery. 1996. *Zapotec Civilization.* Thames and Hudson, London.

Markman, Roberta, and Peter T. Markman. 1992. *The Flayed God: The Mesoamerican Mythological Tradition.* Sacred Texts and Images from Pre-Columbian Mexico and Central America. HarperCollins, New York.

Merrifield, Ralph. 1988. *The Archaeology of Ritual and Magic.* New Amsterdam, New York.

Miles, Elton. 1976. *Tales of the Big Bend.* Texas A&M University Press, College Station.

Monoghan, John. 1990. "Sacrifice, Death and the Origins of Agriculture in the Codex Vienna." *American Antiquity* Vol. 55, No. 3, 559–569.

———. 1991. "Sacrifice, Death, and the Origins of Agriculture in the Codex Vienna." *American Antiquity,* Vol. 55, No. 3, 559–569. Society for American Anthropology.

Newton, John, and Stephen G. Hyslop, editors. 1992. *The American Indians: The Spirit World.* Time-Life Books. Silver Burdett Company, Morristown, New Jersey.

Nuttall, Zelia. 1902. Introduction to *Codex Nuttall: Facsimile of an Ancient Mexican Codex Belonging to Lord Zouche of Harynworth, England.* Peabody Museum of American Archaeology and Ethnology, Harvard University, Cambridge, Massachusetts.

Oudijk, Michel R. 1998. "The Genealogy of Zaachila: Four Weddings and a Dynastic Struggle." In *The Shadow of Monte Alban,* Maarten Jansen, Peter Krofges, Michel Oudijk, editors. Research School CNWS. School of Asian, African, and Amerindian Studies. Leiden, The Netherlands.

Paddock, John. 1985a. "Tezcatlipoca in Oaxaca." *Ethnohistory,* Vol. 32, No. 4 (Autumn), 309–325. Duke University Press, Durham, North Carolina.

———. 1985b. "Covert Content in Codices Borgia and Nuttall." *Ethos,* Vol. 13, No. 4 (Winter), 358–380. American Anthropological Association. 1985.

Parmenter, Ross. 1994. "The Lienzo of Tulancingo, Oaxaca: An Introductory Study of a Ninth Painted Sheet from the Coixtlahuaca Valley." *Transactions of the American Philosophical Society,* Vol. 83, Part 7. Philadelphia.

Pohl, John M. D. 1984. "The Earth Lords: Politics and Symbolism of the Mixtec Codices." Ph.D. dissertation. University of California, Los Angeles.

———. 1991. *Aztec, Mixtec, and Zapotec Armies.* Osprey Men-at-Arms Series, No. 239. Osprey Publishing, London.

———. 1994. *The Politics of Symbolism in the Mixtec Codices.* Vanderbilt University Press, Nashville, Tennessee.

———. 1995. "Notebook No. 2 for the Mixtec Pictographic Writing Workshop at Texas." Fourth Mixtec Studies Group, March 13–18. Maya Hieroglyphic Writing Workshops, Department of Art and Art History, University of Texas, Austin.

———. 2003a. "Creation Stories, Hero Cults, and Alliance Building: Confederacies of Central and Southern Mexico." In *The Postclassic Mesoamerican World,* Michael E. Smith and Frances F. Berdan, editors. University of Utah Press, Salt Lake City.

———. 2003b. "Ritual, Ideology and Commerce in the Southern Mexican

Highlands." In *The Postclassic Mesoamerican World,* Michael E. Smith and
Frances F. Berdan, editors. University of Utah Press, Salt Lake City.

———. 2004. Screenfold Manuscripts of Highland Mexico and Their Possible
Influences on Codex Madrid. In *Codex Madrid: New Approaches to
Understanding an Ancient Maya Manuscript,* Gabrielle Vail and Anthony
Aveni, editors. University of Colorado Press.

———. 2005a. "The Arroyo Group Lintel Painting at Mitla, Oaxaca." In *Painted
Books and Indigenous Knowledge in Mesoamerica: Manuscript Studies in Honor
of Mary Elizabeth Smith,* Elizabeth Hill Boone, editor. Middle American
Research Institute, Tulane University, New Orleans. Publication 69.

———. 2005b. "The Archaeology of History in Postclassic Oaxaca." In
Mesoamerican Archaeology: Theory and Practice, Julia A. Hendon and
Rosemary A. Joyce, editors. Blackwell Publishing.

———. 2005c. "Screenfold Manuscripts of Highland Mexico and Their Possible
Influence on Codex Madrid: A Summary." In *The Madrid Codex: New
Approaches to Understanding an Ancient Maya Manuscript,* Gabrielle Vail and
Anthony Aveni, editors. University Press of Colorado, Boulder.

Pohl, John M. D., and Bruce Byland. 1990. "Mixtec Landscape Perception and
Archaeological Settlement Patterns." *Ancient Mesoamerica,* Vol. 1, No.1,
113–131.

Powell, Christopher. Nd. "The Creation and Ordering of the Mixtec World: An
Analysis of Ten Rituals in the Codex Vindobonensis Mexicanus I." http://
mayaexploration.org/pdg/Creation%20and%20Ordering%20of%20the%20Mi
xtec%20World.pdf.

Prescott, William H. 1934 [1843]. *The Conquest of Mexico.* International
Collectors Library. The Junior Literary Guild, Garden City, New York.

Rabin, Emily. 1974. "Some Problems of Chronology in the Mixtec Historical
Manuscripts, Part 1." Paper presented at the 41st Congreso Internacional de
Americanistas, Mexico.

———. 1976. "Some Problems of Chronology in the Mixtec Manuscripts, Part 2."
Paper presented at the 2nd Cambridge Symposium on Recent Research in
Mesoamerican Archaeology, University of Cambridge, England.

———. 1979. "The War of Heaven in Codices Zouche-Nuttall and Bodley: A
Preliminary Study." In *Actes du XLII Congres International des Americanistes,*
7, 171–182. ICA, Paris.

———. 1980. "Chronology of the Mixtec Codices: An Overview." Paper presented
at the 1980 Annual Meeting of the American Society for Ethnohistory,
Colorado Springs.

———. 1982. "Confluence in Zapotec and Mixtec Ethnohistories: The 1560

Genealogy of Macuilxochitl." In *Native American Ethnohistory,* Joseph Whitecotton and Judith Bradley Whitecotton, editors, 359–368. Papers in Anthropology 23(2). Department of Anthropology, University of Oklahoma, Norman.

Reilly, F. Kent III. 1996. "Art, Ritual, and Rulership in the Olmec World." In *The Olmec World: Ritual and Rulership.* The Art Museum, Princeton University, Princeton, New Jersey.

Renfrew, Colin, and Paul Bahn. 2005. *Archaeology.* Thames and Hudson, London.

Schele, Linda. 1996. "The Olmec Mountain and Tree of Creation in Mesoamerican Cosmology." In *The Olmec World: Ritual and Rulership.* The Art Museum, Princeton University, Princeton, New Jersey.

Schele, Linda, and David Freidel. 1991. *A Forest of Kings.* William Morrow and Company, New York.

Schele, Linda, and Mary Miller. 1986. *The Blood of Kings: Dynasty and Ritual in Maya Art.* Kimbell Art Museum, Ft. Worth, Texas.

Smith, Mary Elizabeth. 1973. *Picture Writing from Ancient Southern Mexico: Mixtec Place Signs and Maps.* Vol. 124, Civilization of the American Indian Series. University of Oklahoma Press, Norman.

Smith, Michael E. 2003. "Small Polities in Postclassic Mesoamerica." In *The Postclassic Mesoamerican World,* Michael E. Smith and Frances F. Berdan, editors. University of Utah Press, Salt Lake City.

Spores, Ronald. 1969. "Settlement, Farming Technology, and Environment in the Nochixtlan Valley." *Science,* New Series, Vol. 166, No. 3905 (October 31), 557–569. American Association for the Advancement of Science.

———. 1974. "Marital Alliance in the Political Integration of Mixtec Kingdoms." *American Anthropologist,* New Series, Vol. 76, No. 2 (June), 297–311.

Steele, Barbara Fitzsimmons. 1997. *Cave Rituals in Oaxaca, Mexico.* Paper presented at the Annual Meeting of the Society for American Archaeology, Nashville, Tennessee.

Steward, James H., editor. 1981. *Irrigation Civilizations: A Symposium on Method and Result in Cross-Cultural Regularities.* Greenwood Press, Westport, Connecticut.

Tate, Carolyn. 1995. "Art in Olmec Culture." In *The Olmec World: Ritual and Rulership.* The Art Museum, Princeton University, Princeton, New Jersey.

Taube, Karl. 1996. "The Rainmakers: The Olmec and Their Contribution to Mesoamerican Belief and Ritual." In *The Olmec World: Ritual and Rulership.* The Art Museum, Princeton University, Princeton, New Jersey.

Tedlock, Dennis. 1985. *Popul Vuh: The Mayan Book of the Dawning of Life*. Simon and Schuster, New York.

Toorians, Lauran. 1983. *Some Light in the Dark Century of Codex Vindobonensis Mexicanus I*. Codices Manuscripti, Graz, Austria.

———. 1984. *Codex Vindobonensis Mexicanus I: Its History Completed*. Codices Manuscripti, Graz, Austria.

Troike, Nancy P. 1974. "The Codex Colombino-Becker." Unpublished dissertation. University of London.

———. 1978. "Fundamental Changes in the Interpretations of the Mixtec Codices." *American Antiquity,* Vol. 43, No. 4 (October), 553–568.

———. 1987. Introduction. Codex Zouche-Nuttall, British Museum London (Add MS. 39671). Vollständige Faksimile—Ausgabe des Codex im Original format. Vorwort Ferdinand Anders. Akademische Druck- u. Verlagsanstalt, Graz, Austria.

Tyler, Stephen A. 1986. "Post-Modern Ethnography: From Document of the Occult to Occult Document." In *Writing Culture: The Poetics and Politics of Ethnography,* James Clifford and George E. Marcus, editors. University of California Press, Berkeley.

———. 1989. "Post-Modern Ethnography: From Document of the Occult to Occult Document." In *Writing Culture: The Poetics and Politics of Ethnography,* Ames Clifford and George E. Marcus, editors. University of California Press, Berkeley.

Whittington, E. Michael, editor. 2001. *The Mesoamerican Ballgame*. Thames and Hudson, London.

Williams, Robert Lloyd. 1991. "Codex Zouche-Nuttall Obverse: Summary of Contents." In *Texas Notes on Precolumbian Art, Writing and Culture,* No. 20 (September). CHAAAC, Department of Art, University of Texas, Austin.

———. 1995. "Topical Outline of Codex Vindobonensis Mexicanus I." In *Notebook No. 2 for the Mixtec Pictographic Writing Workshop at Texas, March 13–18*. Maya Hieroglyphic Workshops at Texas, Department of Art and Art History, University of Texas at Austin.

———. 2006. "The History of Lord Eight Wind of Suchixtlan: A Chronological Analysis and Commentary on Codex Zouche-Nuttall Pages One through Eight." Thesis. Texas State University–San Marcos.

Winter, Marcus. 1989. *Oaxaca: The Archaeological Record*. Indian Peoples of Mexico Series. Minutiae Mexicana. S.A. de C.V. Insurgentes Centro, Mexico, D.F.

Zeitlin, Robert N. 1990. "The Isthmus and Valley of Oaxaca: Questions about

Zapotec Imperialism in Formative Period Mesoamerica." *American Antiquity,* Vol. 55, No. 2 (April), 250–261. Society for American Archaeology.

Zeitlin, Robert N., and Arthur A. Joyce. 1999. "Insights from the Oaxaca Coast." *Current Anthropology,* Vol. 40, No. 3 (June), 383–392.

Codices

Codex Bodley 2858. Introduction and interpretation by Alfonso Caso. Sociedad Mexicana de Antropología, Mexico. 1960.

Codex Colombino. Introduction and interpretation by Alfonso Caso. Sociedad Mexicana de Antropología, Mexico. 1966.

Codex Selden 3135 (A.2). Introduction and interpretation by Alfonso Caso. Sociedad Mexicana de Antropología, Mexico. 1964.

Codex Vindobonensis Mexicanus I. Introduction, history, and description of the manuscript by Otto Adelhofer. Codices Selecti, Photothypice Impressi, Volumen V. Vollstandige Faksimile-Ausgabe in Orignalformat. Akademische Druck- u. Verlagsanstalt, Graz/Austria. 1974.

Codex Zouche-Nuttall. British Museum London (Add. MS. 39671). Introduction by Nancy P. Troike. Codices Selecti, Phototypice Impressi, Volumen LXXXIV. Akademische Druck- u. Verlagsanstalt, Graz/Austria. 1987.

Codices Becker I–II. Kommentar und Beschreibung by Karl A. Nowotny. Codices Selecti, Phototypice Impressi. Vol. IV. Museum fur Volkerkunde WEin Inv. Nr. 60306 und 60307. Akademische Druck- u. Verlagsanstalt, Graz/Austria. 1961.

The Dresden Codex. 1973. A Commentary on the Dresden Codex by J. Eric S. Thompson. Vol. 93, Memoirs of the American Philosophical Society Held at Philadelphia for Promoting Useful Knowledge. Independence Square, Philadelphia.

Electronic Documents

CNN. "Earliest Mayan Writing Found Beneath Pyramid." January 2006. www.cnn.com

Foundation for the Advancement of Mesoamerican Studies, Inc. www.famsi.org

The Mexico Network. "Oaxaca State Profile." http:www.mexconnect.com/amex/tmn/oaxacaprofile.htm

The Sacramento Bee. http://www.sacbee.com

The Splendors of Thirty Centuries. http://www.humanities-interactive.org/splendors/ex048.html

Index

Page numbers in italics indicate images and tables.

Achiutla, 18, 19, *20,* 47, 65–66, 67, 69, 81, 84, 151, 154
allegories, 13, 16, 22, 33, 36, 39, 40–41, 42, 61
alliances, 4, 16, 18, 19, *20,* 47, 113, 149
ancestors, 1, 14, 16–18, 21–22, 123, 129; born from nature, 6, 69, 95; burial cults of, 79, 148; spirits of, 4, 74; supernatural qualities of, 95. *See also* mummy bundles
Añute. *See* Jaltepec
Apoala, 9, 19, *20,* 36, 61, 66, 67, 84, 106, 111, 137, 144, 157, 181, *189;* cave at, 80, 81, 87, 99, 139, 141, 158; and Eight Wind, 7–8, *9,* 62, 80, *94,* 95, 98, 99, 100, 106, *113, 130,* 138, 139, 141, 142, *142,* 156, 158, *187;* lineage rivers of, 65, 141, 158; plants at, 65; river birth at, 18, 19, 66; tree birth at, 54, 62, 65–66, 69, 81, 97, 99, 106, 110, 111, 122, 138, 139, 141, 142, 158, 159, 181
axis mundi. *See* world tree
Aztecs, 1, 2, 4, 8, 49, 53, 71, 89, 142, 160; codices of, 30; defeat of Mixtecs, 1–2, 3, 41n2, 45, 52, 143; writing system of, 49

ballcourts, 64, 71, 82, 83, 84, 103, 109–110, 127, 153, 167, *168,* 176
bards, 6, 38, 42, 62, 117
Battle in the Sky, 170, *174,* 175–176
books. *See* codices

cacicazgos, 14–15, 18, 19
calendars, 39, 40–41, 72, 88; European, 39–40, *94,* 98, 129, 142, 163; Mixtec use of, 21, 39, 164; reading of, 58, *58, 59;* sacred (260-day), 36, 37, 40–41, 99, 164, 165, 190; solar (365-day), 36, 40–41, 164, 190

Caso, Alfonso, ix, 9, *10,* 13, 32, 34, 52, 112, 154, 180
caves: attributes of, 79, 86–87, 88, 96; in codices, 79–88; and Eight Deer, 81–84, 85, *168;* and Eight Wind, *9,* 66, 69, 80–81, 96–97, 99, 116, 139, 146, 157–158; as entrances to underworld, 73, 96, 116; iconography of, 69–71, 73–77, 79, 81, 157; mummy bundles in, 14, 87, 123, 148; in sky, 69, 87, 108; as transportation through earth, 24n4, 70, 80, 87, 96, 102, 157–158; and Two Rain, 126, 150, 177, 183
Cavua Colorado, 54, 96, 148
Ceremonial Complex, 9, 70, 83, 88, 156–161
Cerro Jasmin, 7, 8, *9,* 11, 13, 14, *17,* 23n2, 80, 95, 157, 186; Eight Wind at, *8,* 9, *9,* 13–14, 80, 97, 100, 116, 139, 146, 150, 177, 186; location of, *8;* as Monkey Hill, 7, *8,* 97; Suchixtlan on, 7, *8. See also* Eight Wind; Monkey Hill
Chalcatongo, 18, 47, 56, 148, 149, 150, 151, 154, 166, 167, 170, 171, 178, 179, 180, 183, 185. *See also* Nine Grass
Chalcatzingo, 69, 71, 80, 123; monuments of, 72–78, *73, 75, 77, 78,* 80, 83, 87, 88, 89, 96
Classic period, 1, *2,* 4, 7, 9, 13, 14, 16, *16,* 37, 41, 42n3, 49, 51, 54, 64, 71, 79, 87, 105, 156
clouds, 7, 67, 69, 72, 74, 108
Codex Alfonso Caso, 4–5, 51, 80, 88, 126, 164, 165; chronology in, 36, 41–42; date of, 83; Eight Deer in, xii, 124, 126, 164, 166, 170, 185; Six Monkey in, 126, 179, 185

Codex Becker. *See* Codex Alfonso Caso

Codex Bodley, 4–5, 18, 20, 43, 51, 82, 139, 185; caves in, 79, 97; chronology in, 36, 39, 41–42; and Codex ZN, 83–84, 85, 112–114; date of, 79–80, 83; Eight Deer in, xii, 82, 83–84, 85, 87, 149, 156, 165, 166, 177; Eight Wind in, 6, 118; Eight Wind's kingdom in, 7–8, 97; Four Wind in, 177, 186; genealogy in, 6, 18, 19, 118; Nine Grass in, 84, 113, 154; Nine Wind Quetzalcoatl in, 99–100; Six Monkey in, 126, 179; Two Rain in, 23n2, 126, 127, 150, 179; War from Heaven in, 54, 62, 112–114

Codex Borgia, 24n3, 41

Codex Colombino-Becker. *See* Codex Alfonso Caso

Codex Egerton, 4–5

Codex Muro, 10

Codex Selden, 4–5, 20, 42, 51, 67–68, 80, 89, 116, 139, 177, *178,* 185; chronology in, 36, 39, 41–42; and Codex Vienna, 67–68; and Codex ZN, 150; date of, 51, 80, 83, 165; Eight Deer in, 87, 149–150, 164, 165, 166, 178; Eight Wind in, 6, 80–81, 97, 100, 177; Eight Wind's kingdom in, 7–8, 81, 97, 179; genealogy in, 19, 67–68, 84, 118, 120; as Jaltepec document, 67, 126, 139, 147, 149, 150, 154, 165, 179, 180–186; Six Monkey in, 102, 126, 164–165, 179–186

Codex Vienna, 4–5, 11, 30–31, 39, 51, 54n1, 63, 64 66, 72, 81, 96, 98, 111, 123, *140, 143,* 157; chronology in, 36, 39, 142; and Codex Selden, 67–68; and Codex ZN, 31, 32, 33–34, 36, 39–40, 52–53, 64, 104, 105, 110–111, 112, 135–145, 156, 159, 160; creation of world in, 68, 141, 142–144; date of, 83; Eight Deer in, 165; Eight Wind in, 6, 81, 97, 99; historicity of, 144; as map, 140–141; Nine Rites in, 135–139; Nine Wind Quetzalcoatl in, 64, 67, 96, 111–112, 116, 138, 139, 141–143, *143,* 157; plants in, 64–65, 104–105, *104,* 109, 137–138, *140;* resistance of, to analysis, ix; tree birth in, 53, *55,* 105, 122; Yucuñudahui in, 9–10, 67, 99, 141

Codex Vindobonensis Mexicanus. *See* Codex Vienna

Codex Zouche-Nuttall (Codex ZN), 4–5, *43,* *44,* 46, 47, 51, 52, 53–56, 57, 60, 63–64, 66, *93, 94, 101, 107, 115, 121, 122,* 124, *125,* 126, *128,* 141, *168, 174,* 179; caves in, 79–83, 87, 99, 157; chronology in, x, 33–34, 36, 39, 41–42, 144; and Codex Bodley, 83–84, 85, 112–114; and Codex Selden, 150; as Codex Tonindeye, 159; and Codex Vienna, 31, 32, 33–34, 36, 39–40, 52–53, 64, 104, 105, 110–111, 112, 135–145, 156, 159, 160; date of, 79–80, 83, 96, 144, 146; eclipsing of pages in, 61–62, 159; Eight Deer biography in, xii, 32, 52, 81–83, 85, 126, 142, 144, 146, 149, 151–154, 156, 164, 165, 166, 190, *190–198;* Eight Wind saga in, 6–8, 31–32, 36–37, 46, 47, 60, 80, 93–100, 115–120, 121, 129, 131, 146–147, 153–154, 157–159; as history, 20, 35, 39, 144; history of, 52–53; as map, 140; narrative structure of, 60–62, 159; and Nochixtlan Valley, 11–13, *16;* as performance narrative, 37; plants in, 64–65, 99; purpose of, 36, 52–53, 64, 104, 105, 110–111, 112, 135–145, 156, 159, 160; reading order of, 93–95, 97–98, 101–103, 110, 113–114, *113, 118,* 121, *130,* 188, *189;* relation between obverse and reverse of, 56, 126, 128, 129, 144–145, 148–149, 152–154; resistance of, to analysis, ix, 32, 156; reverse of, 36, 39, 40, 42, 53, 56, 123, 124, 127, 129, 148–149, 151, 158 (*see also* Codex Zouche-Nuttall: Eight Deer biography in); scribal errors in, 43–44; tableaux on, 57, 65, 93–95, 97–98, 101–103, 107–111, 115–117, 121–125, 144, 156; as Tilantongo document, 18, 149, 150; toponyms in, 8, 14, 70–71; War from Heaven in, *15,* 54, 54n1, 61–62, 101–114, 156, 157

codices, 5, 6, 14, 16, 24n3, 34, 52, 81; Borgia Group of, 5, 30; chronology in, 41–42; comparison among, 32, 33–34, 39, 43; composition of, 5; creation of, by nobles, 5–6, 52; display of, 16–18, 53–54; Eight Deer in, 81, 164, 165; as historical documents, ix, 5, 21, 34, 52, 88, 129, 135, 163; how to read, 57–58, 151; iconography in, 45–46, 71, 79, 88; importance of, ix, 19, 48, 160–161; interpretation of, 32, 38–39, 69–70; Mixtec Group of, 5; Mixtec renown for, 3–4, 30; mythic aspects of, x, 5, 13, 19, 21, 52, 53, 60, 95; performance of, 6, 22, 33, 35, 52, 129; preservation of, ix, 2, 4–5, 30, 36, 51, 52, 160; role of, ix, 22, 30, 88; scribal errors in, 41, 42–44; toponyms in, 7, 10, 14, 24n3, 69, 125, 136–137. *See also under individual names*

Coixtlahuaca, 1, 19, 151

colonial sources, 5, 11, 14, 15, *15,* 16–18, 21, 66, 123, 148

confederacies, 1–2, 5, 7, 14, 79, 86

Cortés, Hernan, ix, 34, 52, 160

costumes, 6, 49–50, 82, 84, 87, 96, 99, 103, 104, 108

coyotes, 82, 172

creation stories, 21, 68, 142–143. *See also* ordering rituals

Cuilapan, 18, 19, *20*

day signs, 58, *59,* 103, 108, 109, 110, 117

de Burgoa, Francisco, 47, 53, 66, 123, 148

de los Reyes, Antonio, 66, 96, 105

dialects, 19, *20*

documents. *See* codices

dynasties, 6, 16, 18, 19, 95, 165; of Cerro Jasmin, 186; of Jaltepec, 55–56, 67–68, 80, 81, 84, 86, 117, 118–*119,* 139, 147, 149, 154, 179–180, 186; of Red and White Bundle, 186; of Tilantongo, 18, 22–23, 23nn1–2, *44,* 61, 81, 82, 83, 106, 118–120, 123, 127, 147, 149, 150, 157, 163, 164, 177, 186; of Wasp Hill, 61–62, 112; of Yucuñudahui, 13–14; of Zacatepec, 165. *See also* lineages

Dzaui (Dzahui), 8, 63, 110, 111, 116; and Eight Wind, 7, 60, 100, 112; personified, 100; and Stone Men, 105, 109. *See also* rain gods

eagles, 96, 103, *104,* 108, 137, 172, 180

earth, birth from, 69, 139; of Eight Wind, 6–7, *8,* 54, 65–66, 69, 80, 96, 98, 99, 105, 106, *130,* 139, 146, 188; of Eleven Wind, 67; of Nine Wind, 99

Eight Deer (m), 6, 14, 45, 89, 123, 124, 144, 158, 159, *168,* 183, 184, 186; death of,

18, 23, 155, 156, 164, 166, 177; in jaguar attire, 82, 84, 87; and Jaltepec, 16, 56, 83, 152, 165; and Red and White Bundle, 85–86, 126, 127, 153, 154, 166, 176, 184, 185; as social changer, 56, 126, 145, 156, 163; and Two Rain's mummy bundle, 127, 128–129, *128,* 149–150, 154, 166, 176, 179; as usurper of Tilantongo, 18, 23n2, 31, 56, 81, 83, 106, 125, 126, 128, 146, 149, 151, 163, 177; as *yaha yahui,* 46, 81, 154. *See also* Codex Zouche-Nuttall: Eight Deer biography in

Eight Wind (m), 6, 16, 31, 36, 103, 159; at Apoala, 7–8, 62, 65, 66, 80, *94,* 97, 98, 99, 100, 106, 110, *113, 130,* 138, 139, *142, 158, 187;* biography of, 33, 54, 60, 61, 95, 98, 114, 115–120, 129, *130,* 153–154, 158; birth from the earth, 6–7, *8,* 54, 65–66, 69, 80, 96, 98, 99, 105, 106, *130,* 139, 146, 188; chronology of, 13, 18, 31, 33, 36, 39, 54, *94,* 98, 117, 138, 142, 159, 163; in Codex ZN (*see* Codex Zouche-Nuttall: Eight Wind saga in); as creation story, 21; death of, 117, *118,* 123, *130;* descendants of, xi, 6, 16, 85, 117, 118–120, 122, 126, 147, 149, 155, 158–159, 165, 179, 186 (*see also* Four Wind; Six Monkey; Two Rain); and Eight Deer, 31–32, 46, 52–53, 56, 126–129, 142, 144; as Eight Wind Twenty, 97, 106, 164, 183; emerging from cave, *9,* 66, 69, 80–81, 96–97, 99, 116, 139, 146, 157–158; emerging from river, 65, 66, 99, 139, 157; as historical personage, 33, 35, 144; identification of kingdom of, 7–8, 81, 97, 179; as lineage founder, 31, 33, 54–55, 62, 66, 80–81, 86, 95, 100, 116, 118, 128, 137, 139, 146, 154, 158–159; marriages of, 7, 81, 97, 116–117, 118–120, *118,* 121, *130,* 146–147, 158, 166; and Nine Wind Quetzalcoatl, 69, 99–100, 112, 137–138, 141–142, 159; as original Mixtec, 106; as personification of the landscape, 22, 102; and plants, 65, 99, 137–138; as rain god, 100; as *santo,* 33, 35–36, 54, 98, 100, 116, 159; as social changer, 54–56, 126, 145, 158; stages of life of, 7, 116, 123, 158–159; as tree born, 54, 66, 69, 81, 99, 139; and Two Rain, 7,

23n2, 31, 60, 117, 123, 124, 126, 127, 144, 147, 148, 149, 150, 152, 154, 166, 177, *187;* and War from Heaven, 62, 106, 139, 146, 158, 164; as *yaha yahui,* 46, 96–97, 98, 116; and Yucuñudahai, 8, 13–14, 62, 64, 80, *94,* 95, 98, 100, 102, 105, 106, 109, 111, *130,* 136, 138, 139, 141, *142, 187*

Eleven Wind (m), 42, 179; defeat by Eight Deer, 85–86, 126, 153, 166, 176, 184, 185–186; genealogy of, 6, 67, *119;* and Six Monkey, 23n2, 85, *119,* 126, 149–150, 153, 166, 179, 183–184, 185

elite, 1, 3, 65, 72, 74, 76, 79, 80, 88, 89, 96, 155; in codices, 57, 141; empowerment of, 69, 70, 77; history, 21, 49

empowerment ceremonies, 79–80, 81–83, 84, 85, 86, 88, *168*

Epiclassic Period, 33, 37, 39, 54, 62, 64, 88, 96, 105, 129, 141, 144, 156, 157, 158

ethnography, 34–35, 41n2, 65, 66, 67, 143

fire drilling, 64, 65, 66, 98, 99, 135–137, 138, 139, 175

Five Alligator (m), 23n2, 43, 82, 83, 167

Five Flower (m), 18, 47, 105, 109, 110, 111, 177, 180, 182, *187*

Five Motion (m), 23n2, *119,* 123, 166

folklore, 32, 66, 96, 105

Four Jaguar (m), 151, 170, 171, 172, 174, 175–176, 186

Four Motion (m), 104, 109–110, 111, *113,* 175

Four Snake (m), 7, 104, 108, 111, 123

Four Wind (m), 6, 16, 18–19, *119,* 166, 177, 185; biography of, 165; consolidates bloodlines, 186; and Eight Deer, 23n2, 85–86, 87, 126, 153, 154, 155, 165, 176; as *yaha yahui,* 46

genealogies, 6, 18, 19; calculating dates from, 13; in codices, ix, xi, 5, 30, 32, 33, 36–37, 52–53, 57, 60–61, 146; as heroic history, 21–22; use of, 18–19

gods, 1, 6, 63, 64–65, 66, 67–68, 74, 78, 95, 99, 100, 104, *104,* 108, 135, 136, 138, 159, 168, 181; at Apoala, 137; of the dead (*see* Nine Grass); of Evening Star, 67; of maguey, 103–105, 109, 110, *113, 130,*

138; of maize, 72, 99n1; residences of, 81; of sun, 47, 67, 124, 151, 171, 175–176; of Venus, 84; of wind, 78. *See also* rain gods; *and under individual names*

grass mats, 68, 82, 103, 109, 116, 168

Grove, David, 71, 72, 77

hieroglyphs, 29–30, 49–51, *50. See also* pictograms

Hill of the Ballcourt, 7, 11, 23n2

Hill of Flints. *See* Mogote del Cacique

Hill of the Flower. *See* Yucuita

Hill of the Jewel—Hill of Feathers, 7, 11

Hill of the Monkey. *See* Monkey Hill

Hill of the Rain God. *See* Yucuñudahui

Hill of the Sun. *See* Achiutla

Hill of the Wasp. *See* Wasp Hill

Hill that Opens-Bee. *See* Wasp Hill

Hua Chino. *See* Red and White Bundle

iconography, 4, 5, 67, 68, 78, 79, 86; of caves, 69–71, 73–77, 79, 81, 88, 157, 158; celestial, 73, 89, 158; in Mesoamerica, 69–70; on monuments, 72–79, 80; Native American use of, 30; of plants, 65, 72, 74, 96, 104; of water, 81, 158

jaguars, 70, 82, 84, 85, 87, 127, 172, 180, 182

Jaltepec, 7, 16, *20,* 148, 151, 157, 177; and Chalcatongo, 154, 180, 183; in Codex Selden, 67–68, 80, 81, 117, 126; first dynasty of, 67, 84, 139, 149, 179–180; and Eight Wind, 80, 81, 117, 139; genealogy of, 19, 67–68; location of, *17,* 48; and Red and White Bundle, 56, 86, 126, 150, 158, 164–165, 179; second dynasty of, 80, 81, 86, 117, 118, *119,* 139, 147, 154, 158, 180; and Tilantongo, 18, 55–56, 82, 83, 86, 87, 117, 120, 124, 126, 147, 149, 150, 154, 158, 164, 166, 177, 178, 183; women ruling, 154, 180, 183. *See also* Nine Wind (f); Six Monkey

kinship, 6, 21–22, 48, 62

ladies. *See under individual names*

La Venta, 71, 72, 76, 77

Lienzo de Zacatepec, 18–19, 165

lightning, 46, 108

lineages, 65, 84, 85, 86, 110, 112, 139, 156, 157, 159; consolidated, 186; founders, 33, 39, 65–66, 80, 81, 85, 95, 100, 116, 151, 154; role of 21–22, 54. *See also* dynasties

lords. *See under individual names*

maguey, 64, 96, 99, 103–105, *104,* 109, 110, 111, 113, *130,* 138. *See also* plants, sacred; pulche

maize, 64, 65, 72, 73, 74, 99n1

manuscripts. *See* codices

marriage alliances, 18, 19, 125, 149; control of, 47, 113, 126, 128, 149–150, 154, 178; of Mixtecs, 1, 18, 45, 47, 79; severance of, 82–83, 86, 126, 127, 154, 158, 164, 178; use of, 6

Maya, 42n3, 68, 87, 88–89, 99n1, 142; calendar of, 40–41, 190; surviving codices of, 30; writing system of, 4, 29, 49–51

metaphors, 36, 39, 40, 41, 85, 95, 98–99, 116

Middle Formative period, 38, 49, 70, 71, 80, 83, 87, 96

Mixteca, 46, 47, 54, 56, 80, 81, 83, 100, 105, 106, 112, 126, 131, 138, 145, 148, 159, 186; Alta, 1, 13, 14, 16, 19, *20,* 47; Baja, 16, 47; Costa, 16, 19, 47

Mixteca-Puebla, 4, 41

Mixtecs, 1, 3, 14, 15, 21, 89, 105, 117; aristocracy of, 6, 16; art of, 3–4; cognition of, 30; communities of, 45–46; concept of time, 36, 40–42, 142; creation chronology of, 13, 14, 41n2, 142–143; Cult of the Dead, 123, 148, 156, 159; defeated by Aztecs, 2, 52, 143; history of, 1, 33, 34, 39, 45–47, 79, 129–131, 158, 159; language of, 3, 35, 48; modern-day, 3, 47, 48, 80, 96; as People of the Rain, 38, 55, 105, 138, 159; role of codices among, ix, 29–30, 52–53; surviving codices of, 4–5, 30, 51, 88; unification of, 1, 56, 144; view of themselves, 21–22, 69; writing system of, 49, 50

Mogote del Cacique, 1, *2, 13,* 14, *17, 20,* 22n1

Monkey Hill, *8,* 13, *15,* 54, 60, *94,* 97, 99,

116, 123, 124, 142, 146, 147. *See also* Cerro Jasmin; Eight Wind

Monte Alban, 4, 10, 16, 22n1, 45, 79

Monte Negro, 16, *44*

Montezuma II, 52, 160

mummy bundles, 111, 117, 126, *130,* 154, 147n1, 177; in caves, 14, 87, 123, 148; of Eight Wind, 60, 123, 124, *130,* 154, 158, 166; of Four Motion, 109–110; of Seven Flower, 109–110; speaking to, 47, 123, 124, 127, 128, *128,* 147–148, 158, 159, 166, 176; of Three Lizard, 149–150; of Twelve Motion, 152, 154, 176; of Two Rain, 60, 67, 124, 127, 128, *128, 130,* 150, 166, 176

mushrooms, 65, 139

Nahuas, 1, 2, 4, 5, 14, 24n3, 50

Nine Grass (f), 84, 151, 154, 157, 183, 184, 185; consulting mummy bundles, 47, 87, 123, 128, 147–148, 149–150; controlling marriage alliances, 47, 113, 126, 128, 149–150, 154, 178. *See also* oracles

Nine Wind (f), 118, *119,* 120, 166, 179, 180, 183

Nine Wind (m), 23n1, 106, 157, 175

Nine Wind Quetzalcoatl (m), 67, 82–83, 111, 112, 116, 139, 169, 171, 177; birth of, 111, 141, 143, 157, 159; and Eight Wind, 69, 99–100, 112, 137–138, 141–142, 159; holding water and sky, 64, 67, 111, 138, 141, *142,* 143, *143,* 164; importance of, in codices, 157; as *yaha yahui,* 96

nobles, 1, 6, 14, 20, 45, 46, 47, 49, 53, 67–68, 79, 81, 95, 99n1, 105, 139, 147; ancestors of, 23n2, 69; composition of codices by, 5–6; as divinities, 6; ethnicity of, 18; mummy bundles of, 14, 123, 148; origins of, 65–66, 69; and supernatural, 6, 74, 129, 148, 155; use of marriage by, 6

Nochixtlan Valley, 15, 62, 64, 112, 156; geography of, *16–17,* 47–48; importance of, in codices, 16; Mixtecs in, 1, 48, 54; original inhabitants of, 105; northern, 7, 8, *8,* 11–13, *13,* 31, 61, 110; southern, *2, 13,* 16, *16–17,* 18, 19, 22–23n1, 54, 61, 157; unification of, 144

nose-piercing, 151, 170, 171, 186

Nuttall, Zelia, 33, 52, 53, 54, 160, 163
ñuu, 68, 95, 105, 106, 180, 182
Ñuu Dzaui, 38. *See also* Mixtecs
Ñuu Tnoo. *See* Tilantongo

Oaxaca, 2–3, 5, 6, 14, 62, 65, 79, 97,
    129–131, 146, 147, 161; confederacies
    in, 5, 19; geography of, 47–48, 151;
    Mesoamerican cultures in, 37, 45, 48;
    Mixtec culture in, ix, 1, 4, 29–30, 48,
    154; Spanish arrival in, 31, 66, 160, 165
    (*see also* Spanish entrada); Valley of, 1,
    16, 18, 19, 48
Olmecs, 29, 45, 49, 65, 70, 71, 74, 76, 87,
    88, 96
One Alligator (m), 86, 87, *119,* 126, *153,*
    155, 165, 166, 177, 185, 186
One Death (m), 47, 67, 84, 89, 151, 171,
    175, 181
One Motion (m), 67, 84, 89, 167, 181
opossums, 103–105, *104,* 109
oracles, 16, 47, 66, 67, 68, 84, 170, 179; of
    dead, 47, 56, 113, 123, 125, 128–129,
    147–148, 150, 156, 163, 164, 170, 178,
    180; in Mixteca, 46–47, 148, 156; of sun,
    47, 84, 151, 154, 171; of Venus, 84; of
    Zapotecs, 79. *See also* Nine Grass
oral histories, 30, 32, 38, 42, 57
ordering rituals, 64, 65, 95, 98, 99, 105,
    109, 111, 135–139, *136,* 141, *142,* 156,
    187

palaces, 1, 9, 11, 15, 20, 45
palimpsests, 51, 67, 165
performances, 6, 35, 37, 52, 57, 64, 67–68,
    126, 129
personifications: of flint knife, 181; of
    maguey, 103–104, *104;* of meteorologi-
    cal phenomena, 7, 46, 108; of nature,
    6, 22, 63, 68, 69, 73–74, 81, 83, 157; of
    rain god, 100, 109, 138; of underworld
    waters, 78
pictograms, 2, 4, 29–30, 38, 48–51, *50,* 53,
    63, 85, 102, 141; guidelines in, 57, 61,
    114, 123; as mnemonic devices, 38, 41,
    42, 57, 61, 63; origins of, 49; reading
    order of, 57, 61, 95, 122–123
place signs. *See* toponyms

Place Where the Sky Was (Place Where the
    Sky Is Held Up), 63, *143,* 151, 164, 174
plants, sacred, 74, 75, 76, 77; at Apoala, 66,
    139; bound, 135, 137–138; in codices,
    64–65, 80, *140;* and Eight Wind, 99,
    137–138; at Yucuñudahui, 64. *See also*
    maguey; maize; mushrooms; tobacco
Pohl, John, 38, 40, 41, 45, 46, 67, 79
Postclassic period, 2–3, 4, 9, 22, 33, 39, 45,
    64, 69–70, 71, 79, 83, 88, 96, 105, 156;
    beginning of, 1; founding of kingdoms
    during, 16, 22–23n1, 62; languages of, 4;
    Mixtec history during, 37, 129, 147, 154;
    Natividad phase of, 13, 157; Yahuitlan
    during, 11–13
priests, 1, 6, 16, 46, 67, 82, 86, 149, 170, 179,
    181, 182, 183; Eight Deer as, 81, 154;
    Eight Wind as, 31, 96, 97, 98, 116; pow-
    ers of, 85, 123, 129, 147–148; Two Rain
    as, 124, 126, 148. *See also* shamans;
    yaha yahui
propaganda, xii, 19, 49
pulche, 64, 103–104, *104,* 110, 138. *See also*
    maguey
pyramids, 1, *13, 15,* 51, 71, 75

Rabin, Emily, 13, 36, 41
rain, 46, 63, 64, 70, 72, 74, 78, 108
Rain God Hill. *See* Yucuñudahui
rain gods, 8, 60, 63, 78, 80, *113,* 116, 117,
    118, 130, 137, 138, 139, 159; Chaac, 78;
    Tlaloc, 8. *See also* Dzaui
Red and White Bundle, 148, 151; claim to,
    7; and Eight Deer, 85–86, 126, 127, 153,
    154, 176, 185; and Jaltepec, 56, 86, 126,
    150, 158, 164–165, 179; war against, 56,
    113, 126, 127, 153, 154, 158, 176, 185. *See
    also* Eleven Wind
river birth, 6, 18, 19, 23n1, 65, 66

sacrifices: animal, 85, 168; bird, 82, 103,
    108, 109, *113,* 116, *130,* 135, 137, 171,
    172, 177, *187,* 188; heart excision, 85,
    108, 124, 152; human, 46, 82, 85–86, 87,
    124, 126, 153, 166, *168,* 169, 172, 175,
    176–177, 179, 180, 183, 184, 185, 186; of
    Stone Men, 7, 11, 102–103, 108, *113, 130,*
    139, *187*

santos, 33, 95, 96, 98, 116, 159. *See also* supernatural; yaha yahui

Seven Flower (m), 79, 104, 105, 106, 108, 109–110, 111, *113,* 123, 175

Seven Motion (m), 7, 11, 102–103, 108, 111, *113,* 123, *130,* 139, *153*

Seven Reed. *See* Two Rain

Seven Snake (m), 7, 102, 104, 108, 111, 169, 188

Seven Wind (m), 7, 11, 66, 103, 104, 111

shamans, 74–75, 79, 96. *See also* priests; yaha yahui

Six Eagle (f), 7, 102, 111, 166, 188

Six Monkey (f), 6, 19, 23n2, 144, 154, 166; biography of, 164–165, 179–186; and caves, 102, 183; and Eight Deer, 19, 153, 154, 165, 166, 167, 184; as Eight Wind's granddaughter, 31, 55, 118, 126, 147; as Eleven Wind's wife, 42, 126, 149, 150, 164, 166, 179, 183–184; as Four Wind's mother, 46, 85–86, 118, *119,* 126, 153, 165, 185; and Tilantongo, 16, 55–56, 126, 147, 179; as War Garment, 184, 185. *See also* Jaltepec

sky, 31, 65, 67, 68, 69, 85, 89, 109, 140, 143, 157–158, 164, 168, 176, 181; birth from, 6, 69, 100, 111, 141; caves in, 69, 87, 108; objects from, 15, 67, 72; people from, 7, 108, *113, 130,* 143, 157; and water held, 64, 67, 111, 138, 141, *142,* 143, *143*

snakes, 67, 68, 72, 78, 85, 96, 127, 182

Spanish entrada, 2, 11, 14, 18, 19, 23n2, 31, 34, 37, 45, 54, 67, 81, 118, 157, 160, 165

spirits, 4, 74, 79, 180. *See also* ancestors; mummy bundles

Spores, Ronald, 9, 10, 14, 46, 48, 117, 157

stone knife birth, 69, 100, 111

Stone Men, 7, 54n1, 60, 62, 102, 111, 126, 159; and Eight Wind, 105, 158; as original people of Mixteca, 54, 64, 105, 112, 138; sacrificed, 7, 11, 102–103, 108 *130,* 139; war with, 102, 103, 112, *113, 130,* 157, 158, 188, *189;* after war, 105–106, 109; at Yucuñudahui, 7, 102, 105, 110. *See also* War from Heaven

Striped Men, 7, 111, 139, 176; lack of names of, 108, 112; war with, 60, 102,

108, 112, *113, 130,* 157, 159, 188, *189. See also* War from Heaven

Suchixtlan. *See* Monkey Hill

sun, 47, 67, 151, 167, 175

supernatural, 78, 81, 98, 148; figures, 79, 82, 87, 95, 96, 109; and Mixtec aristocracy, 6, 155; nature of world, 70, 88, 89; power, 74, 76. *See also* santos; yaha yahui

symbols. *See* iconography

techutli, 146, 151, 170, 186, *195*

temples, 7, 46, 47, 49, *50,* 157, 167, 169, 176, 180, 182; caves in, 84, 96, 116, 157; as celestial, 83, 89; Eight Wind in, 97, 116, 117, 123, 124, 147, *147;* at Jaltepec, 179, 180, 182, 183, 184; of Nine Grass, 84, 123, 148, 151; as residences of gods, 81, 175; Star Temple, 82, 89, *168,* 169; Two Rain in, *124,* 125, 147, 152–153

Ten Deer (f), 123; and Eight Wind, 7, 117, 118, *119,* 146–147, 166, 183; and Jaltepec dynasty, 117, 139, 147, 179, 183

Ten Eagle (f), 67, 97, 117, 146, 181

Ten Eagle (m), 23n2, 118, *119,* 120, *153,* 166, 179, 180, 183

Tey Ñuu. *See* Stone Men

Three Flint (f), *16,* 36, 60, 61

Three Lizard (m), 23n2, 117, 126, 149, 150, 177, 179, 183

thunder, 46, 108

Tilantongo, *2,* 7, 14, 16, 19, *20,* 24n4, 38, 87, 112, 124, 155, 167, 171, 172; councils at, 82, 86, 150; dialect of, 19; first dynasty of, xii, 18, 22n1, 23n2, *44,* 61, 81, 82, 83, 86, 106, 118, *119,* 123, 147, 149, 150, 157, 158, 164, 177; location of, *17;* second dynasty of, xii, 18, 23n2, 118, *119,* 127, 163; and War from Heaven, 112; war with Jaltepec, 55–56, 83, 86, 124, 126, 128, 147, 149, 150, 154, 158, 164, 165, 177–178, 183; war with Red and White Bundle, 55–56, 113, 126, 158. *See also* Eight Deer; Ten Eagle (m); Two Rain

tobacco, 64, 68, 116, 182

Tolteca-Chichimeca, 45, 47, 126, 127, 151, 170, 186

Toltecs, 45, 146, 186

tonindeye, 88, 159, 161, 165
toponyms, 7, 10, 14–16, 21; of Apoala, 141; in codices, 7, 10, 14, 24n3, 69, 125, 136–137; key to, 58, *60;* of Monkey Hill/Suchixtlan, 7, 116; of nature, 76, 81, 108; of Yucuñudahui, 8, 141, *143*
Toto Cuee Cave, 95, 96, 98, *187,* 188
tree birth, 53, 66–68, 81, 105, 138, 139, 141, 181; at Achiutla, 19, 65, 67–68, 69, 81; at Apoala, 54, 62, 65, 66, 69, 81, 99, 110, 111, 122, 138, 139, 158, 181
trees, 65–68, 81, 182. *See also* tree birth
Tututepec, 2, 81–82, 84, 86, 126, 151, 166, *168,* 169, 170
Twelve Motion (m), 23n2, 123, 151, 152, 154, 167, 168, 170, 171, 175, 176
Two Dog (m), 99, 104, 109, 110, 111, 116, 137, 138, 141
Two Rain (m), 6, 144, 166, 183, 185; biography of, 177–179; born as Seven Reed, 164, 177; death of, 18, 23n2, 82, 126, 127, 147, 150, 151, 164, 166, 169, 179; and Eight Wind, 7, 23n2, 60, 117, 123, 124, 126, 127, 147, 148, 149, 150, 154, 158, 166, 177, *187;* as Eight Wind's great-grandson, 31, 55, 117, 118, 147; mummy bundle of, 60, 67, 124, *125,* 127, 128–129, *128, 130,* 148, 150, 152–153, 166, 176, 179; and Tilantongo's first dynasty, 23n2, 56, 118, *119,* 123, 147, 149, 164, 177; and war with Jaltepec, 55–56, 82, 117, 164, 166, 177, 183
Two Snake (f), 117, 118, *119,* 120, 166, 179, 180

underworld, 73, 76, 86, 96, 116, 148; aquatic, 70, 71, 78, 81, 87; as part of cosmos, 65, 68, 70, 80, 83, 87, 89. *See also* caves

War from Heaven, 8, 11, *15,* 18, 157; as allegory, 16, 46, 105; on Codex ZN, 7, 10, *16,* 32, 60, 61, 95, 100, 101–114, *101, 107,* 113, *113,* 146, 157, 158, 159; date of, 100, 146; differing versions of, *16–17,* 32, 164; importance of, 61–62, 112. *See also* Stone Men; Striped Men

War with the Stone Men. *See* Stone Men; War from Heaven
War with the Striped Men. *See* Striped Men; War from Heaven
Wasp Hill, 1, *2,* 14, 23n1, 86, 184; lineage at, 157; location of, *13, 17,* 22n1; war at, 18, 54, 61–62, 112, 139, 186
wind, 74, 76, 78, 108
world tree, 65, 72, 74, 79, 81

Xipe Totec, 47, 64, 79

yaha yahui, 103, 172; abilities of, 46, 85, 147–148; Eight Deer as, 46, 81, 154; Eight Wind as, 46, 96, 97, 98, 116; Four Wind as, 46; Nine Wind Quetzalcoatl as, 96. *See also* priests; *santos;* shamans; supernatural
Yanhuitlan, 8, 11–13, 14, *15,* 16–18, 19, *20,* 48, 66, 157
year signs, 58, *58,* 102–103, 108, 117
Yucu Dzahui. *See* Yucuñudahui
Yucuita, 1, 7, 9, 10, 13, *13,* 14, *15,* 16, *17,* 48, 102, 108, 111, 156
Yucuñudahui, 1, 9, 10, *10, 12–13,* 13, 14, *15,* 64, 156; and Eight Wind, 7, 8, *9,* 62, 80, *94,* 95, 98, 99, 100, 102, 105, 106, 109, 136, 138, 139, 141, 142, *142, 187;* importance of, 64, 111, 138, 141; location of, 8–9, *17,* 48; and Nine Wind Quetzalcoatl, 67, 138, 141–142, *142, 143, 143;* as personification of rain, 63, 108, 138; plants at, 65, 137, 138; as Rain God Hill, 8; as source of Mixtec name, 55; as Stone Men territory, 105, 106, 138; War from Heaven at, 9, 102–103, 105, 110, *113,* 139
Yucu Yoco. *See* Wasp Hill
Yuta Tñohu. *See* Apoala

Zaachila, 18, 19–20, *20,* 79
Zapotecs, 1, 14, 18, 19–20, 45, 46, 47, 48, 54, 79, 89, 112; religion of, 108, 123; writing system of, 29, 49, 50
ZN. *See* Codex Zouche-Nuttall

Milton Keynes UK
Ingram Content Group UK Ltd.
UKHW010705280324
439889UK00010B/156

9 780292 725737